GAMING LAW
IN A NUTSHELL

By

WALTER T. CHAMPION, JR.
George Foreman Professor
of Sports and Entertainment Law,
Texas Southern University
School of Law

and

I. NELSON ROSE
Professor of Law
Whittier Law School

A Thomson Reuters business

Mat #41198183

Thomson Reuters created this publication to provide you with accurate and authoritative information concerning the subject matter covered. However, this publication was not necessarily prepared by persons licensed to practice law in a particular jurisdiction. Thomson Reuters does not render legal or other professional advice, and this publication is not a substitute for the advice of an attorney. If you require legal or other expert advice, you should seek the services of a competent attorney or other professional.

Nutshell Series, In a Nutshell and the Nutshell Logo are trademarks registered in the U.S. Patent and Trademark Office.

ISBN: 978–0–314–27836–4

To Charles, Sarah,
Tommy and Zooey

W.T.C., Jr.

To Patricia, David, Lauren, Mimi
and, of course, Zooey

I. Nelson Rose

PREFACE

It is a great honor to write my second Nutshell. My first Nutshell on Sports Law is now in its fourth edition. To me, the Nutshell is "graduation day." It shows that a particular field has the gravitas to merit a victory lap. If that's the case, and it is, then Gaming Law has certainly earned its stripes. It is the most dynamic field in law today!

WALTER T. CHAMPION, JR.

Houston, Texas
March 2012

ACKNOWLEDGEMENTS

My co-author, Professor I. Nelson Rose just about single-handedly created the field of Gaming Law. In fact, he has a registered trademark for Gambling and the Law®. His name is synonymous with the field. His fifteen minutes of fame, when the Department of Justice on December 23, 2011 gave the gambling world a Christmas gift by declaring that states are now free to legalize almost every form of Internet gambling, has stretched on for three months.

I stumbled on to the field from the relative safety of Sports Law about six years ago when I went to Vietnam in an attempt to develop a casino gambling zone. Sincere acknowledgements must also go to my partner, friend, and former student Michael Hoc Cao.

From that point, I associated myself with the venerable publication, Gaming Law Review and Economics as a member of their editorial board and had the good fortune to meet their co-editors-in-chief, Joseph M. Kelly and Prof. Rose. My insight into gaming law emanates from this publication's cogent articles, not to mention their case selections.

I am also indebted to the following authors and books: Internet Gaming Law, I. Nelson Rose, Martin D. Owens; Blackjack and the Law, I. Nelson

ACKNOWLEDGEMENTS

Rose, Robert A. Loeb; The Wizard of Odds, Charles Rosen; International Casino Law, Anthony N. Cabot, William N. Thompson, Andrew Tottenham; Indian Gaming Law and Policy, Kathryn R.L. Rand, Steven Andrew Light; Gaming Law: Cases and Materials, Robert M. Jarvis, Jr., Shannon L. Bybee, J. Wesley Cochran, I. Nelson Rose, Ronald J. Rychlak; Indian Gaming and the Law, William R. Eadington (editor); Regulating Commercial Gambling: Past Present and Future, David Miers; Going for Broke: The Depiction of Compulsive Gambling in Film, Jeffery W. Dement; Gambling and the Law, I. Nelson Rose; Governing Gambling, John Lyman Mason, Michael Nelson; The Gaming Industry: Introduction and Perspectives, UNLV International Gaming Institute (edited by Vincent Eade, David Christensen); and The Business of Gaming: Economics and Management Issues, William Eadington, Judy Cornelius (editors).

I submitted a rough outline for Gaming Law in a Nutshell to my West editors as a means to save my spot until they decided to publish a nutshell in this field. They suggested that I seek a co-author for marketing purposes. My first and only thought was to seek the guru, I. Nelson Rose, which I did. He was sufficiently amused with my earnest, school-boy demeanor to accept my invitation, and for this I am eternally grateful.

Acknowledgements must also be shared with my assistant, Crystal Graham, my current student, Susan Onyewuchi, and my former student, JoAnn Kvintus, who did yeoman work on the manuscript

ACKNOWLEDGEMENTS

typing, proofing and formatting. Believe me, JoAnn, you are most sincerely appreciated by both co-authors.

WALTER T. CHAMPION, JR.

Houston, Texas
March 2012

I want to thank Walter T. Champion, Jr., for inviting me to be his co-author on this Nutshell. A few years ago, I contacted the largest law book publishers to see about writing a treatise on Gaming Law. I was disappointed to find that there simply are no more treatises being published, because even law schools no long buy them. But the need for a summary of this and other legal topics is essential. As the continuing success of the Nutshell series shows, doing research on the Internet is fine, but it is not a substitute for having a single book explain the law in a way that is understandable for law students and others who are new to the subject, or those who know only one part of the field. So, I purposely wrote this Nutshell as a mini-treatise. It should prove useful for anyone interested in this fast growing and fast changing area of the law.

I cannot hope to thank the many people who helped make this book possible. I have been studying legal gambling for more than 35 years, so I apologize if I left your name out—I do appreciate all the help you have given me over the years. Special thanks to my research assistants, who, starting in 1983, helped me find the cases, statutes and regulations that make up the body of gambling law: Chris Wilson, Beverly Stane, Patricia Kozlowski, Christine Condy, Craig McLaughlin, Bradley J. Quittschreiber, Douglas Bond, David Gary Jones, Daniel B. Herbert, Ranjit Indran, James B. Lewis, John Secco, Michael Shelton-Frates, Michelle Black, David A. Freemon, Kimberly Phillips, Amy Hu, Adam Thomas, John J. Lewis, Chrystal Bobbitt, Joanna Maurer, Alex Yneges, Michael Montrief, John B. Noone, Eric Panitz, Richard Grossman, Brian A. Borba and Nicholas D. Myers; and an outstanding graduate student, Sebastien Gariepy. As always, I thank all of my students over the years. I have learned a lot from you.

There are so many, now, who are studying and writing about gaming law. The leaders in the field in academia include William R. Eadington, Director of the Institute for the Study of Gambling and Commercial Gaming at the University of Nevada, Reno. Bill invited me to be the Institute's first Visiting Scholar, giving me the chance to work with, among others, Mark Nichols, Richelle O'Driscoll, Connie Rehard, and especially Judy A. Cornelius. In the southern part of the state, Prof. William N. Thompson of the University of Nevada, Las Vegas, is one of the most prolific writers covering legal gaming. Others at UNLV who have worked with me include James H. Frey, John Goodwin, Larry A. Strate, Susan Jarvis and the rising young scholars, David G. Schwartz and Bo Bernhard. Other gaming scholars include James Smith at Pennsylvania State University; Tom Hammer at Glassboro State College; David Miers, Cardiff Law School; Jack Samuels, Montclair State College; Jerome H. Skolnick, New York University School of Law; Mark Griffiths, Nottingham Trent University; Kathryn R.L. Rand, University of North Dakota Law School; Jeffrey Derevensky and Rina Gupta, McGill University; Howard J. Shaffer, Harvard Medical School; Steven Andrew Light, University of North Dakota; Kathryn Hashimoto, East Carolina University; and Ricardo C. S. Siu, Davis K.C. Fong and my good friend, Jorge Godinho, at the University of Macau.

There are now thriving organizations for gaming lawyers, including the International Masters of Gaming Law and the International Association of Gaming Advisors. I want to give special thanks to Daniel Schiffman, Bob Faiss, Frank Catania, Tony Coles, Kelly Duncan, Doug Florence, Carlos Fonsca Sarmiento, Morden C. Lazarus, Michael Lipton, Mike McBride, Bob Stocker, Miriam Wilkinson, Andre Wilsenach, G. Michael Brown, Frank J. Fahrenkopf, Jr., Cory Aronovitz, Bud Hicks, Frank A. Schreck, Michael D. Rumbolz, Maria Milagros Soto, John J. Tipton, Trevor Garrett, Nancy J. Goodwin, Russell C. Mix, Michael J. Gough, Gloria E. Soto, Tony Parrillo, David O. Stewart, Kevin F. O'Toole, Fred Gushin, and Andy Schneiderman.

I also want to acknowledge the individuals who have worked with me on gaming law publications. My Co–Editor–in–Chief of the *Gaming Law Review and Economics*, Joe Kelly; the Executive Editor, Heidi Staudenmaier; Editor–at–Large, Sue Schneider; and, Managing Editor, Steve Zweig. My co-

ACKNOWLEDGEMENTS

authors of my prior books: INTERNET GAMING LAW, Marty Owens; BLACKJACK AND THE LAW, Robert A. Loeb; GAMING LAW: CASES AND MATERIALS, Robert Jarvis, J. Wesley Cochran, Ronald Rychlak and the late Shannon L. Bybee, Jr. My Gambling and the Law® column appears in Peter Mead's *Casino Enterprise Management*, Stan Sludikoff's *Poker Player*, Michael Caselli and James McKeown's *iGaming Business* and now *iGaming Business North America*, Mickey Charles' Sports Network, among others.

Most important of all have been my family. My wife, Patricia Prince Rose, a journalist and former professor of journalism, is the best writer I know, and my best friend. She makes it all possible.

I. NELSON ROSE

Encino, California
May 2012

INTRODUCTION

Legal gambling is exploding around the world. In jurisdictions as diverse as Antigua, Mexico and the Peoples Republic of China's Macau, governments are authorizing casinos, running lotteries, licensing racetracks and debating Internet gaming. In the United States, large-scale commercial gambling is in every state and territory, from Maine to Guam, with the sole exceptions of Utah and Hawaii. And, as this is being written, a bill has just been introduced into the Hawaii Legislature to legalize Internet gambling.

Every year Americans spend about $12 billion at the nation's approximately 36,000 movie screens. This includes all ticket sales plus popcorn and other confectioneries. The total for all forms of recorded music is about the same size, less than $14 billion.

By comparison, lotteries operating in all but a half-dozen states sell more than $60 billion in lottery tickets. Add to this parimutuel betting on horses, dogs, and jai-alai; total "action" in casinos and on slot machines; legal wagers on sports; bets made in licensed card rooms; and expenditures before prize payments in charity gaming and Indian bingo, and the total amount wagered legally in the United States is about a trillion dollars. Looking just at revenue, Americans spent more money on gambling than they did on all live events, concerts, plays, all movie theaters, all spectator sports, and all forms of recorded music—combined.

Changes in the law trail changes in society. Although the general public accepts charity bingo, state lotteries and casinos as a normal part of society, ancient statutes and out-of-date court decisions make the law of gambling legally confusing and wildly inconsistent. And it is not just the idea that Utah and Nevada share a border. In Nevada today, a player cannot sue a casino if the casino refuses to pay a winning bet. Internet horseracing is expressly legal, but not Internet dogracing. And the Kansas State Lottery owns all of the state's commercial casinos, since, in that state, all forms of gambling are "lotteries."

Part of the problem is simply historical. This is the third time in American history that legal gambling has swept across the nation. Twice before, the gaming boom crashed down in scandal, leaving anti-gambling laws on the books.

This is the reason the California State Lottery cannot broadcast television or radio commercials in Las Vegas. When the Second Wave crashed in the 1890s, the states asked the federal government for help in preventing the Louisiana Lottery of that era, known as "The Serpent," from advertising in other states. Federal laws were passed, which in modified form are still around, preventing lotteries from using the U.S. Mail. When radio and then television were invented, these anti-lottery prohibitions were added to federal laws regulating those media as well. Then, in the 1960s, the state lottery was rediscovered. Naturally, state lotteries have to be able to advertise in their own states, so exceptions were carved into the laws. But Nevada has no state lottery. So, federal laws today protect the good people of Nevada from hearing about the evils of California's legal gambling.

Americans are not sure of what role law should have in society. Should the law be used only against acts that everyone agrees should be illegal, like murder? Or, should law be used as a tool to enforce morality, like Prohibition? We have the most trouble with the morally suspect industries—alcohol, drugs, abortion and gambling. Although the Prohibition Era is the best example, there have always been limits and prohibitions in American law that have been routinely violated, sometimes unknowingly, by large numbers of the population.

The anti-gambling prohibitions epitomize the traditional approach taken by American laws. These laws are not only designed to protect people from themselves. They are part of a greater moral framework, designed by policy-makers as a reflection of an imagined ideal society. Surveys and election results have shown that voters want most of the anti-gambling laws to stay on the books, even if they do not want those laws actively enforced.

Perhaps our cycles of complete prohibition to complete permissiveness and back again can be explained by the tendency of Americans to go to the limits, and beyond. Congress passed the Indian Gaming Regulatory Act with the image of tribal bingo halls in mind. Entrepreneurs took the poorly written law and used it to create some of the largest casinos in the world.

Gambling spreads in a haphazard manner, with long-term recurring patterns played out against a background of local politics and unpredictable technology. Inventions redefine experience. Modern technology has played havoc with traditional legal categories.

What does the spread of gambling mean for the future? It is important to remember that the prior two gambling waves ended with nationwide prohibitions on virtually all forms of gaming. Is the current boom headed toward the same bust?

About the only certainty is that gaming law is going to remain a continuing growing, and changing, field.

OUTLINE

OUTLINE

OUTLINE

OUTLINE

Page

TABLE OF CASES

References are to Pages

C

D

E

F

G

H

I

J

K

L

M

N

O

P

Q

R

S

T

U

V

W

Y

TABLE OF STATUTES

UNITED STATES

UNITED STATES CONSTITUTION

UNITED STATES CODE ANNOTATED
12 U.S.C.A.—Banks and Banking

TABLE OF STATUTES

UNITED STATES CODE ANNOTATED
18 U.S.C.A.—Crimes and Criminal Procedure

TABLE OF STATUTES

UNITED STATES CODE ANNOTATED
18 U.S.C.A.—Crimes and Criminal Procedure

TABLE OF STATUTES

UNITED STATES CODE ANNOTATED
18 U.S.C.A.—Crimes and Criminal Procedure

25 U.S.C.A.—Indians

26 U.S.C.A.—Internal Revenue Code

UNITED STATES CODE ANNOTATED
26 U.S.C.A.—Internal Revenue Code

28 U.S.C.A.—Judiciary and Judicial Procedure

31 U.S.C.A.—Money and Finance

TABLE OF STATUTES

GEORGIA CONSTITUTION

ILLINOIS CONSTITUTION

ILLINOIS COMPILED STATUTES

ILLINOIS REVISED STATUTES

LOUISIANA CONSTITUTION

LOUISIANA STATUTES ANNOTATED—REVISED STATUTES

TABLE OF STATUTES

LOUISIANA STATUTES ANNOTATED—CIVIL CODE

MONTANA CODE ANNOTATED

NEBRASKA REVISED STATUTES

NEVADA CONSTITUTION

NEVADA REVISED STATUTES

TABLE OF STATUTES

NEW JERSEY CONSTITUTION

NEW JERSEY STATUTES ANNOTATED

NEW YORK, MCKINNEY'S PENAL LAW

OHIO REVISED CODE

SOUTH DAKOTA CODIFIED LAWS

TENNESSEE CONSTITUTION

TABLE OF STATUTES

CODE OF FEDERAL REGULATIONS

FEDERAL REGISTER

GAMING LAW

IN A NUTSHELL

CHAPTER 1

THE WORLD OF GAMING AND GAMBLING

A. The History of Gaming and Gambling

Technically, there are distinctions in the common law among gambling, gaming, lotteries, and wagers, and the distinctions have important differences in the eyes of the law. The entire field should be called "gambling," although it is understandable why the more genteel word "gaming" is used. However, care must be taken in using that term, since "gaming" also can mean children's video games or merely one form of gambling, i.e., where a patron goes to a location like a casino to participate in a gambling game.

In 2010, forty-three states, the District of Columbia, and three U.S. possessions operated lotteries, which combined to sell more than $60 billion in lottery tickets. In Canada, provincial lotteries are operating Internet poker and other games, or are about to. And virtually every state and province has some form of commercial, charitable or tribal gaming, and often many competitors for the gambling dollar: banking table games and slot machines in

1

small casinos and gigantic integrated resorts, or as part of racetracks, i.e., "racinos;" parimutuel betting on horses, dogs, and jai-alai; video poker, linked bingo machines, and video lottery terminals; charity bingo and pull-tabs; legal sports betting; and licensed poker clubs. The total amount bet in the United States each year is well over a trillion dollars.

The trillion dollar figure is a little misleading, since if a player makes a single bet and wins $20 and bets the same again and loses, that would add $40 to the amount wagered. But, the amount wagered does give an indication of the size of the industry. Americans spent more money on gambling than they did on all live events, concerts, plays, all movie theaters, all spectator sports, and all forms of recorded music—combined. Even by the more conservative measure of gross revenue, the only part of the entertainment industry—if that is where legal gambling should be placed—which earns as much money is television, and legal gaming passed the T.V. industry years ago.

This trillion-dollar phenomenon was not created in a day. Gambling has had a recurring, consistent pattern throughout the country's history. When gambling is illegal, there is pressure for legalization, first of one game and then, gradually, of all forms. However, when it is illegal, many people still gamble at social games, particularly poker; underground commercial lotteries, called the numbers game or policy; and sports and race books and casinos. The laws are difficult to enforce and the general population does not want arrests made if it means taking police resources away from more serious crimes. The result is widespread evasion of the law, leading to disrespect, bribery, and corruption. The response by the public is a demand for reform. The perceived solution is often a demand for legalization.

America's First Wave of legal gambling began even before there was a country. The earliest settlements were funded, in part, by lotteries in England. The first racetrack was set up in New York in 1666. Gaming was usually outlawed by statute; the Massachusetts Bay Colony banned the possession of cards, dice, or gaming tables, even in private homes. It appears to have been easier to buy a lottery ticket during George Washington's time than the present; lotteries were everywhere.

The 1820s and 1830s saw the birth of a reform movement. The movement became centered on Andrew Jackson's call for a clean sweep and to "throw the rascals out." Although Jackson himself was a noted gambler, his movement to bring in the common man, and to eliminate corruption, lent support to growing anti-lottery feelings.

The mix of the two—lottery scandals and a newfound morality—led to the near-complete prohibition of lotteries. These reformers coerced the states to write bans on lotteries in their constitutions. These state constitutional prohibitions on "lotteries" still exist 150 years later, and have been used to challenge everything from parimutuel betting on horseraces to riverboat casinos.

The crash of the First Wave also led to the enactment of the first federal anti-lottery statutes. The federal laws were weak because in the 1840s, 1850s, and 1860s, it was widely believed that the federal government did not have much power to affect technically legal interstate commerce.

The Second Wave began with the Civil War and the continuing expansion of the western frontier. The South turned to state-licensed lotteries as a painless way to raise revenue.

Many southern states resumed state-licensed lotteries. Throughout the Wild West, gambling was ubiquitous.

The establishment of permanent cities in the West brought the desire for law and order. Westerners wanted to be viewed as respectable in the eyes of their established East Coast counterparts; with this desire for civilization often came statutory prohibitions on casinos.

Betting on horseraces was not viewed as a problem, considering that bettors had to be physically present at the track. The invention of the telegraph, telephone, and totalizer machines in the late 19th century, however, made it possible for the average working man to bet on races taking place somewhere else. The establishment of "pool rooms" that took these bets led to the passage of anti-bookie statutes prohibiting the transmission of gambling information.

The 19th century ended with a second round of lottery scandals. The Louisiana Lottery, known as "The Serpent," was the greatest, both in the size of its operation and in the magnitude of the scandal. The lottery operators were correctly accused of attempting to buy the Louisiana state legislature.

Some states, like New York, reacted to the opening of the Louisiana Lottery stores in their major cities by enacting statutes which made it a crime to sell a lottery ticket within their borders, even if the lottery was legal where the drawing was held. These statutes still exist today, although they are of questionable constitutionality, since they interfere with interstate commerce.

Because the states were helpless, President Benjamin Harrison asked Congress to pass legislation to close down the Louisiana Lottery. Congress responded by using the various constitutional provisions and federal powers it thought it had at the time to address President Harrison's concerns. Congress first used its power to regulate U.S. mails, which was the federal government's most powerful weapon at the time. In 1890, Congress passed a law barring the distribution of lottery material via the mails. The law, codified as 18 U.S.C.A. § 1302 specifically prohibits the use of the mails for lottery tickets, for checks for the purchase of tickets, and even for "any newspaper, circular, pamphlet, or publication of any kind containing any advertisement of any lottery, gift enterprise, or scheme of any kind offering prizes dependent in whole or in part upon lot or chance."

The rise of Victorian morality, scandals, and the desire for respectability brought the Second Wave crashing down in the West. The territories of Arizona and New Mexico were told if they wanted to become states, they would have to close their casinos. Even Nevada outlawed all gambling. By 1910, the only large commercial gambling operations were racetracks in Maryland, Kentucky, and New York, and in that year, New York closed its racetracks. The United States was once again virtually free of legalized gambling.

The most important legal debris of the crash of the Second Wave was the federal anti-lottery laws passed in response to the Louisiana Lottery scandal. The federal anti-lottery laws were so successful that no legal lottery existed for almost 70 years; these laws also helped to create the modern United States. They remain on the books today, with sometimes bizarre impacts, such as preventing the California Lottery from advertising on T.V. and radio in Nevada, since Nevada has no state lottery.

Congress believed that it was forced to push its constitutional power to the limit to prevent the Lottery from reappearing. Congress specifically turned to the Interstate Commerce Clause to counter these new practices of the Louisiana Lottery. At that time, the prevailing thought of the law was that "interstate commerce" was limited to commerce that was interstate, for example, shipping on rivers between states. The idea that Congress could regulate legal commerce that happened to cross a state line was a truly radical idea for the time. It was now a federal crime to carry or send a lottery ticket, lottery information, or a list of lottery prizes in interstate or foreign commerce. The Supreme Court, in *the Lottery Case*, upheld this great expansion of the federal government's power in 1903. *Champion v. Ames*, 188 U.S. 321, 23 S.Ct. 321, 47 L.Ed. 492 (1903), and its companion case, *Francis v. United States*, 188 U.S. 375, 23 S.Ct. 334, 47 L.Ed. 508 (1903); the plaintiff here, Charles F. Champion, is not related to the co-author's son, Charles H. Champion. *The Lottery Case* gave birth to modern America, allowing the federal government to become involved with legal products and services that crossed a state line or had another impact on interstate commerce.

The Great Depression gave birth to the Third Wave of legal gambling. Nevada re-legalized casino gambling in 1931. Twenty-one states opened racetracks with parimutuel betting in the 1930s, with additional states allowing parimutuel betting in every decade since. Charities played Bingo, at first illegally, until many of the states changed their laws in the 1940s and 1950s to permit charitable and social gambling. New Hampshire re-discovered the state lottery in 1964. New Jersey became the second state to legalize casinos a decade later. And, federally-recognized Indian tribes are allowed to operate any form of gambling permitted by state law.

B. The Elements of Gambling

The definition of "gambling," unless changed by statute, consists of any activity with three elements: consideration, chance, and prize. Generally, "payment for a chance to win a thing of value" sums up the transaction required. If any one or more of these elements is missing, the activity in question, though it may be regulated, is not gambling.

1. Prize

If no prize can be won, the game in question is classified as an amusement game, not gambling. The majority of jurisdictions today understand the differences between a replay, that must be played, and a credit, which can be turned in for cash (ergo, a "prize").

2. Chance

Even if a game costs money to enter, and, therefore, has "consideration," and the winner will receive a thing of value, a "prize," the contest is technically not gambling if skill predominates over luck in determining the winner; contests of skill are by definition, not gambling. At a minimum, the outcome must be determined by chance for a game to be considered gambling. The question is whether chance is involved in any stage of the activity to the point where it can be said, that it was chance not skill, which determined the winner and how much was won.

3. Consideration

The consideration required for gambling is usually more than the peppercorn or inconvenience sufficient for consideration for non-gambling contracts. Players have to pay money to enter for there to be consideration for gambling. Free games lack consideration, while a game that requires all players to bet cash clearly has consideration. For example, online casinos and racebooks operate on an account basis, and, therefore, require an initial "post-up" transfer of funds to a customer's secure online account by credit card, debit card, or wire transfer. Since these funds must be in place before any bets can be taken, this constitutes consideration by any standard. No-purchase-necessary sweepstakes and donation-requested charity raffles, on the other hand, usually are considered to be without consideration, and thus not gambling. See, e.g., *Federal Communications Commission v. American Broadcasting Co.*, 347 U.S. 284, 74 S.Ct. 593, 98 L.Ed. 699 (1954).

4. Common Law of Gambling

To understand the law of gambling in the United States today, one must understand the law of England in the Middle Ages. The common law is still developing today from court decisions and being modified by statutes passed by legislatures. In the earliest days of the common law all games were legal, and a loser had to pay off his debts. Under the common law, however, the courts could close down as a public nuisance any activity that ran the risk of a breach of the peace or of public morals.

Each state is free to experiment and develop its common law as it sees fit, within the limits of our constitutional government. One state, like New Jersey, may say that gambling debts are collectable under certain circumstances in court; a neighboring state, like Virginia, may say just the opposite. The only way to know the common law in any jurisdiction in any particular case is to study the statutes and court decisions of the jurisdiction in which the case is being heard.

It is possible to describe the common law of gambling, at least in general terms. If you know what the common law is you will have some idea of the law of your own state. Most states still have the common law, unchanged from what we call the date of reception. When a state creates its state constitution it includes a clause stating that it has "received" the common law as of a certain date, usually the year it became a state. Because the common law has proved itself over the years and because it usually takes a positive act by the highest court of the state or the state legislature to get the law changed, most states have kept at least the general concepts of the common law unchanged.

5. English Common Law and Gambling Generally

King Richard II of England in 1388 passed a statute that directed all laborers and serving men to secure bows and arrows and to abandon the pursuit of "tennis, football, coits, dice, casting of stone kaileg, and other such importune games." Henry VIII brought all the gambling statutes together in 1541. The Statute of Anne (1710) as interpreted by American common law stands for the principle that gambling debts, in fact all contacts having anything to do with gambling, are not only void, not only illegal, but are treated as somehow unclean, and the courts will not sully their hands with even considering the merits of the claims. A gambling debt is treated exactly the same as a contract for prostitution; the courts will "leave the parties where it finds them" and will automatically dismiss every claim.

When dealing with the law of gambling debts, it pays to divide the cases into two parts: lawsuits brought in the state where the bet was made and lawsuits brought in a different state. If the local law where the casino or other gambling is local makes gambling contracts unenforceable, the operator is out of luck. But, even gambling debts are legally enforceable where incurred, they may not always be collected in courts of other states where the patron is located. If a Nevada casino sues a player on a written marker in Nevada, the court will hear the suit. If the casino wins, it can take that judgment and enforce it in any other court in the U.S. under the federal constitutional and statutory full faith and credit provisions. But, if the casino merely sues the defaulting patron directly in an out-of-state court, the forum court may find that gambling so offends local public policy that it will not hear the case, and leave the parties where the court finds them. The current trend is to find that local public policy does not oppose legal gambling, as evidenced by the local legalizations of lotteries and bingo.

6. American Common Law and Gambling Generally

The Statute of Anne was received as part of the common law either directly, through reception clauses of state constitutions, or by statute in every state of the United States. Gambling, under the common law, is any activity in which: 1) a person pays something of value, called consideration; 2) the outcome is determined at least in part by chance; and, 3) the winnings are something of value. The three elements of gambling, consideration, chance and prize have been the subject of literally thousands of court cases. If even one of the elements can be disproved, the activity is not gambling under the common law. In a criminal prosecution for gambling, the state has the burden of proving beyond a reasonable doubt the existence of all three elements. A criminal defendant does not have to disprove anything; all he has to do to be found not guilty is to raise a reasonable doubt as to any one of the three elements. In a civil suit, such as a local government attempting to close down a game, or a private party suing for a gambling debt, the burden is usually on the plaintiff to prove the existence of the three elements by a mere preponderance of the evidence.

Lotteries are a form of gambling. But, for historical reasons, the law often involves prohibitions on "lotteries," as opposed to "gambling." This has led to confusion and uncertainty. In addition, every jurisdiction is free to decide for itself how to define these terms and what standards to apply. Some state supreme courts have even ruled that "lottery" includes all games with prize, chance and consideration, which makes that term synonymous with gambling. Others have established different definitions. For example, it is common to find that "gambling" requires that the outcome be determined by at least a predominance of chance, while "lottery" means a game that is pure chance: In these jurisdictions, all lotteries are gambling but not all gambling is a lottery.

The consideration necessary to establish an activity as gambling is usually more than the consideration required for a contract. The United States Supreme Court, for example, has held that something more than a player's time and effort is needed to find consideration, at least under the federal anti-lottery laws.

Courts have devised a number of tests for distinguishing a game of skill from a game of chance, although the results are not always consistent. The courts use one or more of the following criteria to determine whether a game is one of skill or luck: 1) a skillful player can continue to play until he has won all that is at risk; 2) skill can be learned from experience, from real or mock play; 3) skill games require a knowledge of mathematics; 4) skill games require psychological skill; 5) player participation changes the result; 6) skill can be learned from reading; and 7) the opinion of the community. For example, in ruling that the card game of bridge was not gambling because it was predominantly skill, the California Supreme Court used the criteria that it can be learned from reading: "The existence of such a large amount of literature designed to increase the player's skill is a persuasive indication that bridge is not predominately a game of chance." *In re Allen*, 59 Cal.2d 5, 27 Cal.Rptr. 168, 377 P.2d 280 (1962).

The last element, prize, has been less of a problem for the courts. In the past, operators offered free replays or credits. But, if a player can redeem those credits for cash, the prize is obviously something of value. A possibly apocryphal story involves a patron of a slot machine in a bar who had to play off the 10,000 "free replays" he won as a jackpot, because a police officer was present, preventing the bartender from paying off the winner. If the prize is not worth winning, the game usually soon ceases to attract customers. However, as the enormous success of Zynga has shown, it is possible to design successful games where players cannot win prizes convertible into cash.

7. The Interface Between Common Law and Legislation

The role of the legislature has greatly increased. In ancient times, a legislature like the Parliament could change the law only with the greatest of effort. Prior to 1700, it was generally accepted that a legislature could not modify the basic principles of the common law. Today, any legislature can pass a statute and modify the common law by a simple majority vote. This is done often in direct response to a ruling by a judge that is unpopular.

8. Nevada Common Law and Gambling

Nevada for 50 years has made casino gambling legal, but still refuses to repeal the Statute of Anne, except in bits and pieces. A casino can now sue a player but a player cannot sue a casino. The Nevada Constitution explicitly prohibits lotteries. The ban is stated in clear, strong language. When the Nevada Legislature re-instituted casino gambling in 1931, it did not amend the Constitution. To this day, Nevada has legal gambling, but does not have a legal lottery, (other than charity raffles, authorized under a constitutional amendment). Casino games of chance, including slot machines and keno, are not lotteries under Nevada state law, and, are therefore, legal. Federal law can treat the same games differently. The Internal Revenue Service, for example, has ruled that keno is a lottery under the federal Internal Revenue Code.

The Nevada Supreme Court was faced with the question of whether slot machines were legal, given the state's constitutional ban on lotteries. The Court held that a lottery is a "widespread pestilence." Since a slot machine is a device that must be located in a fixed spot it must not be a lottery, at least under Nevada law.

9. "Bank Night" Decisions

Plaintiff, *Yellow–Stone Kit*, held a drawing with eight winning tickets out of 8,000 distributed; he put on performances and sold tickets for his show. But, tickets also were given free to anyone who attended. During the 1930s, this came to be known as "Bank Nights," with movie theaters awarding dishes and similar prizes to the holders of winning tickets. But, *Yellow–Stone Kit v. State*, 88 Ala. 196, 7 So. 338 (1890), helped create the rule that if tickets were available for free then there was no consideration, which meant that there was no gambling contract, and therefore, no gambling.

10. The Enforceability of Gambling Debts

The law on gambling debts has been fairly well settled since Queen Anne signed the Statute of Anne in 1710. The question of whether a gambling contract is enforceable is also well-settled. Crooked gamblers became subject to criminal and civil penalties; professional gamblers were subject to special sanctions. Only in the 1980s, did the Nevada Legislature repeal that part of the Statute of Anne that made gambling debts unenforceable. Thus, the law of gambling debts stood for almost three centuries: illegal bets from a debt owed to a bookie, to a check written at a friendly poker game, are void and unenforceable; but so were legal bets under the Statute of Anne.

Under Nevada state law, if a player stopped payment on a check to a Nevada casino, the casino could not use the court system to collect. *Evans v.*

Cook, 11 Nev. 69 (1876). And, since debts can run both ways, players who thought they were owed money by a casino were consistently thrown out of court. *Corbin v. O'Keefe*, 87 Nev. 189, 484 P.2d 565 (1971). In *Flamingo Resort, Inc. v. United States*, 485 F.Supp. 926 (D. Nev. 1980), *aff'd*, 664 F.2d 1387 (9th Cir. 1982), the Court held that Nevada casinos had to report outstanding markers as income, because most debts eventually were collected; this led to the casinos asking the legislature to make their debts legally enforceable. In 1983, the Nevada Legislature changed the law to allow casinos, but not players, the right to collect under certain circumstances through the court system. (Nev. Rev. Stat. § 463.361(1)).

C.   By Definition Not Gambling

The definition of gambling consists of any activity with three elements: consideration, chance, and prize. There are some games, contests, and events that, by definition, are not gambling.

1.   Amusement Games—No Prize

If no prize can be won, the game in question is classified as an amusement, not gambling.

2.   Tournaments of Skill—Not Chance

The usual test is whether skill or luck predominates. Skill and chance are simply two ends of a spectrum; every imaginable activity fits somewhere between the two points. Bets are made on every

conceivable contest and event, by the actual participants and bystanders alike. The deciding factor is
the individual bettor's participation in the event
and control over the results. The less input and
control, the higher the likelihood it is a game of
chance. However, in a true game of skill, there is
usually no "house" participating as a player, and no
third party can place a wager on a contest between
actual participants.

3. Online Skills Games With Mass Media Applications—Fantasy Leagues

There has been much debate about the elements
of chance in online fantasy sports leagues. Where
fantasy leagues are permitted, it is often because of
an implicit assumption that the activity is a controlled skill, and not a form of gambling. The fantasy league is just that, a fantasy, with fictional teams
created out of the statistics of real-world athletics.
The most popular version is fantasy football. Fantasy league players pay an entry fee to become owners
of virtual "dream teams," assembled via a virtual
"draft" and "trades" of players. In Montana, for
example, fantasy sports leagues are specifically authorized. MONT. CODE ANN. § 23–5–802 (2002).

4. Alternate Means of Entry—Donation Requested—No Consideration

There are "free games," offered online, that are
used as a form of marketing. Games that are completely free, like many online bingo games giving
small prizes, are almost universally legal, and in the

few jurisdictions that might still find consideration in the effort players have to make, law enforcement does not care. Some sites allow players to obtain a small number of chips for free, but most play with chips purchased by credit cards. Nonetheless, the free alternative means of entry (FAME or AMOE) make the games non-gambling (like no-purchase-necessary) "sweepstakes," under some state laws and under federal law as well. The important requirement is that anyone can enter for free and that all players, whether they have paid or not, are treated with "equal dignity," meaning they have an equal chance of winning. Having to sit through pop-up ads to play a game does not constitute participation in gambling, either because it lacks technical consideration or perhaps because the gauntlet of online flackery amounts to an appropriate penance.

D. The "Lottery" Problem

The concept of pooling wagers, betting on a winning number or token to be drawn by chance, dates from remote antiquity. Lotteries have come to be identified as a distinct genre, more because of their unique legal position as state-approved and sponsored entities, rather than any major differences between lotteries and other number-picking games (e.g., keno or bingo).

Most states now have lotteries. However, many state constitutions, until recently, banned lotteries. For example, to allow a state lottery, the California Constitution had to be amended specifically to exempt the state lottery from the complete prohibition on lotteries. The ultimate irony is the state of Nevada; its Constitution specifically bans lotteries. When the Nevada Legislature instituted casino gambling in 1931, it did not amend the Constitution. Although Nevada has legal gaming, it does not have a legal lottery (other than charity raffles); casino games of chance, including slot machines and keno, are not lotteries under Nevada State law and are, therefore, legal.

1. Various Definitions

Jurisdictions are free to decide for themselves what is, and what is not, a lottery. Governments have looked at factors such as whether a game is 100% chance, whether there are paper tickets involved, whether players have to go to a particular place to participate in the play of a game, and whether there is pooling of bets to create the prize.

a. Synonymous With Gambling

Since there is a little or no skill involved with lotteries, it can be easily synonymous with gambling. Defining "lottery" as all games of prize, chance and consideration can create both opportunities and barriers for both proponents and opponents of legal gambling. For example, the state of Kansas was able to open and own true casinos through its State Lottery, because in that state "lottery" includes all gambling games.

b. 100% Chance

Federal law has adopted what it sometimes called "the English Rule," or the "pure chance" rule (or

100% chance), meaning "lottery is defined as a game with virtually no skill." When riverboat casinos were challenged in Missouri, that state's highest court ruled the casinos could open with blackjack but not slot machines, because that Missouri Constitution forbid "lotteries."

c. "Widespread Pestilence"

In *Stone v. Mississippi*, 101 U.S. 814, 25 L.Ed. 1079 (1880), the United States Supreme Court indicated us that lotteries are a "pestilence ... [that] infests the whole community; it enters every dwelling; it reaches every class." In modern terms, this means if a player has to go to a specific place to participate in a game, it is not a lottery, under this test.

d. Requires Paper Ticket

When Congress passed laws to eliminate lotteries in the 1890s, including the infamous, though technically legal, Louisiana State Lottery, it used its power to regulate the postal service. Given the law and technology of the time, it did not seem strange that "lotteries" would require a paper ticket. But in jurisdictions that apply this ancient test today, electronic games that most people would see as being lotteries simply do not fall under the jurisdiction's anti-lottery laws.

2. Who Decides?

Even before deciding what test to apply, the law must first determine who has the final say on what is, and is not, a "lottery." Many state courts defer to their state legislatures. Other state supreme courts have ruled that they alone have the power to decide whether an activity can be legalized by the state legislature, in the face of state constitutional prohibitions on "lotteries." These disputes first became widespread with the reintroduction of legal betting on horseracing during the 1930s.

Activities that are clearly lotteries, such as those that involve paper tickets and numbers drawn once a week, clearly require amending state constitutional prohibitions on "lotteries." But electronic games are not so easily classified. There were no legal state lotteries in the U.S. from the end of the 19th century until 1964, when New Hampshire reintroduced America to the state-run lottery. New York followed by introducing a lottery in 1967, and New Jersey introduced one in 1970. These modern lotteries were not highly successful, however, until New Jersey developed a computer-based weekly game in 1971. The success of the New Jersey game was attributed to more prizes, cheaper tickets, convenient sales and a large jackpot. Currently, lotteries are popular forms of generating revenue conducted in at least forty-three states and the District of Columbia. But several state lotteries ran into problems when they tried to introduce video lottery terminals ("VLTs"), where the game is played entirely on a machine, often indistinguishable from a conventional slot machine.

Over the years, all states except Alaska and Hawaii have introduced commercial gambling, including parimutuel betting, landbased and riverboat casinos, and other forms of licensed or state-sponsored gambling. Sometimes these have required amendments to the state constitutions; sometimes not.

Those states that have lotteries actively promote and seek to improve them. Daily drawings (often two separate daily games) are supplemented with weekly or bi-weekly drawings offering a much larger payoff, and some states have banded together to offer even larger jackpot drawings. Subscriptions are sold so that people may play the same numbers for up to a year at a time without visiting a lottery ticket distributor. Instant lottery tickets are available to people who do not want to wait for a later drawing. Some states have introduced a television "game show" component to their instant game. One state even initiated a payroll withholding plan to encourage participation in the lottery. With recent advances in electronics and telecommunications, it is likely that lottery sales will soon reach inside the average home. The advent of Internet gambling has raised again the question of who decides what forms of gambling are permitted in a jurisdiction. In the District of Columbia, for example, the D.C. Lottery was expressly given the right by the district's governing body to offer poker and blackjack, as well as lottery games, over the Internet.

3. Why It Makes a Difference

A secondary purpose of state-sponsored gambling in some states is to compete with illegal gambling and organized crime. Organized crime gained prominence in the United States in the 1920s as the result of Prohibition. These criminal enterprises expanded their areas of influence into extortion, prostitution, public corruption, organized labor and gambling. With the repeal of the Eighteenth Amendment in 1933, crime syndicates found themselves depending primarily on the proceeds of gambling to hold their empires together.

Even today, gambling is an important revenue source for organized crime. Current estimates of illegal gambling run as high as $1 billion annually wagered in New York City alone, and $100 billion wagered nationally. In 1977, the National Institute of Law Enforcement and Criminal Justice estimated that organized crime controlled half of all illegal gambling in the northeastern section of the United States. If state lotteries were able to draw customers from patrons of illegal games, the state could simultaneously raise revenue and fight crime.

a. State Constitutions Ban "Lotteries"

The Great Awakening, when coupled with Andrew Jackson's political reforms of the 1830s, created an anti-lottery mentality. States changed their constitutions in an attempt to ensure that there never would be lotteries again. Some states expressly prohibited state legislators from authorizing lotteries. Settlers carried this anti-lottery feeling west with them. New states, such as Texas and California, also prohibited lotteries in their state constitutions. Even Nevada banned lotteries; a prohibition that is still in the Nevada Constitution today.

b. Racetracks in the 1930s, Casinos Today

Parimutuel betting on horseraces, like all forms of legal gambling, virtually disappeared from the United States with the crash of the Second Wave of legal gambling in the 1890s. The Great Depression forced states to look to new forms of revenue, and many states reopened their racetracks in the 1930s. Charities started offering bingo, at first in violation of state laws. The state lottery was rediscovered by New Hampshire in the early 1960s; and, New Jersey became the second state to legalize casinos, in the 1970s.

The Third Wave of legalized gambling includes the tracks. At the beginning of the 20th Century, racing and bookmaking had been outlawed everywhere, except Maryland, Kentucky and New York. But the Depression of the 1930s forced the states to look to means other than taxes to raise income. A majority of the states now allows betting on races.

4. Federally Recognized Tribes Can Operate "Lotteries"

In the 1970s, Native Americans took a leading role in the expansion of legalized gambling across the United States. The U.S. Constitution expressly declared that only Congress had the power to regulate commerce with Indian tribes. There are two kinds of state law; the first are "criminal/prohibitory" laws, which directly serve policies such as health and safety by banning the given activity altogether. The second sort, however, are "civil/regulatory," when state law generally permits the conduct at issue, subject to regulation. Under federal law, many states have criminal jurisdiction over Indian reservations within their borders; but no state has regulatory jurisdiction without the express consent of Congress or the Tribe itself. The U.S. Supreme Court in *California v. Cabazon Band of Mission Indians*, 480 U.S. 202, 107 S.Ct. 1083, 94 L.Ed.2d 244 (1987), held that where a state licensed gambling outside the reservation, its gambling laws were "civil/regulatory," rather than "criminal/prohibitory," and, therefore, unenforceable on Indian land.

E. Universally Recognized as Gambling

1. Lotteries

The concept of pooling wagers, betting on a winning number or token, to be drawn by chance, dates from remote antiquity and retains its appeal today. Even though most states have a legal lottery, the categorization of which forms of gaming are legal may merely be a result of tradition. However, that categorization is still important in determining whether the game may be legally offered online.

2. Slot Machines

Most slot machines in land-based casinos are set to deliver a random number on each of three or five "reels." In some cases, the images of reels are still actual circular components with numbers and symbols. But today, the majority are mainly computer-generated images. The first slot machines required an insertion of a coin. Modern versions, however, take advantage of computer technology to accept larger amounts in *de facto* accounts.

3. Banked Table Games

Card games in particular can be classified as "banked," on the one hand, and non-banked on the other hand. In a banked, or banking, game, the players compete against one player, usually the gaming establishment, rather than against one another. The term arises from the definition of a bank; in a banking game there is, literally, a fund of money against which players bet. The banker does not initially place a bet. Instead, the banker "fades" or matches, up to the house limits, the bets made by the players.

4. Sports Betting

Contests of speed, strength, and endurance between men, beasts, and machines are a natural subject of wagers, both by participants and onlookers, and the practice dates back to the beginning of human society.

Informal, social wagering is practically universal, and not a particular target of law enforcement. Sports wagering as an organized business is another matter. Periodic attempts by professional gambling rings and organized crime to "fix" or "throw" games in various ways have given the trade a lurid reputation (see The Black Sox Scandal of 1919, where it was alleged that professional gamblers influenced the Chicago White Sox baseball team in such a way that they "threw" the World Series; see the movie *Eight Men Out*).

The question of which states allow sports betting is of more than passing importance. The Professional and Amateur Sports Protection Act (PASPA) (28 U.S.C.A. §§ 3701–3704 (2000)), prohibits any state or Indian tribe from offering sports betting. However, the Act grandfathers in all existing forms of sports wagering, defined as any type of gambling on sports events authorized by a state "at any time during the period beginning January 1, 1976, and ending August 31, 1990." So, the question becomes which states had legal sports betting between 1976 and August 31, 1990. In November 2011 the voters of New Jersey, which had not been grandfathered-in, approved legalizing sports betting. The necessary legislation was passed and signed into law in January 2012, allowing the state to file a constitutional challenge to PASPA in federal court.

5. Bingo

The traditional game of bingo has consistently been viewed as gambling, although many times it remained legal only because it was used for charitable purposes. However, its most recent significance emanates from the ongoing discussion of its legality in the context of Indian gambling under the Indian Gaming Regulatory Act (IGRA), 25 U.S.C.A.

§§ 2701 *et seq.* (2008), and the development of gaming devices that play much like slot machines, although they are technically bingo. Potential difficulties in this area center on the difference between what is categorized as IGRA Class II gambling (bingo and non-banked card games) and Class III (lotteries and the full assortment of casino games including slots, table games, etc.) The legal difference is that a tribe may open Class II gaming without its "home states" permission, provided only that the gambling is permitted by that state's laws. The term "Class II machine" has become so common that it is used in jurisdictions like South America, which have no Class I or Class II games, since they are obviously not covered by the IGRA.

6. Horse and Dog Racing

Parimutuel betting on horse and dograces has a long and somewhat honorable history. Simulcasting, a short hand for "simultaneous broadcast," consists of the broadcast of a live race to a remote site, allowing bettors to wager at that site, as well at the track where the race is being conducted. Simulcasts require the instantaneous transmission of wagering information, so that bettors at one location will not gain an unfair advantage. The parimutuel industry divides simulcasting into two categories: inter-track wagers, where a person has to go to one track to bet on races taking place at another track; and true-off track betting, which includes stand-alone OTB parlors, as in New York City, and at-home wagering. The racing industry usually calls remote wagering on horseracing as Advanced Deposit Wagering, or ADW.

F. Generally Recognized as Gambling

1. Poker

The question of whether poker is a game of skill has resonated throughout the years. Essentially, skillful players will win more often over the long run. The case of *Indoor Recreation Enterprises, Inc. v. Douglas*, 194 Neb. 715, 235 N.W.2d 398 (1975), is a somewhat typical type of case in that it holds that poker is predominately a game of chance using the short-term time frame. Poker is a game of chance in the sense that the next card could be any card among the remaining 51 cards; however, this ignores poker's unique and enduring quality of bluffing. Recent studies have shown that, in fact, most rounds of poker are resolved without players having to show whether or not they have the best hands.

2. Pyramid Schemes Held to be Illegal Lotteries

The classic "Ponzi," or pyramid scheme (see Bernie Madoff), has been held to be "gambling," and an illegal lottery. The Ponzi is a swindle where the initial investors in an "investment opportunity" earn attractive returns, but since there is no underlying business, older investors are paid with the money "invested" by new suckers. The pyramid scheme should probably be more correctly categorized as a fraud, although the argument can be made that it is gambling, since first investors do make money, so long as they do not reinvest their payouts.

G. Generally Not Recognized as Gambling

1. Future and Proposition Betting Generally

Trading on stock and commodities markets appears to be very similar to gambling. In fact, in the eyes of most state laws, it is gambling. For decades, the U.S. Supreme Court struggled to uphold commodities futures contracts against challenges that they were unenforceable gambling contracts under state law, *see e.g., Bibb v. Allen*, 149 U.S. 481, 13 S.Ct. 950, 37 L.Ed. 819 (1893). Congress eventually enacted the federal securities laws, including express exemptions for puts, calls, options, and other securities and commodities traded on a national exchange from being outlawed by state laws (15 U.S.C.A. § 78bb). Even trading in stock index futures, where investors bet on which way the stock market will go and there cannot, by law, be physically delivery of the stock or any other product, by federal statute is not gambling.

2. Day Trading

Speculative trading on foreign legal exchanges are not covered by these federal preemptions of state laws and thus are still illegal under some state anti-gambling statutes. The sellers of shares on foreign exchanges are often called "bucket shops." In a true bucket shop, the order is not actually placed with a foreign exchange; rather the operator simply accepts the bet of the patron on which way the patron thinks the security will go.

Individual investors through Internet access can legally become "day traders" on listed markets, buying and selling securities such as stocks, bonds, and futures in the markets, directly online for their own account. The risks, behaviors, and fates of many online "day traders" are indistinguishable from those of online gamblers.

3. Multi–Level Marketing

Network or multi-level marketing (MLM) has been a feature of the commercial landscape since about 1950. It is allegedly an arrangement of independent sales representatives; it differs from the standard sales organization in that "override" or "downline" commissions are awarded to the initial organizers on the sales of the representatives that are recruited, and those of the sub-representatives that they recruit in turn. Where the right to receive rewards is based solely on recruitment that is completely unrelated to product sales, a company is in danger of violating FTC guidelines for the prevention of pyramid schemes.

4. Prediction Markets

On the other extreme from pyramid schemes, is the experiment, or prediction market. These markets allow you to put up money and win (or lose), when you make a prediction. In 1988, the University of Iowa's Henry B. Tippie College of Business faculty created the Iowa Electronic Market (IEM), which was designed to be an educational and research project. The IEM allows players to bet real money on unpredictable future events in the hopes of winning bigger money, which is the classic definition of gambling. Instead of betting on the future price of commodities or bundles of stock, traders buy and sell events, like the U.S. presidential election. The IEM prices have proven to be amazingly accurate predictors. The federal Commodity Futures Trading Commission (CTFC) issued a "no-action" letter to the IEM, stating that as long as the IEM conforms to certain guidelines, the CFTC will take no action against it.

5. Insurance

Historically, insurance was a form of gambling. The purchaser of an insurance policy pays a small amount, called a premium, and receives a much larger amount if a certain event, outside of the purchaser's control, takes place. Of course, today most of the time the insured does not want that future event to occur. During the 19th century courts developed doctrines like the insured interest rule to distinguish true insurance from mere betting on future events. The insurance industry is almost as regulated as gambling, but, today, it is not viewed as gambling.

6. Auctions

Auctions are another form of activity that resembles gambling, but are not gambling. For example, the auction model of real estate sales, which historically was limited to involuntary sales for past taxes and mortgage loan defaults, but now has segued into the fields of voluntary real estate auctions. Another example is auctions of thoroughbred horses. E.g., the annual thoroughbred auction market in the United States is comprised of the sale and purchase of approximately 20,000 horses at 150 individual sales for gross revenues in excess of 1.3 billion dollars.

H. Internet

1. What Type of Game Is It?

Gambling can be divided into three basic formats based on style of play: lotteries, wagers, and gaming. All lotteries are gambling, but not all forms of gambling are lotteries. The same holds true for gaming and wagering. Lotteries and games of chance depend on the generation of random numbers within set parameters: possible results available from 52 cards, two dice, three reels, etc. Sports betting depends on odds and payoff calculations, measured against results transmitted in real-time. All three formats are readily adaptable to the Internet.

2. Jurisdiction

In the relatively typical situation of four online poker players from four different countries, (including a player from California), using a server based in Antigua, the question is, what nation has jurisdiction over whom, and why? Until December 2011, the position of the United States government was that the operation was technically in violation of American law because all Internet gambling violated the Wire Act (18 U.S.C.A. § 1804). Two days before Christmas, the U.S. Department of Justice announced that it had re-evaluated and was reversing its position that the Wire Act covers all gambling of any kind. With the Wire Act now limited to bets on sports events, prosecutors have to find there is a violation of a specific state law, and an organization involved in interstate commerce, to create a federal crime. See, for example, 18 U.S.C. § 1955.

Even when the federal government tried to eliminate all Internet gaming using the Wire Act, prosecutors had problems. The Wire Act has an exception for bets that are legal on both ends. Online poker is legal *and* licensed in Antigua. So, even if the Wire Act covers poker, criminal liability for the operation depends upon a state gambling law being violated first. And that depends on whether a poker game hosted from Antigua is deemed "a controlled game exposed for play" within, for example, California, *see*, CAL. PENAL CODE § 337j(a)(1) (2008). From there, "exposed for play" must be defined; which causes problems because of the wording of the statute which mimics similar problems that exist in many other states. Another presumption is in play here; namely, whether state statutes like California's anti-gambling laws, reach outside the borders of the state.

3. Online Games

The best known online gaming sites are those that allow poker play. Online poker sites are now a powerful presence in the online gambling market. These sites allow anyone with an Internet connection to download a program that enables them to play poker with other players anywhere in the world. But any form of gambling that exists in the real world also exists in hyperspace.

4. Virtual Worlds

The assorted video/FRPG (fantasy role playing games) combinations, applied to personal computers (''PCs'') have been strengthened by digital technology. Also known as ''persistent games'' or ''synthetic worlds,'' they represent a new social phenomenon whose impact is only now becoming apparent.

5. Massively Multiplayer Online Games (MMOGs)

Massively Multiplayer Online Games (MMOGs), and their successful subset, Massively Multiplayer Online Role–Playing Games (MMORPGs), are server-based mega programs with platforms that accommodate hundreds of thousands of players simultaneously interacting in real time with the ''virtual world'' and with each other. The possibilities of

MMORPGs are as vast as the games themselves. Players purchase the particular software for the world, install it in their PCs and subscribe online via credit card to the online service. Contests and tournaments for cash prizes are now a standard feature of the video gaming world.

I.   Mode of Play

Another means of differentiating various forms of online gambling is how the game is played; with, or against, whom.

1.   Against the House

Most forms of commercial gambling involve patrons betting against the house. With casino and similar games, this is known as a house banking game. Non-banking table games, also known as "round" games are much less common. The one exception is true poker, where the house cannot participate. The most common forms of sports betting involve bettors betting straight up against the bookmaker. There, the sports book acts as the house, setting the odds, collecting from the losing patrons and paying the winners. The sports book makes its money in the same way that a casino percentage game: it pays the winner less than the full odds.

2.   Pooling

Most traditional lottery games involved pools, where the prize was created by the bets, minus a share for the operator. Horse racing took this idea to the next level with the creation first of Calcutta pools or auctions; a primitive form of parimutuel betting, still popular with golf bettors. In a Calcutta, where players bid for the right to "own" a house; the favorite would go for the greatest amount, say $100, while a long-shot might get no bid over $2. The pool of money went to the winner, minus, of course, the operator's percentage. Race wagering today is primarily conducted with computers calculating parimutuel odds.

3. Games With More Than One Characteristic

Bingo, for example, is normally a pooling game. But bingo jackpots commonly have banking game characteristics, with the house putting up the money for a big prize if a difficult to achieve pattern, like a cover-all, is won by a player in a predesignated, small number of balls being drawn.

4. Computer Simulations

Almost all gambling games require some form of random number generator (RNG). Traditionally, these have been dice and cards or spinning wheels. Today, formerly electromechanical slot machines use internal computers as RNGs. An online establishment can simulate the probabilities of any game through computerized RNGs, although the image seen on the bettor's screens appear to be dice, cards, or spinning wheels, creating virtual table games, such as craps, roulette, or blackjack, as well as virtual slots and video poker. An RNG and an animation sequence are combined to furnish a simulation of the dice roll, card draw, slot pull, or what have you, and the process appears as an animated simulation on the player's PC monitor. A great deal of effort is put into reproducing the "look and feel" of a craps table, roulette wheel, or video poker machine.

5. Interactive Person-to-Person

By 1999, enough broadband was available to allow person-to-person (P2P) games to be offered to the general public. Poker was first out, and continues to hold first place in P2P games by its huge popularity. Texas Hold'em became the most popular poker game as the result of being televised in the World Series of Poker. The game was one of the favorite games of the professional poker players in the early games, plus it had up-cards, allowing viewers to have some idea of what was going on. Other poker staples, such as 7–card and 5–card draw, also are easily simulated online. As with other kinds of online gaming, betting is allowed on an account system. The Internet allowed the creation of large-scale, commercial P2P betting exchanges. These provide a neutral service for a private wager between individuals. The service matches, for a fee, two or more patrons who want to wager on opposite teams in an upcoming game, often with point spreads or other inducements to encourage betting on the underdog.

6. Computer Skill Games

Many different computer games and even formats share the confusingly broad appellation of "skill games." It is understandable when the term applies to "first-person shooters" such as DOOM® and arcade-style games which require good hand-eye coordination, and to PC-based military strategy and role-playing games, which emphasizes teamwork and planning. Even more confusing, some of these skill games offer prizes and are part of advertising campaigns. Because the element of chance is not predominant and because there is no history linking them to social problems or criminal activity, skill or amusement games are not considered to be gambling in most U.S. jurisdictions. The lack of gambling "action" limits the direct income from such games. But since they are "clean," the lure of gaming competition and prizes represents a powerful marketing tool with very substantial profit potential.

CHAPTER 2

GAMBLING AND THE LAW®

The phrase, Gambling and the Law® is a federal-ly registered trademark, granted to one of this book's co-authors, Professor I. Nelson Rose. The law of gambling has become an important topic of scholarly interest, mostly as a result of the trend of state after state turning to legal gambling as an important source of revenue. The explosion of legal gambling is a worldwide phenomenon. Today, in 2012, Macau is the preeminent international casino zone, far surpassing Las Vegas, with Singapore, which has only two casinos, not far behind.

A. The Why and How Behind America's Most Regulated Industry (i.e., Gambling)

The federal government has a hand in regulating gambling, but mainly to assist states in enforcing their public policies. Thus, it is state laws and local ordinances that have the most impact on gaming. Most crimes, for example, including most anti-gam-bling laws, are still solely the responsibility of the various states.

No industry in America is as heavily regulated as legalized gambling, including atomic power plants. However, regulation is by no means uniform; startling differences exist between regions of the country, or even between various games played within a single state. The answers to the question, "why regulate at all?" are usually answered by the standard responses that regulations ensure the competency of the operators, while keeping organized crime out. The government has essentially two ways to go: state ownership or private control.

B. Short History of American Gambling

Legal gambling in America began during the Colonial period. Although it is not far-fetched to say that "American" gambling began in England in 1710 when the Statute of Anne was passed, which was designed to attack gambling and protect wealthy landowners by prohibiting winners from using the courts to collect gambling debts; it made all gambling contracts unenforceable in all common law jurisdictions. Thus, this 300–year–old English statute is still of great importance to gamblers in modern America because the Statute of Anne is now a part of the common law of each state.

C. The Waves of Legalization

There have been three distinguishable waves of legalized gambling in the United States; the second period was clouded with scandal, and caused "prohibition"—like reactions that have only ended with the latest legal gambling boom, which includes casino gaming, state lotteries, games on Native American reservations, and Internet gambling.

1. Lotteries and Foundations

The First Wave of legalized gambling ended during those decades immediately prior to the Civil War; in fact, the colonies were partially financed by public lotteries, and notable founding fathers such as George Washington, Benjamin Franklin and Thomas Jefferson sponsored private lotteries.

Following the Revolution, American gambling of all kinds gradually fell into disrepute. Lotteries in particular bred a series of scandals. Cheating and fraud became so widespread that the public demanded that lotteries be outlawed. States changed their constitutions to expressly prohibit state legislators from authorizing lotteries.

2. Federal Intervention and Frontier Gambling

As a reaction to lottery scandals, the federal government intervened; in fact, the federal government still has a law on its books, 18 U.S.C. § 1304, prohibiting the broadcasting of almost all advertising of lotteries in states like Nevada, which do not have a state lottery. (In the past, the Federal Communications Commission used to keep legal casinos and bingo games off of radio and television. The U.S. Supreme Court finally declared this statute unconstitutional, when it prevented a state-licensed casino from broadcasting its commercials in the very state that issued it its license. *Greater New Orleans Broadcasting Association, Inc. v. United States*, 527 U.S. 173, 119 S.Ct. 1923, 144 L.Ed.2d 161 (1999). The federal Department of Justice followed this decision by announcing that it would not prosecute under this statute any television or radio advertisement by a state-licensed casino, even in states without legal casinos.)

The Second Wave of legal gambling ran in the South from Reconstruction to the turn of the 20th Century. Meanwhile, the "Wild West" often had wide-open gambling other than lotteries. Frontier societies always had gambling, although it was sometimes merely tolerated rather than actually legalized.

3. Lottery Scandals and Federal Law

The Second Wave of legal gambling started with the Civil War. The defeated south looked to gambling, and in particular, lotteries, as a painless way to raise needed funds. Unfortunately, this Second Wave broke in scandal after scandal; the largest and most notorious scandal involved the Louisiana Lottery of the 1890s, where the promoters of the Louisiana Lottery, a private company, attempted to bribe the Louisiana State Legislature, which resulted in the imposition of stiff federal laws and state constitutional restrictions. The other states responded with laws against selling lottery tickets within their borders, even if the drawing was legal elsewhere. Territories and states in the western U.S. outlawed their casinos to become respectable in the eyes of the East Coast.

4. Gambling is Reborn

The Third Wave of legislation began in 1931, when the Great Decession devastated the states and Nevada re-legalized casinos. In the 1930s, states reopened their racetacks. The majority of states now allow betting on horses; some states allow parimutuel betting on dograces and jai alai. In fact, most states now allow off-track betting (OTB), also called Advance Deposit wagering (ADW), with New York leading the way. In December 2000, Congress amended the Interstate Horseracing Act to allow states to decide whether they would permit betting by phone and computers; a majority of states have opted in.

In 1964, the state lottery was rediscovered, with the creation of the New Hampshire Sweepstakes. To legalize parimutuel betting on horseraces and later state lotteries, many states had to amend their constitutions. This Third Wave of legal gambling has swept in the charities, and in an unusual development, federally recognized Indian tribes. Developments in the Third Wave have been casino gambling, state lotteries, video machines, Internet gambling, commercial sweepstakes, gambling tournaments, charity and Indian bingo, and the rapid growth of legal card rooms, particularly poker.

D. Whales and the Law

The phenomenon of Las Vegas, Reno, Atlantic City, and international casinos has also developed the phenomenon of luring the high rollers, or big fish (hence, "whales") to a particular casino. All types of inducements (e.g., comp hotels, free first class travel, etc., etc.) will be used to lure these whales. Local ordinances have been promulgated to assist the casinos in catching the whales, who can afford to lose millions in a weekend, and can literally make or break a casino, at least in the short term. There are even "whale hunters," individuals who wrangle the industry's biggest players and set them up to risk millions of dollars in games in which the long-term odds are hopelessly tilted against them.

The misnamed Bank Secrecy Act, which actually requires reporting, not secrecy, was designed to go after drug dealers and other criminals, long before the current pre-occupation with Islamist terrorists. Under the Bank Secrecy Act ("BSA") (31 U.S.C.A. ch. 53) and its regulations (31 CFR Chapter X, 75 FR 65806 et seq.) banks and other financial institutions are required to keep track of and report large and suspicious financial transactions to the federal government. As the U.S. Treasury's main enforcer, the Financial Crimes Enforcement Network ("FinCEN"), puts it, the BSA "requires U.S.A. financial institutions to assist U.S. government agencies to detect and prevent money laundering."

Because American licensed casinos deal with cash, Treasury has defined gaming operators as "financial institutions" under the BSA. They are thus required, by regulation, to file Currency Transaction Reports Casinos ("CTRCs") when patrons have more than $10,000 in cash and Suspicious Activities Reports Casinos ("SARCs") when they know or should know that a financial activity has occurred which the government thinks is suspicious. So, American casinos often have to file reports with government agencies revealing the identities of their high rollers.

Whales also create interesting civil and criminal cases. A former Nebraska philanthropist, turned Whale, who lost hundreds of millions of dollars gambling, was charged with writing bad checks when his final markers for less than $15 million were not honored. Naturally, the casino also filed a civil suit. The Whale filed a counterclaim, alleging the casino, now owned by Harrah's Entertainment, allegedly plied him with alcohol and prescription drugs to keep him on the casino floor. *Watanabe v. Harrah's Entertainment Inc. et al.,* No. A–09–603929–B, *complaint filed* (Nev. Dist. Ct., Clark County Nov. 19, 2009). Terry Watanabe says Harrah's executives knew he had a gambling addiction and took advantage of it by giving him a nonstop supply of booze and painkillers while he lost more than a hundred million dollars at roulette and slot machines.

E. Illegal Gambling

Nowhere are the nation's ambivalent feelings about gambling more evident than with the criminal laws. On their face, criminal laws look pretty tough; almost all forms of public or commercial gambling are illegal, except those specifically licensed. Even most forms of private gambling are criminal, although there has been a great relaxation in the laws against purely social betting.

Illegal Internet gambling appears to come within the reach of the federal Illegal Gambling Businesses Act ("IGBA") (18 U.S.C.A. § 1955). The elements of § 1955 apply to anyone who: (1)(a) conducts, (b) finances, (c) manages, (d) supervises, (e) directs, or (f) owns; (2) all or part of an illegal gambling business that; (3)(a) is a violation of the law of a state or political subdivision in which it is conducted, (b) involves five or more persons who conduct finance, manage, supervise, direct, or own all or part of such business, and (c) has been or remains in substantially continuous operation for a period in excess of 30 days or has a gross revenue of $2,000 in any single day. The section bars only those activities that involve illegal gambling under applicable state law and that meet the statutory definition of a business. Although this federal statute requires that there be five or more individuals involved, charges can also be brought under theories of accomplice liability and for the separate crime of conspiracy, 18 U.S.C.A. § 371. The IGBA can be applied only to offshore Internet gambling operations when the gambling activity is illegal under a state law where either the bettor or the gambling operations are located.

The Organized Crime Act of 1970, Pub. Law 91–452, 84 Stat. 922, enacted by Congress on October 15, 1970, added the IGBA and contains additional legislation pertaining to many facets of organized crime. These include making syndicated gambling and racketeer-influenced and corrupt organizations a crime, authorizing special grand juries, protecting housing for government witnesses, and imposing special offender sentencing. The House Report on the Organized Crime Control Act of 1970 states that the intent of the IGBA was to deal only with illegal gambling activities of major proportions and with corrupt state and local officials who make it possible for them to operate.

It has been held that one who participates in the operation of a gambling business may be counted toward the five-person requirement of the statute whether or not he had knowledge of the involvement of five or more persons in the operation of the business (§ 5); whether or not he has been named, indicted, or convicted in a criminal prosecution (§ 6); and whether or not he had any control of the gambling business (§ 8). The five-person requirement of the statute may also be affected by the provision of 18 U.S.C.A. § 1955(b)(1)(iii) that a gambling operation is only prohibited by the statute if it has been or remains in substantially continuous operation for at least 30 days or has a gross revenue of $2000 on any single day (§ 7).

1. Crime Organizations

Senator Estes Kefauver's well-publicized investigation in 1950 of organized crime and gambling, as featured in *Godfather II*, created the Johnson Act, 15 U.S.C.A. §§ 1171–1178, which makes it a federal crime to transport an illegal gambling device across a state line.

2. Wire Schemes

Wire schemes, as showcased in *The Sting*, was made a crime as part of Attorney General Robert F. Kennedy, Jr.'s war on organized crime in 1961. The Wire Act, 18 U.S.C.A. § 1084, was designed to go after "the Wire," i.e. the telegraph wire services illegal bookies used to get horserace results before their patrons. David G. Schwartz, CUTTING THE WIRE: GAMING PROHIBITION AND THE INTERNET (Reno: University of Nevada Press, 2005). This can be seen in the operative language of the first section of the statute; it is a crime if anyone "engaged in the businesses of betting or wagering knowingly uses a wire communication facility for the transmission in interstate or foreign commerce of bets or wagers or information assisting in the placing of bets or wagers on any sporting event or contest..."

Criminal prosecutions require a statute making the activity illegal. Lacking anything better, until 2011, the federal Department of Justice has mainly relied on the Wire Act in its fight against Internet gambling. One of the most widely known of federal Internet gambling prosecutions, *United States v. Cohen*, 260 F.3d 68 (2d Cir. 2001), *cert. den.*, 536 U.S. 922, 122 S.Ct. 2587, 153 L.Ed.2d 777 (2002), involved the conviction of a licensed offshore, online sports book under the Wire Act. However, the "Black Friday" indictments, revealed on Friday, April 15, 2011, against the founders and principals of the largest online poker operators then taking money bets from the U.S., did not mention the Wire Act. Instead, the U.S. Attorneys relied on the Illegal Gambling Businesses Act and the more recently passed Unlawful Internet Gambling Enforcement Act ("UIGEA") (18 U.S.C.A. §§ 1563 and 1566). And in December 2011, Justice announced that it had reevaluated its position and would only apply the Wire Act to interstate sports betting.

3. Official Corruption

An example of official corruption would be bribes to government officials to allow licenses or to remove people from the Black Book, etc. There were many examples of official corruption in the movie, *Casino*, a slightly fictional version of the non-fiction book by the same name.

F. How Internet Gambling Developed

Online casinos and sports books operate on an account basis and therefore require an initial "post-up" by credit card, debit card, wire transfer or other means. Since these funds must be in place before any bets can be taken, this would constitute consideration by any standard in a civil suit. There are, on the other hand, "free games," offered online, used as a form of marketing by various sites. Games that are completely free, like many online bingo games giving small prizes, are almost universally legal, and in the jurisdictions which might still find consideration in the effort players have to make, law enforcement does not care. Some sites allow players to obtain a small number of chips for free, but most play is with chips purchased by credit cards. Nonetheless, the free alternative means of entry (FAME or AMOE) makes the games non-gambling, like no-purchase-necessary sweepstakes, under some state laws and under federal laws as well. Participation in these "free" games often involves transfer to one or more additional web sites, with attendant barrages of "pop-up" ads, banners, and assorted other come-ons. This should not constitute participation in gambling, because it lacks consideration. With the widespread availability of free Internet access in libraries, every state has held that merely being required to play online by itself does not amount to consideration.

G. The State as Operator and the Internet Revolution

American gambling's "Third Wave" had its roots in the Depression. Searching for revenue without raising taxes, 21 states once again moderated their opposition to gambling and opened racetracks with parimutuel betting in the 1930s; additional states have added parimutuel betting in every decade since. Nevada brought back casino gambling in 1931. New Hampshire re-instituted a state lottery in 1963. New Jersey legalized casinos in 1976; the Indian Gaming Regulatory Act solidified the rights of Federally recognized tribes to do the same in 1988. The legacies of the Third Wave seem to be the entry of U.S. state governments into the gambling market as participants, further presence of the federal law, and use of the Internet. The Third Wave coincided with and was accelerated by the advent of computers, world telecommunications networks, and finally the Internet and mobile phones. Modern technology makes borders between states and nations little more than lines on a map, while bringing gambling into everyone's home. The Internet cannot be stopped or blocked; gambling is an established feature of a global economy.

CHAPTER 3

THE U.S. CONSTITUTION, FEDERAL LAWS AND GAMING

An original idea inherent to our democratic form of government is that the federal government cannot always do something because the states have not yet agreed to relinquish or delegate that particular power. The federal government is a government of limited power; limited not only by the Bill of Rights, but also because the people and the states have not authorized that power in the U.S. Constitution. Of course, many of these limitations have been eroded away by acts of Presidents, Congress passing laws creating a massive federal bureaucracy, and opinions of the U.S. Supreme Court.

For gamblers, the expansion of federal jurisdiction means that the use of a means of interstate commerce, such as a telephone line, gives the federal authorities the power to intervene; and the federal courts are even more creative in finding federal jurisdiction. There are two major restrictions on federal power: one is the Constitution, and the other is the practical restriction of the limits that face Congress due to a lack of time, interest and politics.

Federal laws are the supreme law of the land; in a direct conflict between a valid act of Congress and a state law, the state law must give way. But even federal laws are subject to the restrictions imposed by the Constitution.

A. Fundamental Rights

1. The Power to Regulate Interstate Commerce

Although it appears that the Interstate Commerce Clause of the Constitution may have lost most of its practical and immediate thunder, there are still parts of the Constitution that have great practical force. For example, Congress cannot violate an individual's right of free speech; of course, it is up to the courts to decide whether free speech has been violated. The second, practical limitation on the federal government's power is relevant because there is only a limited amount of time to deal with a tremendous number of pressing problems, and gambling is almost never a high priority. Even matters solely under the control of Congress, such as Indian gaming, might not always be deemed a pressing political priority. In fact, when it finally was forced to face the question of what to do about tribal gaming, due to a U.S. Supreme Court case, Congress decided to let the public policies of the individual states determine what forms of gambling tribes in those state could operate.

Even with the help of the federal bureaucracy, not every matter of potential federal interest can be studied and dealt with; additionally there are political pressures, and some issues, like gambling, seem to be best left with the states. A co-author asserts that "I have no doubt that Congress could completely outlaw virtually every form of gambling overnight, simply by declaring every commercial bet illegal under its power to regulate interstate commerce. Such a complete prohibition would not violate the Constitution; Congress would not be taking away a fundamental right like free speech, it would only be taking away your privilege to gamble. But rest assured fellow gamblers, this will *never* happen because of those political pressures just mentioned."

2. Due Process and Equal Protection

It is often alleged by unsuccessful applicants for casino licenses, that they were denied due process of the law. E.g. *Jacobson v. Hannifin*, 627 F.2d 177 (9th Cir. 1980). But there is no property right in merely applying for a license, and states have enormous power to decide whether and how gambling will be regulated, under their police power. A gambling license is a privilege, not a right. *Barry v. Barchi*, 443 U.S. 55, 99 S.Ct. 2642, 61 L.Ed.2d 365 (1979). There is an important factor of timing. There is no property right in a mere application for a casino license. *Rosenthal v. Nevada*, 514 F.Supp. 907 (D.Nev. 1981). However, once a license has been issued, it cannot be taken away without first giving the licensee due process notice and hearings required by the U.S. Constitution.

Another common claim is that the unsuccessful applicant was denied equal protection, usually with similar unsuccessful results in the courts. And many who are included in state "Black Books," which exclude individuals from entering on casino property, often argue that their inclusions violates the equal protection clause of the 14th Amendment; again, these legal arguments do not normally succeed.

Consistency is not always required. For example, in *Brainerd Area Civic Ctr. v. Commissioner of Revenue*, 499 N.W.2d 468 (Minn. 1993), the court upheld a graduated gross receipts tax on charitable gambling under the federal equal protection clause, distinguishing it from a similar tax on for-profit gambling that had been held unconstitutional.

Although most government classifications must meet only the "reasonableness" test, suspect classifications such as race, religion, and national origin which infringe upon a "fundamental right" such as travel, privacy, and speech must survive the more rigorous "strict scrutiny" test. Under that test, the classification must be "shown to be necessary to promote a *compelling* government interest" and must be "closely tailored to effectuate those interests."

Those included in the "Black Book" do not appear to belong to a particular racial, ethnic, or religious group and thus, will not constitute a suspect classification. This classification does infringe on the fundamental rights of association and travel and the protection from punishment on the basis of status; however, these interests do not appear sufficient enough to counterbalance the ends of the state in protecting the credibility and reputation of a state-run industry, which appear to be compelling.

Governments' police power can often seem nearly limitless. The power and perhaps obligation of a government—usually a state but also the federal government—to protect the health, safety, welfare and morality of its residents usually trump constitutional rights.

For example, in *Carroll v. State*, 361 So.2d 144 (Fla. 1978), the Supreme Court of Florida, held that a statute permitting non-profit and veterans' organizations to hold bingo games does not violate Due Process or Equal Protection Clauses and is constitutional despite the contention that it constitutes class legislation that is discriminatory, arbitrary, and without any reasonable relationship to the police power of the state. And, in *United States v. H.M. Branson Distributing*, 398 F.2d 929 (6th Cir. 1968), the Court of Appeals upheld the Gambling Devices Act against a challenge by a manufacturer and distributor of coin activated electrically operated pinball machines. That Act, which authorizes the seizure and forfeiture of gambling machines, was held to be not so vague and ambiguous as to violate the Due Process Clause of the Fifth Amendment (Gambling Devices Act of 1962, §§ 1–9, 7, 15

U.S.C.A. §§ 1171–1178, 1177; U.S.C.A. Const. Amends. 5–7).

B. First Amendment Freedom of Speech

The U.S. Supreme Court in *Greater New Orleans Broadcasting Ass'n v. United States*, 527 U.S. 173, 119 S.Ct. 1923, 144 L.Ed.2d 161 (1999), held that the federal prohibition on radio and television broadcast advertisements of private casino gambling violates the First Amendment where the advertisements are carried by radio or television stations in states where gambling itself is legal. The main reason was that there were so many exceptions to the ban, including the right of identical, but tribally owned, casinos to use T.V. and radio, that the federal statute, 18 U.S.C.A. § 1304, was legally irrational. The federal Department of Justice announced after the Supreme Court decision that it would not enforce those prohibitions even in states that did not have licensed casinos.

C. Federal Taxes and Mail Systems

The U.S. Treasury, mail systems, and federal taxes have also had their impacts on the legal status of gaming in the United States. Of course, 26 U.S.C.A. § 61 of the I.R.C. provides the basis for taxation of all income including gambling winnings. The main mail fraud statute, 39 U.S.C.A. § 3005, also gives the Postal Service the authority to intercept and return lottery mail. Although only state lotteries are exempted by the language of the statute, the Postal Service seems to be concerned primarily with illegal schemes, and not legal gambling. The government is greatly restricted under the Constitution from opening private mail.

D.   Internet Gambling

1.   Problems With Enforcement

Internet gambling allows people the comfort of gambling in their own homes. But, Internet gambling critics note that the nature of the Internet makes it easier for compulsive gamblers and children to gamble and increases the potential for money laundering.

In 1999, the National Gambling Impact Study Commission ("NGISC") found that a prohibition on Internet gambling would be the best solution in preventing problematic use by minors and pathological gamblers, as well as in curbing criminal activities. This recommendation, like all others from this Commission, has been completely ignored. The NGISC was filled with political appointees, including pro- and anti-gambling activists, and has been generally discredited. The NGISC's Final Report contains numerous misstatements of fact. Still, the NGISC did note, correctly, that current gambling laws are too ambiguous to cover Internet gambling or will soon be obsolete due to technological advances. Also the NGISC noted that ambiguities in the Indian Gaming Regulatory Act could lead to inconsistent state court interpretations on whether tribes have the ability to offer Internet gambling to individuals outside their reservations.

Even if the federal government prohibited Internet gambling, there would be major obstacles in enforcing such a ban. One of these obstacles is the international nature of the Internet gambling business. In 1999, at least 25 countries permitted Internet gambling. That number has now grown to more than 200 jurisdictions. The U.S. federal government would be infringing on the sovereignty of these foreign nations if it tried to unilaterally impose its anti-gambling laws on Internet operations conducted in those nations. Thus, without the support of these countries, it would be difficult to enforce an American prohibition on Internet gambling operated from abroad, even if gamblers from the United States were to place bets or wagers on these sites.

Part of the problem is also jurisdictional. The U.S. does not allow trials in absentia; it is both a constitutional and statutory right for a criminal defendant to confront witnesses. So, a criminal defendant must appear in court before he can be found guilty. There are almost no extradition treaties covering illegal gambling. And even if they did, extradition requires dual criminality: The activity must be a crime both in the foreign country and the U.S. No nation would extradite someone it licensed to stand trial in the U.S. for the very activity that the license was for.

There are many other plausible actions both Internet casino users and operators might take to remove themselves from the jurisdiction of the United States. Plus, there are additional problems with going after legal, overseas operator. Many are licensed by foreign countries, or even operated by those countries themselves. Finally, prohibiting Internet gambling might infringe on United States citizens' First Amendment rights.

2. The Wire Act, 18 U.S.C.A. § 1084

It is a crime if "anyone engaged in the business of betting or wagering knowingly uses a wire communication facility for the transmission in interstate or foreign commerce of bets or wagers on any sporting event or contest..." This was the major anti-gambling statute used by the federal Department of Justice in its war of intimidation against Internet gambling. But in a case involving consolidated class actions from across the U.S., a District Court and federal Court of Appeals ruled the Wire Act was limited to bets on sports events and races. *In re MasterCard International Inc.*, 313 F.3d 257 (5th Cir. 2002), affirming 132 F.Supp.2d 468 (E.D.LA. 2001). For ten years, the federal Department of Justice contended that it was not bound by this decision, because it had not been a party to the suit. But, in December 2011 the DOJ announced that it had officially reevaluated its position and that the Wire Act did not apply to information or wagers sent over telephone lines, including the Internet, except those related to sports betting.

The Wire Act applies to any wire communication across state lines. In *Martin v. United States*, 389 F.2d 895 (5th Cir. 1968), the defendants were a group of entrepreneurs: Some took sports bets in Texas, made phone calls to their partners in Las

Vegas, who then placed the bets with licensed bookies. The Court upheld convictions under the Wire Act, ruling Congress has the power to prevent all interstate wagers, even to Nevada where the bet would be legal. The federal statute was originally passed to help the states' enforce their anti-gambling policies. Today Nevada has to enforce special regulations to prevent out-of-state phone bets to prevent violations of the federal law.

3. UIGEA

The Unlawful Internet Gambling Enforcement Act ("UIGEA"), 31 U.S.C.A. §§ 5361–5367, was signed into law by President Bush on Friday October 13, 2006. The Act is title VIII of a completely unrelated bill, the SAFE Port Act, HR 4954, dealing with port security. Senate Majority Leader Bill Frist (R.–TN) rammed the UIGEA through Congress, apparently without even being proofread. According to Sen. Frank R. Lautenberg (D–NJ), the Republican leadership refused to let members of Congress read the final version, or even have the author or anyone else explain what the UIGEA would do.

Although the UIGEA scared all of the publicly traded Internet gambling operators out of the American market, the law actually does only two things. It creates one new crime, being in the business of gambling and accepting funds from bettors in connection with an unlawful Internet gambling transaction. And it called upon federal regulators to make regulations requiring money transferors to identify and block transactions to unlawful gambling websites. The regulators, the Board of Governors of the Federal Reserve System and the Secretary of the Department of the Treasury in consultation with the Department of Justice, found it was impossible to issue those regulations, since it is so difficult to determine whether a particular Internet gambling transaction is illegal. So, they issued final regulations, which went into effect on January 19, 2009, that merely require banks and other payment processors to do due diligence when setting up new commercial accounts. 12 C.F.R. Part 233 duplicated at 31 C.F.R. Part 132. (Banks and other payment processors were given an additional six months, until June 1, 2010, to implement procedures to comply with the final regulations).

The UIGEA expressly does not change state or federal substantive law; it is merely, as the name implies, an enforcement statute. But it was rushed through so quickly that it has actually led to an expansion of Internet gaming. Some forms, including fantasy sports, inter-tribal gaming and intrastate gaming, are expressly excluded from the UIGEA. Others, including contests of skill and games with free alternative means of entry, have expanded, since they are not considered gambling.

E.   Gambling on Indian Land

Gaming on Indian land involves difficult legal issues, many dating back to before the creation of the United States itself. States usually want their anti-gambling laws to apply to all land within their borders, including reservations. But the unique status of tribes as domestic nations complicates the relationship between tribes and the states, even if the gaming is restricted to Indian land. When tribal gaming seeks to include patrons outside the tribes' land, additional cross-border issues arise. In part due to the requirements of federal law, particularly the IGRA, tribes have had to often behave not as separate sovereigns, but as active participants in state-level politics, to protect their gaming markets.

For two centuries, Indian tribes had to be mostly concerned with their relationship with the federal government, and were much less concerned about their relationships with state governments. Indian tribes counted on the federal government to protect them from the rapacious settlers that sought to overrun Indian lands, as well as from the state governments that sanctioned such activity.

IGRA intentionally created a paradigm shift in Indian policy in the United States. In light of aggressive state political activities, the federal-tribal relationship has given way to a state-tribal relationship that has had far greater economic importance to many Indian tribes. For many tribes, legal gambling is the most significant economic resource available; it is the single most effective economic development mechanism that Indian country has ever known. The rise of Indian gaming has also forced the states to recognize and respect tribal governments and negotiate as equals, as required by IGRA.

F. The U.S. Supreme Court in the "Lottery Case" (1903)

The "Lottery Case" expanded the meaning of "interstate commerce." Decided in 1903, the Supreme Court ruled that the federal government had the power to regulate legal state lotteries, because the lottery tickets were shipped from one state to another, *see Francis v. United States*, 188 U.S. 375, 23 S.Ct. 334, 47 L.Ed. 508 (1903); and *Champion v. Ames*, 188 U.S. 321, 23 S.Ct. 321, 47 L.Ed. 492 (1903). This was the first major expansion of the power of the federal government to regulate a legal product, merely because it had an impact on interstate commerce. The result was the birth of modern America, where Congress, the President and the federal regulatory agencies have become involved in almost all areas of the life of the citizenry, even when little or nothing involved actually crosses a state line.

G. The Johnson Act, 15 U.S.C.A. §§ 1171–1178

The Johnson Act, created out of Senator Estes Kefauver's well-publicized investigation in 1950 of organized crime and gambling—the first televised Congressional hearings—makes it a federal crime to transport an illegal gambling device across a state line. The law requires that even legal manufacturers must register with the Attorney General and keep complete records of all buyers. The law applies to "any person engaged in the business of manufacturing gambling devices, if the activities of such business in any way affect interstate or foreign commerce." Section 1175 prohibits the use of gambling devices in the District of Columbia, within Indian country, and within U.S. territorial waters. Violations of the law result in confiscation and forfeiture, up to two years in prison, and a $5,000 fine.

H. Interstate Horseracing Act, 15 U.S.C.A. §§ 3001–3007

As regards to federal regulation of interstate off-track betting, Congress specifically found that "the states should have the primary responsibility for determining what forms of gambling may legally take place within their borders," and, "the federal government should prevent interference by one state with the gambling policies of another." Congress passed the Interstate Horseracing Act ("IHA") in 1978 to set up the framework so that states could decide for themselves whether they wanted to allow wagers on races taking place in other states. In December 2000, Congress amended the IHA to expressly give the states the power to decide whether they wanted their residents to be able to bet on horseraces by phone and computer. The federal government has no interest in horse racing beyond facilitating interstate bets. The statutes set up all sorts of requirements for legal, interstate OTB. For example, the law requires that an OTB office obtain the prior consent of the "host" racing association, the host racing commission, off-track racing commission, and all currently operating tracks within 60 miles of the OTB office; and, if there are no currently operating tracks then the closest currently operating track in an adjoining state. The federal Department of Justice has taken the position that the IHA does not "overrule" the Wire Act, and that it only authorizes remote wagering within a state: According to the DOJ, bettors can set up Advance Deposit Wagering accounts with OTB offices only if they are in the same state as the office, though they can bet on races taking place in other states. Everyone else who has looked at the IHA, including the World Trade Organization, in resolving a complaint by Antigua against the U.S., and the state racing commissions, have come to a completely different conclusion: that the IHA allows interstate wagers. In fact, if it did not, then all the state racing commissioners, who have approved cross-border wagers, would be committing felonies under the Wire Act.

I.   Casino Ships, 18 U.S.C.A. §§ 1081–1083

It used to be unlawful for a U.S. citizen, or anyone on an American vessel, or anyone on any vessel inside U.S. waters, to set up a gambling ship. This is an American law which had worldwide impact in the 1980s and 1990s; the gambling ships that ply the Caribbean could not be American flagships. It was passed in 1948 for the much more limited purpose of outlawing casino ships that anchored just outside the territorial waters of California. The Johnson Act also applies to slot machines onboard ships in U.S. territorial waters. Exceptions have now been carved out to allow day-trips to nowhere, outside the three-mile limit of state and federal jurisdiction. In 1991, U.S. flagships were allowed to operate casinos in international waters, but states could prevent the gambling, if the ship docked in that state's ports. In 1996, Congress again amended the Johnson Act to exempt certain cruises from state regulations. States still have some power to control gambling on the high seas through their power to regulate their docks.

J. Anti–Lottery Laws, 18 U.S.C.A. §§ 1301–1307

These are the main federal anti-lottery laws. Section 1301 makes it a federal crime to carry or send a lottery ticket, or lottery information, or a list of lottery prizes in interstate or foreign commerce. The statute was amended to allow states to operate interstate lotteries. Section 1302 specifically prohibits the use of the mails for the checks for the purchase of tickets, and for "any newspaper, circular, pamphlet, or publication of any kind containing any advertisement of any lottery, gift enterprise, or scheme of any kind offering prizes dependent in whole or in part upon lot or chance..." Postal employees cannot sell lottery tickets (§ 1303), and neither can other specified federal agencies (§ 1306). The Postal Service mainly limits its enforcement powers to illegal lottery-type schemes.

The FCC has not felt its power to be so limited. Section 1304 makes it a federal crime to broadcast "any advertisement or any information concerning any lottery, gift enterprise, or similar scheme," etc. The FCC has promulgated a formal ruling stating that radio and TV broadcast stations cannot carry lottery information. Informally, the FCC has interpreted the prohibition to apply to virtually every form of gambling, including all legal games such as bingo, and all casino advertising. Horseracing was exempted as a game of skill or a sport. Some casinos had taken to cable television since the FCC defined "broadcast" as not covering cable.

The Supreme Court's decision in *Greater New Orleans Broadcasting Ass'n v. United States*, 527 U.S. 173, 119 S.Ct. 1923, 144 L.Ed.2d 161 (1999), discussed above, greatly reduced the reach of these statutes. Today, tribal and state-licensed casinos can advertise over television and radio in every state; although, there are still some state anti-gambling laws, of questionable constitutionality, that might apply. But state lotteries are still limited to TV and radio stations with broadcast towers in states which have state lotteries. *United States v. Edge Broadcasting Co.*, 509 U.S. 418, 113 S.Ct. 2696, 125 L.Ed.2d 345 (1993). This creates the bizarre situation where Nevada casinos can run commercials over the air in Los Angeles, and California tribal casinos can advertise in Las Vegas; but the California State Lottery cannot run ads in Nevada, because Nevada does not have a state lottery.

The federal anti-lottery laws were so pervasive that Congress found it necessary to pass two special statutes, § 1305, exempting fishing contests, and § 1307, which is a limited exemption for legal state lotteries and promotional sweepstakes.

K. The Racketeering Statutes, 18 U.S.C.A. §§ 1951–1955

Federal laws are designed to help the states in their public policies toward gambling. The main target of the anti-gambling laws are organized crime. So, all federal statutes, except the Wire Act and the anti-lottery statutes, are expressly limited to gambling that is illegal under some other federal or state law. The Racketeering Statutes include the Hobbs Act (§ 1951) and the Travel Act (§ 1952); these statutes make it a federal offense to travel or use any facility in interstate or foreign commerce, including the mail, with intent to promote or carry on any unlawful activity. Section 1953 covers the interstate transportation of illegal wagering paraphernalia. Section 1955, part of the Organized Crime Control Act of 1970, makes it a federal crime to conduct or own a gambling business outlawed under state law.

L. Rico, 18 U.S.C.A. §§ 1961–1968

The Racketeer Influenced and Corrupt Organizations Act makes it a new federal crime if you commit two other specific crimes within the last ten years (one plus one equals three). The other crimes may be state or federal and include § 1955, or the use of threats to collect illegal gambling debts (§ 1951, the Hobbs Act). RICO also creates a new civil cause of action, and private companies have been suing each other, charging RICO for such things as violations of the federal securities laws.

M. Taxes on Wagering, 26 U.S.CA. §§ 4401–4424, 4901, 4902, 4904–4906, 6419, 7262

Sections 4401 to 4424 are Chapter 35 of the IRC, entitled "Taxes on Wagering." This chapter sets up special taxes on gambling both on bets placed and on the business side of the operation. There is an excise tax imposed on wagers; ¼ of 1% of the amount bet legally and 2% of illegal bets. The operator who runs the gambling game is liable for the tax, much the way a store owner acts as the tax collector—additionally, gambling operators must pay an occasional tax of $500 per year for illegal games and $50 per year for legal operators.

Every person required to pay these special taxes must register with the IRS and keep a daily record showing the wager's gross amount. The excise and occupational taxes apply to everyone who is engaged in the business of accepting wagers, except licensed parimutuels, coin-operated devices, and state lotteries. Games such as craps and poker are exempt under the strict definitions contained in § 4421, which defines "wager" and "lottery." The law is mainly concerned with bookies; however, § 6419 allows a credit for wagers laid-off to another.

N.   Professional and Amateur Sports Protection Act, 26 U.S.CA. §§ 3701 et seq.

This statute, known as PASPA, was added by Congress in 1992 expressly to prevent the proliferation of gambling games tied to sports events. Specifically, the states of Delaware and Oregon had begun taking bets on National Football League games through their state lotteries. Although the games did not attract large numbers of players, the NFL and other professional sports leagues and the National Collegiate Athletic Association fought these lotteries in court cases and through the political law-making process.

The PASPA expressly prohibits states from authorizing lotteries and other forms of gambling that are based on the outcomes of sports events or the performances of athletes. The language is as broad as possible, without being unconstitutionally overbroad. PAPSA does contain a number of express exceptions. Parimutuel betting on jai alai and on horse and dograces and sports betting does not fall under the PASPA and thus can continue and even proliferate. New Jersey was given one year to legalize sports betting in its casinos in Atlantic City, which it failed to do. Existing legal sports betting was grandfathered-in. No definitive list has ever been created as to what states had sports betting. The Third Circuit has ruled that states are limited to the specific form of sports wagers they were conducting in 1992. *ofc. Comm. Baseball v. Markell*, 579 F.3d 293 (3d Cir. 2009). It appears that the following have been grandfathered-in: Delaware and Oregon, State Lottery games based on parlays of three or more real-world games; Montana, State Lottery may run games based on sporting events and licensed operators may conduct other sports games, including sports tabs and sports; Nevada, licensed sports books with heads-up and parlay bets; New Mexico, "keirin," the Japanese word for parimutuel wagering on bicycle races; North Dakota, nonprofit organizations may run sports pools on professional sports events; Washington, anyone can conduct low-limit sports pools; qualified organizations may conduct calcuttas on amateur sports events.

The voters of New Jersey legalized sports betting in November 2011, and a statute authorizing the wagering was signed into law in January 2012. This allows a federal lawsuit to resume, which challenges the constitutionality of PASPA's ban on new games. A member of Congress from New Jersey has filed a bill to amend to PASPA to allow that state to have sports betting, and another would allow any state to legalize. Either of these would resolve the immediate dispute, but not answer the question of whether Congress has the power to discriminate in favor of a few states and prevent states from changing their public policy toward gambling.

CHAPTER 4

STATE CONSTITUTIONS, STATE LAWS, AND GAMING

The constitution of each state, along with state and federal laws, and to some extent, the U.S. Constitution, establish the parameters of the discussion of the legality of gaming in each jurisdiction. For example, according to the Georgia Constitution, all net proceeds from the State Lottery must be used to support educational programs and purposes, GA. CONST. art. I, § 2, para. 8. The Constitution specifies that Lottery proceeds be appropriated to the following five areas of educational programs: (1) university, college, and technical school tuition scholarships, loans, and grants; (2) pre-kindergarten programs; (3) one or more educational shortfall reserves, capped at 10% of the prior year's net Lottery proceeds allocable to educational programs; (4) costs of providing certain computer and technological training to educators; (5) and educational facilities capital spending. The greatest portion of Lottery proceeds has been spent for the scholarships, loans, and grants category; under which $3.6 billion has been appropriated for the Helping Outstanding Pupils Educationally (HOPE) program since the program's inception in 1993.

A. The Range of State Constitutions and State Laws Generally

In determining the meaning of a statute, the conditions under which the statute was adopted and the evil intended to be cured may be considered as materially explaining the purpose of the Legislature.

Under old slot machine laws in New York, the machine itself had to emit something in order to constitute a violation. The slot machine statute was enacted to completely suppress, and not to regulate, gambling of the type that existed at the time, by eliminating the machines manufactured and leased for gambling purposes. When the statute was updated, an amendment omitted the phrase, "from which [machine] ... may issue." Therefore, under the amendment it is no longer necessary that the machine be capable of emitting anything in order to be a slot machine and constitute a violation, N.Y. Penal Law, § 982, subds. 1(a), 2. Today, the possession of a coin-operated pinball game which has scoring method and register which can keep record of amount paid out, constitutes a violation of the statute prohibiting possession of a "slot machine," even though the device has no slot.

B. How State Constitutions Deal With Gaming

State constitutions are usually intentionally made difficult to amend; though not impossible. When there is strong public sentiment, such as when legal gambling crashed at the end of the fall of the First and Second Waves of Legal Gambling, prohibitions are often written into state constitutions. Because the particular form of gambling that was seen as creating problems in the 1840s and 1890s were lotteries, it is common to find language that states that the legislature shall never authorize a lottery. See, e.g., TENN. CONST. art. XI, § 5. A century or more later, these prohibitions have to be interpreted to determine whether a different form of gambling is a "lottery."

The two most important questions are what does a state constitutional prohibition on lotteries cover, and who decides. In the 1930s, these questions reached many of the states' highest courts, when legislatures attempted to legalize parimutuel betting on horseracing. In a typical case, the Illinois Supreme court ruled that the statute legalizing parimutuel wagering on horseraces did not contravene Illinois' constitutional prohibition against lotteries, *People v. Monroe*, 349 Ill. 270, 182 N.E. 439 (1932). Fifty years later, similar questions arose over riverboat casinos. Today, the disputes involve Internet gambling.

Fights have arisen over every conceivable form of gambling, and even activities that do not have chance, prize and consideration. For example, a statute exempting bona fide coin-operated amusement machines from criminal anti-gambling statutes went all the way to the Alabama Supreme Court, when entrepreneurs attempted to introduce amusement machines that played a lot like slot machines. The Court held the statute cannot be construed so as to legalize games in which skill does not predominate over chance in determining the outcome, since that construction would contravene Alabama's constitutional ban on lotteries. Const. Art. IV, § 65; Code 1975, §§ 13A–12–20 to 13A–12–76; *State ex rel. Tyson v. Ted's Game Enterprises*, 893 So.2d 355 (Ala. Civ. App. 2002), reh'g denied, (Mar. 21, 2003) and judgment aff'd, 893 So.2d 376 (Ala. 2004).

State lotteries are, of course, now legal. But states are desperate for additional sources of revenue. Governors and legislators have been looking to their state lotteries to bring in more money, either through new games, such as video lottery terminals ("VLTs"), or by the state selling the entire lottery to a private operator. The Rhode Island Supreme Court ruled that a proposed casino bill was valid, since it vested operational control in the State as required by the State constitution, where the bill allowed the State Lottery Division to hold the daily net gaming income, empowered the Division to monitor all gaming devices, and reserved for the Division the power to set the number of VLTs and non-slot table games to be played at the casino and to set the odds of winning. Const. Art. VI, § 15; *In*

re Advisory Opinion to House of Representatives,
885 A.2d 698 (R.I. 2005).

Other state constitutional provisions are often
raised by opponents of legal gambling. Many state
constitutions forbid "special legislation." The Illinois Supreme Court upheld an amendment to the
Riverboat Gambling Act requiring the Gaming
Board to allow only a single licensee, that was not
operating on January 1, 1998, to renew its license
and relocate its gambling operations. The Court
declared the amendment was rationally related to
the Act's economic goals of assisting development,
promoting tourism, and generating revenue for education; an amendment did not have to promote all
of an Act's goals to pass the rational basis test.
S.H.A. Const. Art. 4, § 13; S.H.A. 230 ILCS
10/11.2(a); *Crusius v. Illinois Gaming Bd.*, 216
Ill.2d 315, 297 Ill.Dec. 308, 837 N.E.2d 88 (2005).

Because most state constitutions have prohibitions on lotteries, the drive to legalize state lotteries
over the last half century has required amended
those state constitutions. But, even the express
authorization of a state lottery does not eliminate
problems later; for example, when the lottery wants
to introduce VLTs. And politically, proponents have
often had to include other language when proposing
a state lottery, to convince voters that this was not
opening the door for casinos. In *Hotel Employees
and Restaurant Employees Intern. Union v. Davis*,
21 Cal.4th 585, 981 P.2d 990, 88 Cal.Rptr.2d 56
(1999), the California Supreme Court was faced
with a state constitutional prohibition on "casinos

of the type currently operating in Nevada and New Jersey." Cal. Const., art. IV, § 19, subd. (e), added by initiative, Gen. Elec. (Nov. 6, 1984). The Court decided that the word "currently" meant the restriction was limited to what was a casino in 1984. It looked to a book written by one of this nutshell's co-author's, Professor I. Nelson Rose's 1986 GAMBLING AND THE LAW, and concluded that the blackjack and slot machine games proposed by the state's tribes were not "lotteries," but rather constituted casino banking games in violation of the State Constitution.

C. State Constitutions, State Laws and Gaming

Gambling is usually considered as being against public policy. So, exceptions are often read narrowly. Even if a state constitution allows legalization of a form of gambling, and the state legislature makes that gambling legal, it does not necessarily mean the gambling business has all the rights of other legal businesses. A casino license is often seen as merely protection from criminal prosecution, and does not give the license holder the right to sue to collect gambling debts. As far back as 1872, the Nevada Supreme Court interpreted a gaming statute in *Scott v. Courtney*, 7 Nev. 419 (1872), and held that the statute licensing gaming did not legalize gaming so as to render a debt recoverable. By the terms of the statute to restrict gaming, Stats. 1869, 119, Sec. 3, the legislature specially declared its intention, which was to protect any person having a license from criminal prosecution, and nothing more.

D. State Constitutions, State Laws and Lotteries

The first Nevada Constitution, originally adopted in 1864, stated that, "No lottery shall be authorized by this State, nor shall the sale of lottery tickets be allowed." NEV. CONST., art. 4, § 24 (amended 1990). But, this state constitutional ban on lotteries has not prevented Nevada from legalizing other forms of gaming, from time to time. Casinos were technically illegal when Nevada was a territory, and even after it became a state. But in its very first year, the State Legislature tried to legalize non-lottery gaming. It failed, but did reduced penalties for operators and completely exempted mere players. Five years later lawmakers succeeded in making casino gaming legal. Act of March 4, 1869, 71, Nev. Laws 119. But Nevada again outlawed all of its casinos in 1909, at the end of the Third Wave of Legal Gambling. Act of March 24, 1909, ch. 210, Nev. Laws 307. Then, in 1915, the Legislature made an exception for slot machines, that paid in cigars and drinks. Stats. 1915, c. 284. The rest of Nevada's gaming prohibition lasted until the Great Depression. In 1931, Nevada relegalized casinos, Act of March 19, 1931, c. 99, Nev. Laws 165 but, except for charity raffles, it has never allowed lotteries.

The state's constitutional ban on lotteries was tested in a friendly case in 1919. The Supreme Court of Nevada ruled that the Legislature did have the power to legalize "nickle-in-the-slot machines," because, under their interpretation, slot machines are not lotteries. The Court deferred to the decision of the Legislature. *Ex Parte Pierotti*, 43 Nev. 243, 184 P. 209 (1919). By pointing out that the Legislature has consistently had separate laws over other forms of gambling, the Court logically concluded that, at least under Nevada state law, lottery was not synonymous with gambling.

Nevada's construction of its constitution is perhaps best illustrated by its immediate legislative response to the enactment of the federal Johnson Act. Nevada took advantage of the provision in the Act that the sovereign states could enact laws excluding themselves from the application of the Act. The rationale for Nevada's exemption from the Johnson Act was a state legislative determination that gambling was "vitally important," as a matter of public policy, to the Silver State's economy and the general welfare of its inhabitants. The state Gaming Control Board, created in 1955, was specifically given the power to enforce Nevada public policy. Nevada then enacted legislation creating a gaming commission, *see* NEV. REV. STAT. § 463.022 (1991). This commission has the power to act as a quasi-judicial agency for licensing, determining factual issues, and making decisions on violations and punishment.

Nevadans amended their Constitution in 1990 by adding a provision that allowed the legislature to authorize persons to operate a lottery, provided that the net proceeds went directly to a charity or non-profit organization, *see* NEV. CONST. art. 4, § 24, cl. 2. But, the first sentence of Article 4, Section 24 still contains a prohibition on lotteries: "Except as otherwise provided in subsection 2, no lottery may be authorized by this State, nor may lottery tickets be sold," *see State ex rel. Murphy v. Overton*, 16 Nev. 136, 142 (1881). So, all the bingo and keno games and linked progressive slot machines found in Nevada casinos must not be "lotteries" under Nevada state law.

Other jurisdictions are free to define "lottery" differently. The federal government, for example, has held that the identical keno games are lotteries, at least for income tax purposes. And while Nevada courts have deferred to the State Legislature and decided the test for a "lottery" is whether a person can play the game without having to go to a particular place to participate, as in a casino, other states have imposed other tests.

In 1994, the Missouri Supreme Court had to decide whether that state's constitutional ban on lotteries precluded the statute legalizing riverboat casinos. The Court decided that the test for a lottery, at least in Missouri, is whether a game is pure chance. This opinion knocked out slot machines. What probably swung the Court was the inclusion by the Missouri Legislature of bingo in the list of permitted casino games. *Harris v. Missouri Gaming*

Com'n., 869 S.W.2d 58 (Mo. 1994). Missouri river-boat casino operators tried to operate with only blackjack and other gambling games which had elements of skill, although still predominantly chance. But they finally had to give up and sponsored more elections to amend the State Constitution to expressly allow casino "boats in moats."

E. State Constitutions, State Laws and Bingo

Gambling is not a constitutional right. As the Kansas Supreme Court declared in *Bingo Catering and Supplies, Inc. v. Duncan*, 237 Kan. 352, 699 P.2d 512 (1985), upholding a statute limiting bingo games on any one premise to three calendar days per week: No one has a constitutional right to operate bingo games every day.

Bingo has been one of the most important games in determining the limits of state constitutional prohibitions on "lotteries." The highest courts of states have split on whether bingo is a lottery, depending upon the test used. Compare *Secretary of State v. St. Augustine Church*, 766 S.W.2d 499 (Tenn. 1989) with *Greater Loretta Imp. Ass'n v. State ex rel. Boone*, 234 So.2d 665 (Fla. 1970).

Even the time of adoption of the prohibition on lotteries can made a difference. The Mississippi Supreme Court decided that its State Constitution was a living document. Rejecting the idea that it should look at what was meant by "lottery" when the Constitution was adopted, the Court ruled that bingo was not a lottery, and could thus be legalized by the State Legislature, because citizens of Mississippi today would not think that bingo was a lottery. *Knight v. State of Mississippi*, 574 So.2d 662 (1990).

Bingo was also the game most instrumental in the creation and expansion of Indian gaming. In one of the first important cases, *Seminole Tribe of Florida v. Butterworth*, 658 F.2d 310 (5th Cir. 1981), the Seminole Indian tribe of Florida brought a declaratory judgment and injunction action concerning application of Florida bingo laws to operation of a bingo hall on the Indian reservation. The Court held that the statute permitting bingo games to be played by certain qualified organizations and subject to state restrictions is "civil/regulatory," rather than "criminal/prohibitory," and therefore, cannot be enforced against the tribe. States lack jurisdiction over Indian reservation activity until granted such authority by the federal government. Even if the restrictions on bingo are in the state penal code, that alone is not determinative of whether the restrictions are civil/regulatory or criminal/prohibitory. The test is whether the state has a public policy completely outlawing the particular gambling game, and the test cases are usually bingo. Act, Aug. 15, 1953, §§ 1 *et seq.*, 67 Stat. 588; 18 U.S.C.A. § 1162; 28 U.S.C.A. §§ 1360 note; West's F.S.A. §§ 285.16, 849.093.

F. State Constitutions, State Laws and Internet Gambling

As of 2010, eight states have directly outlawed Internet gambling businesses which they do not license; these states have express prohibitions which use the word "Internet" and gambling. The numbers of states that expressly outlaw Internet gambling do not tell the entire story; at the same time, 29 states license web-based businesses to take bets on horseraces at their respective tracks—and this test includes seven of the eight states with prohibitive legislation. There are inherent areas of conflict between the regulated gambling permitted by the laws of the states and the largely unregulated gambling that can be engaged in on the Internet.

Most state statutes dealing with gambling were enacted long before the Internet was invented. This causes problems for governments that want to enforce their criminal restrictions. For example, there is a strong presumption that no state statute has extraterritorial reach, unless the statute expressly says it does. So, it is not clear that even a strict prohibition on poker would apply to an operator who is outside the country with all players, except one, being also outside the state.

Even laws designed to legalize gambling are normally not designed for the Internet. Colorado's statute authorizing low-stakes casinos is typical. The basic goal of Colorado's Limited Gaming Act is to produce a gaming industry in Colorado that is profitable and beneficial to both the communities where the gaming takes place and to the state as a whole. In order to achieve that goal, the statute states that the public must have confidence and trust in this industry. The Act is concerned mostly with ways of fostering public confidence in the integrity of casinos and casino employees. The Division of Gaming and the Gaming Commission are given wide latitude by the Legislature in its licensing and revocation powers. In addition to overseeing the licensing of casino employees, the Division of Gaming and the Gaming Commission are also responsible for the licensing of the casinos and gambling machine manufacturers. Foreign Internet casinos, even those strictly licensed by developed nations, would not meet the regulatory standards that have been established for land-based casinos in Colorado, because the state's regulators have no involvement in the control of the online gaming.

G.   State Constitutions, State Laws and Casinos

The gaming industry has been among the strongest growing industries in America, and casinos have experienced the fastest growth rates in terms of revenue. Local and state budget problems have also helped spread legal gaming, including casino gambling. Casinos are controlled by state gaming regulators, with, usually, an assist from local ordinances. The commissions are empowered by the state constitution and particularized by state statutes.

The power to regulate gambling derives from the state's police power. Every state has the power, and perhaps even the obligation, to protect the health, safety, welfare and morality of its residents. The most common exercise of this power is with fire, food safety and disease control. But gambling has always fallen under the police power, which gives the state extraordinary power to regulate, even when it makes the activity legal. In fact, the police power normally trumps constitutional rights. When an Islamist terrorist is about to blow up a building, law enforcement shoots to kill, without there first being a trial.

If life can be taken without due process, other constitutional rights are obviously also subject to a state's police power. New Jersey courts, for example, have held that a person involved in the state's licensed casino business has given up her right to free speech, including the right to be involved in political campaigns. *Petition of Soto*, 236 N.J.Super. 303, 565 A.2d 1088 (A.D. 1989), cert. denied 121 N.J. 608, 583 A.2d 310, cert. denied 496 U.S. 937, 110 S.Ct. 3216, 110 L.Ed.2d 664 (1990).

The Supreme Court of Nevada went even further. In *State v. Rosenthal*, 93 Nev. 36, 559 P.2d 830 (1977), appeal dismissed, 434 U.S. 803, 98 S.Ct. 32, 54 L.Ed.2d 61 (1977), the Nevada Supreme Court issued the amazing ruling that the regulation of legal gambling is purely a state legislative issue, with no room for federal or state constitutional rights. Theoretically, the state could discriminate on the basis of race. The case involved the state's denial of a license to Frank "Lefty" Rosenthal, one of the main characters in the movie "Casino," a fictionalized account of events that actually happened, as told in the nonfiction book CASINO: LOVE AND HONOR IN LAS VEGAS. It should be noted that the Nevada Court's assertion in *Rosenthal* that there are no federal civil rights with legal gambling has been rejected by other courts, for example, a federal court in Michigan in *United States v. Goldfarb*, 464 F.Supp. 565 (E.D.Mich. 1979). Even the Nevada Supreme Court has held that state regulators must follow their own rules and procedures and that a licensee does have a constitutionally property right, once a license has been issued.

H. State Laws and Tribal Casinos

The basic principle of all Indian law is the principle that those powers which are lawfully vested in an Indian tribe are not, generally, delegated powers granted by express acts of Congress, but rather inherent powers of a limited sovereignty which has never been extinguished. This derives from cases from the 1830s. In the most important of the three cases, *Cherokee Nation v. Georgia*, John Marshall faced one of the most difficult tests as Chief Justice of the still fairly young U.S. Supreme Court. His landmark declaration that tribes are "domestic dependent nations" does have considerable legal justification, even though there seems to be no dispute that the decision was based at least as much on politics as on law. Tribes are redefining their place in society based on the influx of money and power that has come with tribal gaming; a right afforded to only federally-recognized tribes. The history of Indian gaming is the history of a cross-border issue: the unsuccessful, then successful, and now somewhat uncertain attempt by state governments to extend their gaming laws into Indian reservations.

Indian gaming began modestly in the 1970s with high stakes bingo operations in California and Florida. Although more limited forms of bingo were lawful in each of those states, state and local officials raised stronger and louder objections, as Indian bingo operations grew larger and more successful. Local officials in California believed that they had a particularly strong basis for challenging the Indian bingo operations because, in 1953, Congress enacted Public Law 280 that recognized state criminal jurisdiction over Indian reservations within California and several other states. Public Law 280 dramatically changed the federal common law of Indian nations.

In California, state officials believed that state gaming laws extended into Indian reservations; accordingly, Indian tribes sought declaratory relief to quiet California's regulatory intentions. The case reached the Supreme Court in 1987, resulting in *California v. Cabazon Band of Mission Indians,* 480 U.S. 202, 107 S.Ct. 1083, 94 L.Ed.2d 244 (1987). In *Cabazon*, the Court construed Public Law 280 to recognize that Congress had given California the authority to apply its criminal laws and to exercise civil adjudicatory jurisdiction on Indian reservations, but had not given California the authority to exercise regulatory authority on Indian reservations.

For Indian tribes, the *Cabazon* decision spurred grandiose plans for economic development on Indian reservations across the country, which have sometimes come true. After *Cabazon*, California, and any other state with Public Law 280 authority over Indian tribes, had the theoretical power to prohibit Indian gaming altogether. But this would require the state outlawing all forms of gambling and making the prohibitions criminally enforceable. Such an action would render gaming a subject of state criminal-prohibitory law, rather than tribal-regulatory law. But any state authorization, even for low-limit charity games, meant that the state had merely a civil/regulatory attitude toward gambling. Thus, after the *Cabazon* decision, Indian gaming was lawful only if the state allowed some form of gaming; tribes in Utah today cannot operate any form of gambling. State governments, however, were not willing to end all charitable gaming simply to stop Indian gaming. Congress worked out a political compromise in the Indian Gaming Regulatory Act, which can be seen as codifying the *Cabazon* decision. The result is that it is still state laws that determine whether federally recognized tribes in a state can operate legal gambling, even though the statutes that are directly applicable to those tribes are federal, not state.

CHAPTER 5
CHARITIES AND GAMING

A. Charities and Gaming, Generally

In many jurisdictions, religious, charitable, educational, fraternal, or civic organizations were exempted from anti-gambling statutes. An exempting statute typically requires that all or nearly all the proceeds of the gambling activities be devoted to specified charitable purposes.

State constitutions often put restrictions on what forms of gambling charities can and cannot offer, or even if the state legislature can give charities special rights. For example, in *Fairchild v. Schanke,* 232 Ind. 480, 113 N.E.2d 159 (1953), the Indiana Constitution's prohibition to the general assembly from granting to any class of citizens privileges that do not belong equally to all citizens, trumped a statute that exempted from penal and property seizures "bona fide religious, patriotic, charitable, or fraternal clubs." On the other hand, a state statute permitting non-profit and veterans' organizations in existence for three years and which are engaged in charitable, civic, community, benevolent, religious or scholastic works or other similar activities, to conduct bingo games provided that their proceeds

93

are donated to their respective endeavors and permitting any other non-profit organization, to conduct bingo games provided all proceeds are returned to players in form of prizes, was held to be broad enough to cover any group not organized for profit, and was not unconstitutional class legislation. *Carroll v. State*, 361 So.2d 144 (Fla. 1978). Similarly, in *Mosley v. State*, 255 Ala. 130, 50 So.2d 433 (1951), a statute declaring as contraband, lottery papers and paraphernalia, except those issued by and bearing the name of a religious, charitable, or veterans' organization, and subjecting to condemnation such contraband materials, as well as the automobile carrying them in the state, was held valid. And in one of the leading bingo cases, the Florida Supreme Court ruled that a statute exempting from the general prohibition against gambling the conduct of bingo by nonprofit or veterans' organizations engaged in charitable activities, if those groups existed for more than three years, where the entire proceeds were donated, was constitutional. *Greater Loretta Improv. Assoc. v. State*, 234 So.2d 665 (Fla. 1970).

B. Bingo and Charities

The Florida Bingo Statute § 849.093, Florida Statutes (1975), is a typical charity gambling statute. It permits only non-profit and veteran's organizations to operate the games, which are limited to bingo. The charities must have been in existence for three years and must be engaged in charitable, civic, community, benevolent, religious or scholastic works. Proceeds from the bingo games must be donated to charities' charitable endeavors. Subsection (2) of Section 849.093, Florida Statutes (1975) permits any other non-profit organization also to conduct bingo games, provided all of the proceeds are returned to the players in the form of prizes. Taken together, these subsections permit non-profit or veterans' organizations to conduct bingo games so long as the purpose is either to raise money for certain broad categories of social welfare or for the pure recreation and enjoyment of their members.

The Constitution of Florida puts limits on the Legislature's power. Lotteries are expressly forbidden. But, the Legislature has inherent power to regulate or prohibit all other forms of gambling. In exercising this power, the Legislature has seen fit to permit bingo as a form of recreation, and at the same time, has allowed worthy organizations to receive the benefits. When the statute was challenged, Florida's Supreme Court ruled it was constitutional, because, at least in Florida, bingo is not a lottery. *Greater Loretta Imp. Ass'n. v. State ex rel. Boone*, 234 So.2d 665 (Fla. 1970).

The Legislature has written into § 849.093, Florida Statutes (1975), strict limitations against abuse. For example, the authorized bingo may be conducted only two nights a week and the prizes are limited to $50.00 each, except three jackpots of $250.00 per night.

C. Bingo and the Law

The federal statute, 26 U.S.C.A. § 513, allows charities to run for-profit bingo games without losing their status as tax-exempt charities. But as with most commercial gaming, statutes allowing charities to conduct bingo games are only protections against criminal prosecutions, and do not change the civil laws against enforcement of gambling debts. In *Kennedy v. Annandale Boys Club, Inc.,* 221 Va. 504, 272 S.E.2d 38 (1980), the Court held that even though the taint of illegality had been removed from charitable bingo games, a participant who alleged that she won $6,000 in a bingo game could not use the courts to enforce her gaming contract.

And charities, like commercial operators, usually find that the state's police power trumps all claims of violations of constitutional rights. Nonprofit organizations which had conducted bingo games brought action challenging most of the provisions of Georgia's "1977 Bingo Act." The Superior Court found that certain sections of the Act were unconstitutional restrictions on the right to operate bingo games; however, the Supreme Court of Georgia, in *St. John's Melkite Catholic Church v. C.I.R.,* 240 Ga. 733, 242 S.E.2d 108 (1978), held that all challenged sections of the Bingo Act were constitutional.

D.   Charitable Lotteries and the Law

Although bingo is the most common game operated by charities, the opportunities for gambling have expanded beyond five-by-five bingo cards. Pull-tabs are usually defined as a form of bingo by state statute. And in some states, charities can operate lotteries. These are often instant tickets, which take the form of paper scratchers or pull-tabs. These are sometimes called "pickle jars," from the days when gamblers chose their pull-tabs by reaching into pickle jars filled with the instant tickets. Some charities are putting these games on video screens, often creating games that are indistinguishable from slot machines.

An example of the legal treatment of charitable lotteries can be found in the Nebraska statutes, which require that income from gaming activities be used for the benefit of non-profit organizations, *see* NEB. REV. STAT. §§ 9–211, 309. In *Southeast Rural Volunteer Fire Dep't v. Nebraska Dep't of Revenue, Charitable Gaming Div.*, 251 Neb. 852, 560 N.W.2d 436 (1997), the Nebraska Supreme Court interpreted the "lawful purpose" provisions of the Nebraska Bingo Act and the Nebraska Pickle Card Lottery Act. The Court held that the Southeast Volunteer's use of gaming proceeds for the benefit of private individuals violated the "lawful purpose" provisions.

E. Charitable Raffles and the Law

Raffles are legally a form of lottery. They have traditionally been smaller scale, in terms of the number of players participating, limited to paper tickets, and restricted to recognized charities. Unless there has been a complete preemption by state law, cities and counties are free to impose additional restrictions on charitable games, even when those games are made expressly legal under state law.

In *Theriot v. Terrebonne Parish Police Jury*, 436 So.2d 515 (La. 1983), an owner/lessor of an arena used for charitable bingo sought a temporary restraining order enjoining enforcement of a parish ordinance that restricted use of facilities for raffles and bingo to only two days per calendar week. The Supreme Court of Louisiana held that the ordinance was rationally related to the control and supervision of charitable raffles, bingo, or keno games within the parish and did not offend constitutional guarantee of substantive due process. A provision in the Louisiana State Constitution that requires the Legislature to define and suppress gambling was held not to conflict with parish police jury ordinance restricting use of facilities for raffles, bingo or keno games to two days a week. The Court upheld the local ordinance even though it is more restrictive than its legislative authorization, which does not itself limit the number of times charitable bingo may be held in a given facility in a given week.

F. State Legislation and Charitable Gaming Enterprises

In most states, there is a constitutional prohibition on "lotteries." So the most common fight is over whether bingo is a lottery. Often this is resolved by amending the state constitution to expressly allow charities to operate bingo. In some states, the constitution or statute spells out in detail what is required to meet the definition of nonprofit organization. But in other states, the word "charity" is used, giving local authorities the right to issue licenses to any group that calls itself a charity.

Louisiana's constitutional provision is different, in that it requires the State Legislature to define and to suppress gambling. The Legislature has taken this to mean that it can legalize just about any form of gambling, commercial or charitable. The Legislature can even delegate this power to local jurisdictions. The Louisiana Supreme Court upheld a scheme set out by the Legislature in which local governing authorities determine whether and how to authorize charitable bingo. LSA–R.S. § 33:4861.1 *et seq.*, LSA–Const. Art. 12, § 6.

In Alaska, a nonprofit organization's use of gaming proceeds for a free bicycle program was held not to violate the gaming statute's limitations on the use of proceeds provision. The giving away of bicycles was held to be consistent with the organization's stated purpose: "to awaken groups to the importance of a clean environment and to teach lifestyles which support a clean environment;" plus, bikes provided a benefit to the community by promoting health and alleviating traffic. AS 05.15.150(a); *Roberts v. State, Dep't of Revenue*, 162 P.3d 1214 (Alaska 2007).

Similarly, charitable organization did not violate a statute providing that the entire proceeds of bingo games, less actual business expenses for articles designed for and essential to the operation of the game, must be donated to specified charitable endeavors, where 80% of bingo proceeds were returned to players, and other proceeds were used to pay rent and utilities.

But restrictions on payments for workers are common in charity gambling laws. These are almost never enforced, because police and other government officials understand that no charity is large enough to have unpaid volunteers for all positions for all games. Charitable gaming, like all legal gambling, is an exception to the general rule prohibiting gambling. The statutes are thus normally strictly construed. So when legal actions are taken against charities, game operators are often found to not be in compliance with the applicable statutes and regulations.

For example, in Ohio, a nonprofit organization's bingo games were held to be violating the state's "Charitable Bingo Act," which prohibited payment of compensation or fees by charitable organization conducting game. The charity was using only 9% of the proceeds from its bingo games charitable purposes, while approximately $140,000 was used for annual wages of persons engaged in the operation of the bingo games. *Brown v. Marine Club, Inc.*, 51 Ohio Misc. 51, 2 Ohio Ops. 3d 364, 365 N.E.2d 1277 (1976).

Similarly, a member and "club manager" of a Disabled American Veterans chapter was held to have been properly convicted of promoting unlawful gambling where, although profits went to chapter's charitable and building funds, the fact that members who were not players received wages for assisting in operation of games took the games out of the exclusion in the statutory definition of gambling for games by charitable, fraternal or religious organizations "when no person other than the organization or a player profits." *State v. Johnston*, 56 Or.App. 849, 643 P.2d 666 (1982).

However, in Vermont, the state statute excepting nonprofit organizations from the state's gambling prohibition was held to be too vague to support the prosecution of a veterans' organization for paying workers at bingo games, where the statute was silent on whether proceeds could be used to cover overhead. The Court held that statutory silence invited courts to draw lines between permitted and forbidden worker payments. *State v. Frechette*, 161 Vt. 233, 637 A.2d 1080 (1993).

The statutory language must be examined in detail. Colorado, for example, had a statute outlawing gambling but excluding from the definition of gambling games, wagers that are "incidental to bona fide social relationship," so long as no one is engaging in "professional gambling." Such vague language invites entrepreneurs, and controversy. A Colorado Court of Appeal held that an opera house association's charitable activity, in which participants engaged in casino games and auction in which play money was wagered, was not illegal gambling where all proceeds from the benefit were applied solely to charitable purposes of the association. *Central City Opera House Assoc. v. Charnes*, 743 P.2d 58 (Colo. App. 1987).

Fact that raffles may only be conducted by not-for-profit organizations, in which no part of the profits inure to the benefit of any person, provided reasonable basis for exclusion of raffles from definition of "amusement" under county amusement tax, as required to justify differential treatment under Equal Protection and Uniformity Clauses. U.S. Const. Amend. 14; S.H.A. Const. Art. 1, § 2; Art. 9, § 2; S.H.A. 230 ILSC 15/0.01 *et seq.*; *DeWoskin v. Loew's Chicago Cinema, Inc.*, 306 Ill.App.3d 504, 239 Ill.Dec. 750, 714 N.E.2d 1047 (1st Dist. 1999), appeal denied (Ill. 1999).

Most states that define what is a charity require that the nonprofit organization have been in existence for three or five years before being allowed to offer bingo games to the public. At least one court has held this unconstitutional. In Indiana, a charity gaming statute required that the nonprofit organization had to be in existence in the state for a period of five years before it could get a bingo license. A charity that did not meet this standard and that had its license revoked, sued. The Court held that construing the statute to require an organization to be in existence for five years in Indiana would discriminate against interstate commerce. *Department of Revenue v. There to Care,* 638 N.E.2d 871 (Ind. App. 1994), transfer den. (Ind. App. 1994).

Even the most legitimate charities have found it difficult to live with the strict raffle and bingo laws. But enforcement against charities for technical violations of state and local anti-gambling laws are relatively rare. And convictions usually amount to no more than a fine.

G.   Gambling on the Reservation

In the celebrated case of *California v. Cabazon Band of Mission Indians*, 480 U.S. 202, 107 S.Ct. 1083, 94 L.Ed.2d 244 (1987), two tribes in California operated bingo halls and a card club on their reservations. California law permitted charitable bingo games, but restricted the amount of jackpots to $250 per game and the use of gaming profits to charitable purposes. (The argument has been made that Indian bingo is for charitable purposes, especially if any revenue raised from the games goes to benefit residents of the reservation, and tribes are governments. But, a federally recognized tribe is not subject to state regulatory laws covering charities. So, apparently no court has accepted tribal bingo as being legal as a form of charity gambling.) The U.S. Supreme Court concluded that because

California permits a substantial amount of gambling activity, including bingo, and actually promotes gambling through its state lottery, then it can be inferred that California regulates, rather than prohibits, gambling in general and bingo in particular. Similar results have come from courts throughout the nation. The only way for a state to prevent tribes within its borders from operating gambling games is for the state to outlaw all of its own permitted gaming, including all charity bingo.

CHAPTER 6

NEVADA

A. The History of Nevada Gambling

Nevada was settled mostly by seekers after gold and silver from the eastern United States in the 1850s. It appears that casinos were technically illegal when Nevada was a territory; although, gambling, especially casino gaming, is almost always legal, or at least tolerated, in frontier towns. The mostly young and male miners of the Gold and Silver Rushes openly played faro, monte, roulette and poker, for money. But, they brought with them their first-hand memories of the East Coast lottery scandals of the 1830s and '40s. So, the framers of the first Nevada Constitution, originally adopted in 1864, wanted to make sure that there would never be legal lotteries again. Like virtually all of the state constitutions of the era, the Nevada Constitution stated that, "No lottery shall be authorized by this State, nor shall the sale of lottery tickets be allowed." NEV. CONST., art. 4, § 24 (amended 1990).

Following statehood, there were immediate attempts to legalize casinos. A bill failed to pass the first State Legislature, but the lawmakers did reduced penalties for operators and completely exempted mere players of non-lottery gambling games. Within five years of becoming a state, proponents succeed in convincing the Nevada State Legislature to make casino gaming legal. Act of March 4, 1869, 71, Nev. Laws 119.

The crash of the Second Wave of Legal Gambling in the 1890's–1910, hit Nevada as hard as every other state. In 1909, the territories of Arizona and New Mexico were told if they wanted to become states they would have to outlaw their casinos. That same year, the Nevada Legislature ordered all of its casinos closed. Act of March 24, 1909, ch. 210, Nev. Laws 307.

But gambling continued in Nevada; mostly illegal, but open and tolerated. Movements to bring legal gambling back continued. In 1915, the Legislature legalized slot machines, so long as they paid out only cigars and drinks. Stats. 1915, c. 284. In a friendly test case, the Nevada Supreme Court upheld the limited nickle-in-the-slot machine law, on the grounds that this type of gaming device could be legalized by the State Legislature, because it was not a lottery. The Court ruled that decisions of the Nevada Legislature as to what was, and was not, a lottery would be given great deference, in part because the Legislature had been treating lotteries different from other forms of gambling for half a century. The Court ruled that, in Nevada, a gambling game, even one of pure chance, was not a lottery if a person had to go to a particular place to play and had to participate in the playing of a game. *Ex Parte Pierotti*, 43 Nev. 243, 184 P. 209 (1919).

Nevada suffered as much, if not more, than other states during the Great Depression. In 1931, desperate to bring in tourists and some revenue, Nevada legalized the easy divorce industry. Almost as an afterthought, it also made casinos legal once again. Act of March 19, 1931, c. 99, Nev. Laws 165.

The 1931 statute that legalized gambling in Nevada provided that gaming control within incorporated areas was the duty of city officials. Usually the sheriff's office was empowered to regulate gaming outside these incorporated areas. Until 1945, that regulation was minimal and was concerned primarily with the collection and the control of drunks and cheaters.

In 1945, the Nevada legislature shifted responsibility for gaming regulation to the Tax Commission, which was made responsible for issuing gaming licenses and collecting taxes from the gaming establishments. In 1949, the Tax Commission began to investigate gaming license applicants; this was necessary to stave off the federal level proposals to substantially tax gambling receipts.

World War II and the building of Hoover Dam brought life back into the Nevada economy. But it was really the development of the trans-continental freeways connection with southern California and the widespread use of air conditioning that allowed southern Nevada to boom and Las Vegas to become the gambling capital of the world.

From 1950 to '51, the U.S. Senate Special Committee to Investigate Crime in Interstate Commerce, commonly known as the Kefauver Committee, held the first televised congressional hearings in the United States. The Committee was chaired by Senator Estes Kefauver, who later went on to run for president and vice-president. The focus of the Kefauver Committee was organized crime. Hearings in Las Vegas drew special attention to the connection between the state's licensed casinos and the Mob.

Nevada politicians and business leaders feared that the federal government would take over regulation of the gaming industry, or even close it down. In those days of extensive federal power, the thought was that the federal government might be able to use its constitutional power to regulate interstate commerce, or even to control the nation's currency, to preempt the laws of the only state with legal casinos. So, efforts were made to clean up the industry, and kick out the "wise guys."

A Gaming Control Board was established within the Tax Commission in 1955 and given independent status in 1959, concurrent with the creation of the Nevada Gaming Commission. Pursuant to the Nevada Gaming Control Act, NEV. REV. STAT. §§ 463.010–463.155, members of both these bodies are appointed by the governor to serve four-year staggered terms of office. The three-member Gaming Control Board is an administrative body that oversees six staff divisions: Investigations, Enforcement, Audit, Tax and License, Economic Research, and Administration. The Board recommends to the Gaming Commission which licenses should be granted and brings gaming law violators before the Commission for a hearing. The five-member Gaming Commission, a bipartisan rulemaking body consisting of business and professional leaders, considers recommendations from the Board and sets the state's gaming policy.

B. The Nevada State Gaming Regulators Generally

The Commission has wide discretion in licensing decisions, the only caveat being that its decisions must be reasonable, *State v. Rosenthal*, 93 Nev. 36, 559 P.2d 830 (1977). However, the Commission must follow its own mandates, *Nevada Gaming Comm'n v. Consolidated Casinos Corp., Tahoe Div.*, 94 Nev. 139, 575 P.2d 1337 (1978), and must establish a factual basis for excluding potential licensees, *Spilotro v. State*, 99 Nev. 187, 661 P.2d 467 (1983).

In 1959, authority over licensing and regulation shifted from the Tax Commission to the newly-formed Nevada Gaming Commission. The enforcement responsibilities remained with the state Gaming Control Board. The two regulatory agencies began employing a rigorous application and investigation process.

Over the years, the standards have been toughened. At first, Nevada regulators were willing to give licenses to individuals with felony convictions. The thought was that since gambling was illegal in every other state, the only people with experience running casinos would, by definition, be criminals. It is worth noting that New Jersey, the second state to legalize casinos, rejected that theory, and showed that the market would take of supplying individuals with expertise without criminal backgrounds.

In the 1960s, Howard Hughes discovered Las Vegas. He bought up so many casinos that he was the subject of a federal antitrust investigation. At the time, everyone thought Hughes was a genius. Companies, particularly hotel operators, who had never had an interest in legal gaming, looked into buying hotel-casinos in Nevada. But Nevada law, at the time, required that every owner had to be licensed, and regulatory approval was required before any ownership interest could be transferred. Since holding even one share of stock technically gave an individual an ownership interest, casinos could not be owned by publicly traded corporations. In the late 1960s, following the entry of Hughes into the market, the Nevada Legislature allowed public companies to own casinos without having to license each shareholder.

The statute created the idea of key shareholders. Although Nevada regulators can investigate anyone associated with a casino, they normally do not bother with any individual or company owning less than 5%. Any person, defined as including corporations, who acquires 5% of the voting shares of a Nevada casino company must file a report with state regulators and may be subject to licensing. A person who owns more than 10% of any class of voting shares almost always goes through full licensing. Regulators do have power to make exceptions, even for large shareholders. An institutional investor, such as a well-known bondholder, who unexpectedly becomes the owner of equity through a bankruptcy reorganization will normally get a waiver if it has less than 15% of a casino company's stock.

The toughened regulatory system, along with the addition of respected corporations (e.g., Hilton and Ramada) and individuals (e.g., Steve Wynn and Donald Trump) helped to all but eliminate the threat of federal intervention. This, plus the rise of sources of legitimate funding, contributed to the growth and respectability that Nevada casinos continue to enjoy.

C.   Nevada Gambling Regulations

Over the years, the State Gaming Control Board has come to exercise most of the power when it comes to regulating Nevada's casinos. The Nevada Gaming Commission has deferred, because it lacks the large full-time staff and expertise of the Board. The Commission often still has the final say, but usually accepts the recommendations of the Board.

Nevada's gaming regulations cover all aspects of legal gambling in the state. Control is maintained by doing background investigations and licensing anyone who has a significant ownership interest or control over the conduct of the games. This includes individuals, like dress shop owners on the premises, if it appears that those individuals are exercising secret control or skimming profits. There are detailed requirements for the conduct of every part of the gaming operation. Recent scandals have led to the Board sending notices and even imposing fines on casino operators for activities taking place in swimming pools and nightclubs on the casinos' grounds.

D. The Nuts and Bolts of the Regulators' Day-to-Day Activities

The case of *State v. Rosenthal*, 93 Nev. 36, 559 P.2d 830 (1977), held, rather extraordinarily, that the regulation of gambling was an issue left entirely to the states, not subject even to the protections of the U.S. Constitution. Even the Nevada State Constitution and courts had no role to play, so long as state regulators followed the requirements laid down by the State Legislature and their own rules. The Court expressly discussed the power and focus of the State Gaming Control Board's and Nevada Gaming Commission's responsibilities: (1) gaming is a matter of privilege conferred by the state rather than a matter of right; (2) the licensing and control of gaming requires special knowledge and experience; and (3) the members of the Board and Commission must have special qualifications suited to their important duties and their powers are comprehensive, and, therefore, court intrusion is limited.

In patron disputes, generally, the issue is whether the contract concerning a gaming transaction is enforceable. For more than a century, Nevada law was clear: Gambling debts were not collectable in court. Then, the State Legislature passed a law allowing casinos to sue on written markers, but players could not. A patron who feels he has been wrongfully deprived of the payout on a winning bet can only file a complaint with state regulators. Most disputes concern slot machines. Courts will uphold decisions of the administrative agency if they are supported by any evidence. If the amount in controversy is over $500, the casino must notify the Gaming Board, which will investigate and its agent will issue a written decision within 30 days. An aggrieved party may request a full hearing and the decision is subject to very limited judicial review.

In *Sengel v. IGT and the Silver Legacy–Reno*, 116 Nev. 565, 2 P.3d 258 (2000), the reels stopped with three jackpot symbols appearing in an uneven line across the pay line. The State Gaming Control Board agent concluded there was a malfunction and an uneven alignment of the jackpot symbols. The entire Gaming Control Board then affirmed the agent's recommendation and the player requested judicial review. The Nevada Supreme Court concluded the proper standard of review was whether the agency's decision was supported by *any* evidence. While great deference is given to the finding of fact by the administrative agency, "this court is free to examine purely legal questions decided at the administrative level," though it almost never does.

In *Erickson v. Caesar's Palace*, 106 Nev. 1021, 835 P.2d 36 (1990), the Nevada Supreme Court concluded that the casino did not have to pay a jackpot of over $1 million won by a Tennessee resident aged 19, because it was an unenforceable gaming transaction. Erickson, the plaintiff, then sought relief in federal court, but in *Erickson v. Desert Palace*, 942 F.2d 694 (9th Cir. 1991), the Court held that an unpaid slot jackpot was a gaming debt not evidenced by a credit instrument, and therefore, the sole remedy was administrative procedures. In *Chen v. Nevada State Gaming Control* Board, 116 Nev. 282, 994 P.2d 1151 (2000), $40,000 in winnings to a blackjack player who had produced a fictitious passport in order to purchase $29,000 in casino chips was enforced by the Nevada Supreme Court, which found that there was no fraud by Chen because the casino neither detrimentally relied upon his misrepresentation nor was it the proximate cause for the casino loss.

All persons engaged in the operation of gaming must obtain a license. There are two types of operator licenses: restricted and nonrestricted. Restricted licenses are for the slot machines, usually limited to 15 maximum, found in bars and grocery stores throughout the state. Nonrestricted licenses are issued to full casinos.

The types of licensing include operators, landlords, gaming employees, junket representatives, information services, service industries, race books and sports pools, disseminators, gaming devices, lenders, and labor organizations. There are pertinent qualifications and particular applications that apply. Agents of the Board conduct the investigation. An investigator generally consists of interviews of the applicant, a review of financial records, a check of police records, a review of civil and criminal court records, interviews with business and personal associates, and an examination of business methods. The cost can be many hundreds of thousands of dollars and must usually be borne by the applicant. At the conclusion of the investigation, the agents will again interview the applicant and explain any areas of concern. Areas of concern will be included in a confidential report to the Board. The applicant is not entitled to see this report. Then there also is an approval process, which includes a Board hearing, after recommendation by the Board, the Commission will hear the application. The Commission has the final authority to approve or deny the license. If the Board recommends approval of the application, then a simple majority of the Commission is necessary for licensing. If the Board recommends denial, then unanimous Commission approval is required for licensing.

The Commission has full and absolute power to revoke, suspend, limit, or condition any gaming license, and to fine any gaming licensee for any cause deemed reasonable. This includes the violation by a licensee's agent or employee of any provision of the Gaming Control Act or the regulations of the Commission or Board.

E. The Black Book

One of the more controversial controls is the "Black Book," officially titled the "List of Excluded Persons." This list contains individuals who, because of their "notorious or unsavory reputation," are prohibited from entering any Nevada casino. As sometimes happens, state regulators created the black book without any express statutory authorization.

After a long series of federal court battles, the Nevada legislature in 1967 passed a law specifically authorizing the "Black Book." NEV. REV. STAT. §§ 463.151–463.155 (1985). In order to avoid the problems of due process, the legislation required that candidates from the "Black Book" be notified of their possible inclusion by personal service, certified mail, or by publication. Furthermore, once listed, an individual could demand a hearing from the Commission in order to show cause why he should have his name taken from the list.

In addition to these requirements of notice and hearing, the Nevada Gaming Control Act provided for judicial review of the administrative hearing. Other provisions in the Act allowed the Commission to revoke, limit, condition, suspend, or fine an individual licensee or licensed gaming establishment that failed to exclude or eject from their premises those listed in the "Black Book."

It was not until 1972 that the Gaming Commission exercised the power given it by the Legislature to adopt regulations effectuating the Act. Regulation 28 delineates those eligible for "Black Book" inclusion as anyone who is of notorious or unsavory reputation, convicted of a moral turpitude felony, or whose presence in casino is inimical to the interests of the state. In 1977 and 1981, the legislature passed amendments that expanded the basis for "Black Book" inclusion, *see* NEV. REV. STAT. §§ 463.154 and 463.151.

F. Local Ordinances

Gaming licenses are granted to private enterprises. The licensing and regulation of gaming are bifurcated between state and local governments having concurrent jurisdiction. In most areas of the state, a small business can receive a restricted license to operate up to 15 gaming devices. A local government can prohibit or restrict gaming within its city or county limits. Local governments can license and regulate gaming. Local governments often use licensing primarily for taxation and rarely use their powers in a regulatory fashion, except in Las Vegas. In Clark County, which includes Las Vegas, casinos are restricted to operators that have open and operating hotels with a minimum of 300 rooms. Clark County Ordinance 8.04.310.

G.   The Future of Nevada Gambling

Nevada laws allow all forms of gaming, except lotteries. Authorized games include live table games, slot machines and other gaming devices, race books, sports pools, jai alai, and dog and horse racing. A casino may offer virtually any type of game played for money or property, including baccarat, blackjack, bingo, chemin de fer, keno, klondike, monte, pai gow, panguingui, roulette, twenty-one, poker, and wheel of fortune. The Nevada Gaming Commission can also approve a new game after a short field test. There are two operators of Internet sports books, and other sports books allow people to bet by phone and closed loop systems on their computers, so long as the bettors are physically in the state. Nevada regulators have approved remote wagering on handheld devices on casinos' grounds, though not in hotel rooms. Some of these devices are linked to cameras trained on real slot machines; others replicate slot machines, banking table games and poker tables on the computer screen. The State Legislature has passed laws allowing its licensed operators to take bets from everywhere in the world, so long as they are not sports bets and are legal in the other jurisdictions. None are presently operating, except online sports and horse betting. But the Legislature has called upon the state's regulators to set up standards for Internet poker, and the regulators have responded by putting in place a licensing system that will be issuing online poker licenses in 2012. Operators will then undoubtedly push to be able to form pools of players with other states and nations that have legalized Internet poker, to create more liquidity for the online games.

CHAPTER 7

NEW JERSEY CASINO REGULATORS

In 1976, New Jersey became the first state in the history of the United States to approve high stakes casino gambling at the ballot box. The Nevada State Legislature had approved casinos in 1931, but without a vote of the people. The initiative in New Jersey required an amendment of the State Constitution, and so had to be approved by the electorate. It was not really a contest. The opposition were so over-confident, having defeated casinos at the polls by 60% only two years earlier, that they literally ran no campaign against the Atlantic City proposal: Committees opposing casinos took in only $23,230 and did not even spend it all! Proponents spent $1,330,615.

To implement the Constitutional amendment allowing casinos only in Atlantic City, the New Jersey Legislature enacted the New Jersey Casino Control Act, N.J. STAT. ANN. §§ 5:12–1 to –152. It was passed in 1977, after extensive public and legislative debate. The statute attempted to codify the goals of the campaign for casinos: to tap a viable source of state revenue while curtailing the influx and influence of criminal elements naturally attracted to the cash-rich casino industry. New Jersey lawmakers decided that it was not necessary to license individuals who had been involved in illegal gambling. Unlike Nevada, New Jersey expected the market to create expertise, by bringing in experienced casino companies and individuals from jurisdictions where gaming was legal, and by establishing dealer schools to train casino employees. The Casino Act was designed to establish a strict and extensive regulatory scheme that severely limited the participation in the industry by persons with known criminal records, habits, or associations. To achieve these goals, the Casino Act created a New Jersey Casino Control Commission ("NJCCC"), with broad regulatory power over gambling institutions and related industries. The Casino Act also directs the Division of Gaming Enforcement ("DGE"), under the State Attorney General in the Department of Law and Public Safety, to investigate all applicants for licenses, certificates, or permits, and to prosecute violations of the Act and its regulations either before the Commission or in the state criminal courts. So, the DGE was designed to act like an investigator and prosecutor, and the NJCCC would be the final judge, jury and, sometimes, executioner.

A.   The Rise and Fall of Atlantic City

New Jersey's first legal gaming casino opened on May 26, 1978. To open so quickly after the 1976 vote and 1977 statute, the company, Resorts International, bought and refurbished an old hotel. The

Casino Act required, among other things, that a casino be inside a hotel with a minimum of 500 rooms. Although casinos were legalized mainly to revitalize the tourist economy of Atlantic City, the laws also provided that all tax revenues from the casinos would benefit senior citizens and the disabled by reducing their real estate taxes and utility fees and expanding their health benefits. Over the years, Atlantic City's casinos have raised billions of dollars for the state. Legal gaming does contribute significantly to the state economy, both directly and indirectly. It has also provided employment: more people work in Atlantic City's casinos than live as full time residents of the city. Unfortunately, casino gaming and tourism is not large enough to drive an economy as large as that of the state of New Jersey. In fact, the casino experiment in New Jersey showed that the casino gaming industry cannot even, on its own, revitalize a resort community as small as Atlantic City.

The legalization of casinos has proven that the prohibition on gambling creates pent up demand, but that that demand has its limits. Suppose Prohibition of alcohol had just been repealed. The hypothetical owner of the first and only liquor store in a state would make a fantastic return on investment. But soon, if there were no government controls, there would be liquor stores throughout the state, as there are few barriers to entry. Excess profits would disappear and returns on investment would descend to normal levels, after a large number went bankrupt and that over-supply disappeared. Government makes the situation worse. The fantasy that there is an infinitely inelastic demand for gambling seems to hit politicians harder than entrepreneurs. Sin taxes are always the easiest to raise. Casinos, like liquor stores and tobacco retailers, are easier targets than more politically acceptable businesses. Government's thinking is that people should not be gambling anyway and they will continue to make wagers, no matter how much the cost. So, even though a quarter of the gaming establishments in a jurisdiction might go bankrupt, the state continues to consider raising taxes on gaming.

Resorts International opened the first legal casino on the East Coast on May 26, 1978, spending $45.2 million to refurbish the old Chalfonte–Haddon hotel in Atlantic City. Its first year gross revenue of $224.6 million made it the most profitable casino in the world, at the time. The state of New Jersey, for merely allowing the casino to open, collected $18 million in taxes that first year.

But, twelve more casinos quickly followed. The Trump Taj Mahal, the thirteenth Atlantic City casino to open, cost over $1.1 billion, in 1990 dollars. The Taj opened in April 1990; it declared bankruptcy in July 1991. Of the thirteen casinos that had opened in Atlantic City, eight had been involved in formal bankruptcy proceedings.

Atlantic City was hit harder than Las Vegas by the Great Recession that started in 2007. Even with casinos, Atlantic City still had many of the problems that had originally hurt its tourist economy:

Harsh weather in winter and competition from tropical resorts that could be cheaply and easily reached by plane. The law requiring massive hotels with casinos resulted in island fortresses, with every accommodation a visitor could require. There was thus no need for tourists to leave the buildings; so non-casino restaurants and stores saw few of the tens of thousands of new visitors. But worse was the birth of casino style gaming in nearby states. In 2012, Pennsylvania passed New Jersey as the number two casino state, after Nevada. For many potential patrons living in cities like Philadelphia, there was now no reason to travel more than an hour to Atlantic City to place a bet.

Some casino companies continue to have faith in Atlantic City, and are pouring in billions of dollars in an attempt to revive the casino industry. The newest casino, Revel, is costing $2.4 billion and is instituting the unique policy of hiring workers only for four or six year terms, after which they will have to reapply to keep their current jobs.

The state is also taking a more active role, and the Legislature has attempted to reorganize and streamline the casino regulatory process. In addition, the state has created a state-run tourism district of approximately 1,700 acres in Atlantic City. The Casino Reinvestment Development Authority took control of the district, designed to help boost tourism and gaming.

B. Atlantic City Casinos as a Panacea

The goal of the Casino Act was to prevent the infiltration of organized crime and to provide revenue and revitalize the city. Legalized casino gambling attracts organized crime because casinos contain vast amounts of cash and gaming chips susceptible to misappropriation—the goal of organize crime's infiltration is this "skim"—and because millions of dollars continually change hands among thousands of people on the casino floor without any paper record showing where or from whom the money came.

The State Commission of Investigation explicitly recognized the necessity of state control over casino-related labor unions, asserting that organized crime attempts to gain a stranglehold on an entire industry will be through labor racketeering. If organized crime were able to use extorted funds to finance the operation of ancillary services and exert pressure through the union to gain service contracts, it would, in effect, have the casinos in a stranglehold.

The Casino Control Act, as a whole, has been upheld as constitutional by both the New Jersey and U.S. Supreme Courts. However, in *In the Matter of the Application of Martin*, 90 N.J. 295, 447 A.2d 1290 (1982), applicants for nonsupervisory casino licenses challenged certain questions they were required to answer in order to apply for a license.

The New Jersey Supreme Court held that the challenged provisions of the Casino Control Act application forms were constitutional and that the Casino Control Commission could require applicants to sign release authorizations if they were evaluated as promptly as possible to insure confidentiality. But it was going too far to require the boyfriend of a cocktail waitress, who did not even go onto the casino floor, to fill out a multi-page form with detailed questions about his personal finances.

In *Brown v. Hotel & Restaurant Employee & Bartenders Int'l Union Local 54*, 468 U.S. 491, 104 S.Ct. 3179, 82 L.Ed.2d 373 (1984), the U.S. Supreme Court held that states' regulation of the qualifications of union officials did not conflict and was not preempted by the NLRA. Similarly, a slot machine manufacturer challenged the Commission's requirement that casinos obtain no more than 50% of its slots from any one manufacturer. This regulation—one of the first to expressly limit economic concentration of casinos in the hands of only a few companies—was held to have a rational basis and thus did not violate state or federal antitrust acts. *Bally Mfg. Corp. v. New Jersey Casino Control Comm'n*, 85 N.J. 325, 426 A.2d 1000 (1981).

New Jersey was also one of the first casino jurisdictions to adopt the idea of corporate banishment. The theory is that it is possible to license a company, even if individuals running it were unsuitable, if those individuals were cut out. The State Supreme Court upheld the Commission's removal of two important officials of Caesars Palace, holding the ruling bore a rational relationship to a legitimate state interest and did not violate due process. *In the Matter of the Application of Boardwalk Regency Corp. for a Casino License*, 90 N.J. 361, 447 A.2d 1335 (1982).

C. Regulations Affecting Atlantic City Casinos

New Jersey lawmakers decided to go further than Nevada in their attempt to keep the industry clean. The state even licenses garbage collectors and others who contract to provide goods and services with the casino industry. A casino license is required to own or operate a casino; however, only owners, operators, or landlords may hold a casino license. Operators, landlords, gaming employees, junket representatives and enterprises, service industries, race and sports books, gaming devices, lenders, labor organizations, and gaming schools all are required to obtain some form of licensure. Individuals desiring to hold a license must be licensed to the standards applicable to casino key employees, except for residency. The Commission has no restrictions on foreign investment. But, the Commission will demand the use of particular application forms, along with an investigatory arm. There are accounting requirements, including audits, taxes and fees, gaming equipment, and the stipulation of the form of gaming contracts, which will include credit controls, credit collection, player disputes, etc. Following Nevada's example, the New Jersey Casino Control Act empowers the Casino Control Commission to establish a list of persons who are to be excluded or ejected from any licensed casino establishment.

New Jersey originally placed burdensome requirements on casino companies. Because there were regulations about how much space could be taken up with gaming, hotel-casinos had to submit detailed plans even when they were remodeling non-gaming areas, such as kitchens. New Jersey politicians didn't like the "Loosest Slots" signs they saw in Las Vegas, so they forbad Atlantic City casinos from telling players about the odds of winning, probably the one piece of information gamblers most need. And casinos could not be visible from the street; instead, they were required to be isolated in separate rooms without windows and with guards at the door. Due at least in part to competition from neighboring states, New Jersey has loosened its regulations in both law and practice, in an attempt to make the state more friendly for casino companies to do business.

D.   The Future of Atlantic City Casinos

The future of Atlantic City casinos is linked to the continued success of the regulators. So far, so good; however, it is undeniable that Atlantic City itself and the inhabitants thereof do not appear to be measurably enriched by the casino development boom.

New Jersey legalized casino gambling as a "unique tool of urban redevelopment" in 1976. The move was described as a great social experiment. Rather than use government money to stimulate redevelopment—whether through a housing development or a large public works project like a sports arena or performing arts center—this experiment was designed to use private investment in casino hotels as the catalyst to draw additional investment and rebuild a decaying city.

Atlantic City, a century ago, was the seaside escape for people from Philadelphia and New York with enormous ocean-front hotels and top name entertainment. The city fell on hard times after World War II.

When the voters of New Jersey were asked to legalize casinos, the only significant example they could look to was Nevada. But Nevada's casino industry was notorious, at that time, for having been controlled by organized crime.

The New Jersey Casino Control Act was quite specific about licensing and operation of casinos, casino employees, and the companies that did business with casinos. The Act's details were designed to give comfort to New Jersey residents that casinos would be tightly controlled.

The legislature decided to create two agencies—the Casino Control Commission and the Division of Gaming Enforcement. The Commission would set the rules and issue the licenses. It would have a full-time chairman and four part-time commissioners. The Division would conduct investigations and prosecute cases before the Commission. It would be a division of the Attorney General's Office and headed by an assistant attorney general. The commissioners and the division director would be appointed by the governor to set terms and could only be removed for cause.

The agencies quickly tried to establish a reputation as being tough. Hilton Hotels was denied a license, because it did not take serious obviously false allegations about the company's ties to organized crime. Because the burden is on the applicant in New Jersey to prove that it is suitable by clear and convincing evidence, Hilton failed to get a majority of votes in the NJCCC.

It did not take long for pressure to build to amend the Casino Control Act. However, efforts at deregulation were derailed before they got started. The Abscam investigation in 1980 tainted the Commission when it was alleged that the vice chair had accepted a payoff from a fake Arab sheik who wanted a casino license. The legislature responded by revamping the commission. The four part-time commissioners were replaced with full-time members and the chairman was stripped of much of his executive authority.

By 1990, a variety of other states had started to legalize casino gaming. Casino companies now had alternatives of where to invest their capital and that capital was going anywhere but Atlantic City. To respond to the dramatic change in the business landscape, New Jersey started to implement a series of legislative and regulatory changes that reinvented the way New Jersey regulated gaming. Over the next five years, the regulators and legislators made it easier to introduce new table games, permitted casinos to operate around-the-clock and eliminated many of the facility requirements, such as the amount of various kinds of public space. The effort to give casino operators more discretion in how they run their business and get regulators out of making business decisions reached its peak in 1995 and again in 2010–11, with packages of regulatory reform measures. The legislature eliminated requirements for hotel workers to register with the state, lifted the limit on how many licenses an individual can hold, eliminated experiential requirements for casino employees and reduced duplication between the Commission and the Division of Gaming Enforcement.

One look around Atlantic City today shows that the "experiment" of using casino gambling for urban redevelopment purposes has not been completely successful.

The Casino Control Commission is allowed to legalize any game it finds suitable for casino use and to permit the simulcasting of horseraces. Sports betting was not permitted until 2012. In November 2011, the voters of the state approved legalized sports betting. The State Legislature enacted the necessary enabling statute, which was signed into law in January 2012. However, a federal statute, the Professional and Amateur Sports Protection Act

("PASPA"), 26 U.S.C.A. §§ 3701 et seq., locks in the sports betting that existed when it was enacted in 1992. New Jersey was given special consideration, and had one year to legalize sports betting, which it failed to do. So, now a federal lawsuit will determine whether Atlantic City casinos may also have sports betting, or whether Congress has the power to prevent states from changing their policies on gambling.

New Jersey will also probably be one of the first states to legalize Internet casinos. A bill by Democratic State Senator Ray Lesniak passed both houses, controlled by Democrats, in early 2011. But Governor Chris Christie, a Republican who would like to run for President, vetoed the bill. One of his reasons was legal: The State Constitution allows casinos to only be in Atlantic City. Sen. Lesniak has a new bill, which he thinks gets around this restriction by requiring the servers for online gaming be located in Atlantic City. He may also decide to go with a more clear legal cleanup: a constitutional amendment to expressly allow Internet betting from anywhere in the state. Even Gov. Christie understands the need for additional revenue; he signed the bill legalizing sports betting, and he has come out in favor of Internet casinos in New Jersey.

CHAPTER 8

TRIBAL GAMING

A. Terminology—"Indians"

The legal term has traditionally been "Indian;" even though the only connection most Native Americans have to India was the mistaken belief by Christopher Columbus that he had discovered a new route to Asia. "Indian" is still found in statutes, cases and regulations. For example, the most important law dealing with tribes' rights to offer legal gambling is the Indian Gaming Regulatory Act, commonly called "IGRA," Pub.L. 100–497, § 2, Oct. 17, 1988, 102 Stat. 2467, codified at 25 U.S.C. §§ 2701–2721 and 18 U.S.C. §§ 1166–1168. IGRA does not contain the term "Native American." Thus, this area of the law is usually called Indian gaming. This adds an additional element of confusion: Not only does Indian gaming have no connection with the country of India, but the right to operate legal gambling is based on the sovereignty of tribes, the fact that tribes are legally governments, not on the ethnicity of individuals.

However, it should go without saying that individuals are not free to rename statutes, even if they are offended by the title. Thus, the law should always be called the Indian Gaming Regulatory Act, not the Native American Gaming Regulatory Act, or any other variation.

The term for tribal governments is usually "tribe," although "band," "pueblo," and "rancheria" are often found in federal statutes and some tribes have "Nation" as part of their official name. In Canada, the most common terms are "band" and "First Nations." "Aboriginal" and "indigenous" also frequently appears in Canadian law, particularly in the term "aboriginal rights," although the word almost never appears in U.S. Indian gaming law.

Until 1988, federal law almost always referred to land held in trust for tribes as "Indian Country." IGRA introduced a new term of art: "Indian lands," with a complex definition which differs only slightly from "Indian Country." Compare 25 U.S.C.A. § 2703 with 18 U.S.C.A. § 1151. But even IGRA used the more traditional term when making it a federal crime to violate state anti-gaming laws in "Indian Country." 18 U.S.C.A. § 1166. Tribal land is most commonly called a "reservation," but is also referred in statutes as "dependent Indian communities" and "Indian allotments." See, e.g., 15 U.S.C. § 1175.

B. Tribal Sovereignty Generally

Tribal sovereignty is the doctrine that recognizes tribes' inherent rights as independent nations that preexisted the United States and the U.S. Constitution, and is the primary legal and political foundation of federally recognized Indian law and policy, including tribal gaming. The doctrine of tribal sovereignty was established by Chief Justice of the United States John Marshall of the U.S. Supreme Court in the "Marshall Trilogy" (*Worcester v. Georgia*, 31 U.S. (6 Pet.) 515, 8 L.Ed. 483 (1832); *Cherokee Nation v. Georgia*, 30 U.S. (5 Pet.) 1 (1831); and *Johnson v. M'Intosh*, 21 U.S. (8 Wheat) 543, 5 L.Ed. 681 (1823)). The Court was faced with the question of how to classify, and protect, tribes and their members in the face of sometimes genocidal policies by states. The Indian Commerce Clause in the United States Constitution reaffirmed that tribes were sovereigns of some type, placing them in the same clause with states and nations: "Congress shall have Power... To regulate Commerce with foreign Nations, and among the several States, and with the Indian Tribes." U.S. Const. art. I § 8, cl. 3. Justice Marshall concluded the tribes were "domestic dependent nations" possessing some limited sovereignty, but subject to the plenary power of Congress.

Federal policy toward Indians has shifted dramatically over the years. At its worst, Indian policy could be characterized by General Amherst's "admonition that could it not be contrived to send the small pox among those disaffected tribes of Indians?" (Jeffery Amherst to Henry Bouquet as quoted in Walter Thomas Champion, Jr., Lament of the Iroquois: Participation of the Six Nations in the French and Indian War, M.A. in History, Western

Illinois University (May 1975)). During the civil rights movements of the 1970s, the federal government initiated a new policy of tribal self-determination which essentially encouraged economic self-sufficiency. Some tribes saw gaming on reservation land as an integral part of an economic development strategy. The United States now recognizes tribes as dependent sovereign nations, which means that their location within a state does not subject them to state law; however, tribes are still subject to Congress' plenary power. In short, the tribes have the unique status of semi-sovereignty under federal laws, subject to regulation by the U.S. Congress.

C.　Indian Gaming Before 1988

Two landmark legal events, the U.S. Supreme Court's decision in *California v. Cabazon Band of Mission Indians*, 480 U.S. 202, 107 S.Ct. 1083, 94 L.Ed.2d 244 (1987), and the passage of the Indian Gaming Regulatory Act of 1988 (P.L. no. 100–497, 102 Stat. 2467 (Oct. 17, 1998), codified at 25 U.S.C.A. 6 §§ 2701–2721), ended an era of Indian gaming which could be characterized as traditional tribal games, mostly limited to tribal members. These traditional tribal games viewed gambling as a part of their society and cultural heritage. During the 1970s and early 1980s, some tribes opened parts of their reservations to the general public when they developed bingo halls and card rooms as a nascent means of tribal economic development.

1. Reservation Economic Development

In those early days of gambling operations on reservations, some tribes developed high-stakes bingo halls as a means to raise revenue, in those states where bingo was already legal. The tribes offered bingo games that did not comply with that state's gaming regulations, including maximum prizes and operators having to be state-recognized charities.

Although tribes were not subject directly to state laws, Congress had plenary power over Indian country. Rather than pass hundreds of separate laws for each reservation, Congress took the short-cut of applying the public policies of the state where the tribe happened to be located. In a series of statutes, the most important of which was Public Law 280, Congress decreed that if an activity was criminal under a state's law, it would also be criminal under federal law, if the activity took place on a reservation. So, if the killing of a human being with malice aforethought was murder, it was also murder in Indian country. However, mere civil regulations under state law, like zoning, would not apply to tribes.

In *Seminole Tribe v. Butterworth*, 658 F.2d 310 (5th Cir. 1981) and *Barona Group v. Duffy*, 694 F.2d 1185 (9th Cir. 1982), the courts held that since the states generally allowed bingo games, it could be construed that these games did not violate public policy and, therefore, the state lacked the authority to enforce their bingo regulations against the tribes' bingo halls and palaces. In Florida, charities could only offer bingo jackpots of a maximum of $200; the state's tribes could, and did, operate games with jackpots of $50,000 and more. The gist of these decisions is that it augured in a mentality of a number of tribes to explore gaming in general as a means to enhance reservations' economic development and as a panacea to cure all the myriad of economic and social ills that befuddled Native American tribes in the 1980s.

2. California v. Cabazon Band of Mission Indians

In *California v. Cabazon Band of Mission Indians*, 480 U.S. 202, 107 S.Ct. 1083, 94 L.Ed.2d 244 (1987), two local tribes near Palm Springs, California, operated high-stakes bingo halls and a card club on their reservations. These operations were opened to the public and catered to non-Indians that came on the reservations. Although California law allowed charitable bingo games, the jackpot was restricted to $250.00. The tribes challenged the enforcement of the state and county regulations. The Supreme Court reviewed California's gaming policy and concluded that since "California permits a substantial amount of gambling activity, including bingo, and actually promotes gambling through its state lottery, we must conclude that California regulates rather than prohibits gambling in general and bingo in particular." (480 U.S. at 210–211). The Court rejected the argument that California's limits on bingo were criminal, despite the fact that they were found in the state's penal code. The majority reasoned that if that was the test, states would simply put all of their regulations into their penal codes. On balance, the Court decided that compelling federal and tribal interests outweighed California's interest and thus preempted state regulations (480 U.S. at 221). In his dissent, Justice Stevens reasoned that the "precise contours" of Indian gaming "should be made by the Congress of the United States." (480 U.S. at 227 (Stevens, J., dissent)).

D. The Indian Gaming Regulatory Act

Congress reacted to the *Cabazon* decision by rushing through the Indian Gaming and Regulatory Act. The purpose of IGRA, as expressed in its Declaration of Policy, was to provide a statutory basis for gaming operations "as a means of promoting tribal economic development self-sufficiency and strong tribal governments." Other IGRA policy goals are to shield the tribes from organized crime and "to ensure that the Indian tribe is the primary beneficiary ... and to assure that ... [it] is conducted fairly and honestly.... And, to establish an independent federal authority and standards Commission... to protect such gaming as a means of generating Tribal Revenue."

1. Indian Tribes and Indian Land

IGRA provides that "Indian gaming" is to be conducted by an "Indian tribe" on "Indian Lands." To be eligible for federal Indian programs, a tribe ordinarily must be recognized by the federal government. A tribe may be federally recognized through a variety of methods including treaty, statute, executive or administrative order, or long-standing practices of the federal government treating the tribe as a political entity. The lands within the boundaries of current reservations qualify as Indian Lands under IGRA, as do "trust" and restricted lands (*see* 25 U.S.C.A. § 2703(4); 25 C.F.R. § 502.12; 18 U.S.C.A. § 1151). However, IGRA generally prohibits gaming on "after-acquired lands" (acquired after IGRA was signed into law on October 17, 1988); however, there are a number of general and state and tribe specific exceptions (*see* 25 U.S.C.A. § 2719(a), (a)(1), (a)(2)(A), (a)(2)(B), (b)(1)(A)). The most important is the "two-part test," which requires the Secretary of Interior to certify that gaming on after-acquired land would be in the best interests of the tribe and the community; and that the governor of the relevant state agreed to the acquisition.

2. Classes of Gaming

IGRA attempted to balance the tribes' interest in sovereignty with the interest of states in protecting themselves from the impacts Indian gaming would have on state lands and residents. It divides all gambling into three classes, and provides different rules for the different classes.

Class I games are low-stakes social, traditional and ceremonial games; these forms of gambling remain entirely within the control of the tribes. IGRA §§ 2701(a) and 2703(6).

Class II is bingo, very broadly defined, and non-banking card games, like poker.

Class III is the residual Class and includes all other forms of gambling, specifically slot machines, lotteries, parimutuel wagers and casino table games, including roulette, craps and banking cards games like blackjack and baccarat.

IGRA expressly states that tribes may only operate Class II or Class III forms of gambling if the state where the tribe is located "permits" that form of gaming. The most important difference between Class II and Class III gaming is that a tribe may only offer Class III gambling after the tribe enters into a compact with the state. See, IGRA's Findings and Declarations of Policy, 25 U.S.C. §§ 2701 and 2702.

3. The National Indian Gaming Commission

IGRA established the National Indian Gaming Commission (NIGC), which is an independent federal regulatory agency. Although IGRA empowers the NIGC to enact "such regulations and guidelines as it deems appropriate to implement the provisions of" the Act, 25 U.S.C.A. § 2706(b)(10), the NIGC is mostly concerned with Class II gaming; Class III is to be co-regulated by the state and tribe pursuant to a compact. For example, in 1999, the NIGC created "minimum internal control standards"

(MICS) for all tribal gaming operations. The MICS regulated specific games, as well as cage and credit internal audits, surveillance, electronic processing, and complimentary services and items (25 C.F.R. Pt. 542). In a careful reading of IGRA, District Court Judge John D. Bates ruled the NIGC did not have the statutory authority to issue MICS over Class III gaming, *Colorado River Indian Tribes v. National Indian Gaming Commission*, 383 F.Supp.2d 123 (D.D.C. 2005), and the Court of Appeals for the D.C. Circuit agreed, 466 F.3d 134 (D.C. Cir. 2006).

The NIGC does have some authority to enforce IGRA's provisions, the NIGC's federal regulations, and the tribes' own gaming regulations, ordinances, and resolutions. Before using its enforcement powers, the NIGC must issue a written complaint in "common and concise language." 25 U.S.C.A. § 2713(a)(3). The NIGC has the authority to conduct investigations, demand access to all papers, subpoena witnesses, hold hearings, and receive testimony and evidence. 25 U.S.C.A. §§ 2713(a)(3); 2706(b)(4), and 2715.

4. Scope of Gaming

Much of the fighting over what types of gambling are allowed on Indian land revolves around the question of Class II versus Class III. Class III games require a tribal-state compact and states often put limits on the numbers of machines and ask to share in the tribes' gaming revenue. Class II games do not require a compact, or any other approval by the states. Class II games are often referred to as bingo-type but they also cover non-banked card games. Poker is a non-banked card game; in poker, players play against each other, rather than against the "house" or a "bank." These card games are classified as Class II as long as the card games are in compliance with state law on hours of operation and wager and pot limits. Class II also allows video or computer versions, so long as the games, primarily bingo and paper pull-tabs, are merely being played with "electronic, computer, or other technological aids." A facsimile of a game, such as a stand-alone bingo machine where the player plays against the house, is Class III. IGRA allows Class II games on tribal lands in states that permit this type of gaming for any purpose by any person.

Before a tribe opens a Class II casino, it must adopt a regulatory ordinance approved by the NIGC chair, which will issue licenses for each Class II bingo hall and card room. Class II-gaming is self-regulated by the tribes with NIGC oversight. The NIGC may also inspect and audit Class II gross revenue records. After three years of satisfactory operations, a tribe may request complete self-regulation.

5.   Class III

All other forms of gambling are Class III. These include what are considered the more dangerous games, including slot machines; banking table games, blackjack, craps and roulette; lotteries, sports betting and pari-mutuel wagering on jai alai and horse and dograces. By far the most profitable forms of Class III gaming are casino-style gambling, particularly slot machines. IGRA's Class III requirements echo, in large part, the Class II requirements. Tribes can operate Class III gaming only in those states that allow such gaming for any purpose by any person. Many Class III-type games are illegal under the Johnson Act, 15 U.S.C.A. §§ 1175(a), 1171(a). However, IGRA specifically waives application of § 1175 to any gaming conduct in connection with a valid tribal-state compact in a state in which gambling devices are legal, 25 U.S.C.A. § 2710 (d)(6). A tribe must adopt an NIGC chair-approved ordinance before opening a Class III casino. This ordinance must incorporate Class II provisions; and the tribe has "sole discretion" in revoking ordinances authorizing Class III gaming. The tribe must enter into an approved management contract for operation of a Class III casino and also must enter into an agreement with the State, which is called a "tribal-state compact."

6. Tribal–State Compact

Before a tribe can open a Class III gaming facility, it must enter an agreement, a tribal-state compact, with the state on how the gaming will be regulated. IGRA requires the state, though not the tribe, to negotiate in good faith. IGRA gives the state, along with the tribe, the power to sue in federal court to enforce the compact by enjoining any Class III gaming activity that violates the tribal-state compact. In *Florida v. Seminole Tribe*, 181

F.3d 1237 (11th Cir. 1999), the Court held that a state's right of action extends only to gaming activities that violate an existing compact; the state does not have the authority to seek to enjoin Class III games conducted in the absence of a tribal-state complex. The tribe must first formally request that the state enter into compact negotiations; once the state receives the request, "the state shall negotiate with the Indian Tribe in good faith..." 25 U.S.C.A. § 2710(a)(3)(A). In *Match–E–Be–Nash–She–Wish Band of Pottawatomi, Indians v. Engler*, 304 F.3d 616 (6th Cir. 2002), the Court held that before a state's good-faith duty is initiated, the requesting tribe must possess qualifying Indians lands; that is, a state has no duty to negotiate with any tribe that lacks a reservation or other land that constitutes Indian land under IGRA.

However, the U.S. Supreme Court in *Seminole Tribe v. Florida*, 517 U.S. 44, 116 S.Ct. 1114, 134 L.Ed.2d 252 (1996), invalidated IGRA's mechanism to enforce the state's obligation of good faith. Basing the decision on not only the Eleventh Amendment, but also the sovereignty of states, the Court ruled that Congress did not have the power to allow a tribe to sue a state without the state's consent. In practice, the *Seminole* case only affected a few states, since others, such as California, had consented to be sued in test cases under IGRA. Important questions still remain, particularly whether federal regulations created subsequent to *Seminole* are constitutional when they authorize tribal Class III gaming in a state which has refused to negotiate a compact.

IGRA authorizes three federal causes of actions: (1) failure to negotiate the compact in good faith, (2) the Secretary of the Interior may sue to enforce compact procedures developed through a tribe's suit against the state and (3) either a tribe or the state may sue to stop a Class III gaming activity which violates the governing compact.

7. Criminal Provisions

Prior to the passage of IGRA, the jurisdiction over crimes committed in what is legally called "Indian Country" varied from state to state and depended in part on who the defendants were. Tribes have limited rights to enforce their own criminal laws, especially against members of their own tribe. But, Public Law 280 allowed some states to have criminal jurisdiction, but not others.

That mishmash still exists. But at least for gambling crimes the situation has been clarified. Today, 18 U.S.C.A. § 1166 makes it clear that "all State laws pertaining to the licensing, regulation, or prohibition of gambling, including but not limited to criminal sanctions applicable thereto, shall apply in Indian country in the same manner and to the same extent as such laws apply elsewhere in the State." There are two important exceptions. Gambling conducted pursuant to and meeting all of the requirements of IGRA cannot be prosecuted, because it has been defined as not being "gambling" under this statute. And the federal government has "exclusive jurisdiction over criminal prosecutions of violations of State gambling laws that are made applicable under this section to Indian country," unless the tribe and state agree in their compact that the state will have criminal jurisdiction "with respect to gambling on the lands of the Indian tribe."

These are many federal criminal statutes of general applicability that could conceivably apply to tribal gaming operations. Some examples are the sports bribery law, which prohibits bribery to influence sporting contest outcomes, 18 U.S.C.A. § 224; lottery statutes that prohibit mailing (non-state) lottery tickets, 18 U.S.C.A. § 1301; the Gaming Ship Act, which prohibits "gambling ships" in U.S. waters, 18 U.S.C.A. §§ 1081–1083; in 1992, Congress allowed gambling in U.S. flag vessels in limited circumstances, 15 U.S.C.A. § 1175; the Wire Act, which prohibits use of wire communication to transmit sports bets, 18 U.S.C.A. § 1084; the Travel Act, that generally prohibits interstate travel or use of the postal system in carrying out illegal activities, 18 U.S.C.A. § 1952; the Paraphernalia Act, prohibiting interstate distribution of illegal gambling aids, 18 U.S.C.A. § 1953; the Illegal Gambling Businesses Act, 18 U.S.C.A. § 1955; and RICO, which prohibits racketeering activity, 18 U.S.C.A. §§ 1961–1968. Legal tribal gaming, including Class III conducted pursuant to a compact, would probably be exempt from these statutes. IGRA expressly allows such gaming to be advertised over television and radio. And the legislative history of IGRA makes it clear that Congress did not want any of these other federal anti-gambling statutes to apply to Class II gaming, even if conducted across state lines.

Two statutes that specifically apply criminal sanctions to Indian gaming are IGRA's criminal provisions and the Johnson Act. IGRA created three new criminal provisions: (1) "Gaming in Indian Country," 18 U.S.C.A. § 1166 generally prohibits gaming in violation of state law on tribal lands; (2) § 1167 makes it a federal crime to steal money or property from a gaming facility on tribal land; and (3) § 1168, which applies to officers, employers, and individual licensees, makes it a federal crime for them to embezzle money from a tribal casino.

The Johnson Act prohibits interstate transportation of illegal gambling devices, 15 U.S.C.A. § 1172, and the possession or use of these devices in Indian Country (this part of the Johnson Act is called the Indian Gambling Act, 15 U.S.C.A. § 1175(a)). Prior to IGRA, the Johnson Act clearly prohibited slots on reservations. However, after the Supreme Court's decision in *California v. Cabazon Band of Mission Indians*, 480 U.S. 202, 107 S.Ct. 1083, 94 L.Ed.2d 244 (1987), federal regulations, including the Johnson Act, would apply to tribal casinos. Although *Cabazon* allowed tribes to conduct bingo and card games, the Johnson Act prohibited gambling devices. But, IGRA effectively expanded the types of gambling allowed on reservations by exempting Class III gaming from the Johnson Act. In *Seneca–Cayuga Tribe v. NIGC*, 327 F.3d 1019 (10th Cir. 2003), the Court held that Class II electronic, computer, and technologic aids are shielded from the

Johnson Act on the basis that a contrary conclusion would expose users of Class II technologic aids to Johnson Act liability for the exact conduct that is authorized by IGRA. However, the Eighth Circuit in *United States v. Santee Sioux Tribe*, 324 F.3d 607 (8th Cir. 2003), reasoned that a tribe must comply with both IGRA and the Johnson Act in operating Class II games; the Court held that the technologic aid in *Santee* did not qualify as a gambling device.

E. State Sovereign Immunity

Some states challenged IGRA's cause of action to enforce the good faith duty as an unconstitutional infringement of state sovereignty. In *Seminole Tribe v. Florida*, 517 U.S. 44, 116 S.Ct. 1114, 134 L.Ed.2d 252 (1996), the U.S. Supreme Court sided with the states and held that the inherent sovereign immunity of states, as exemplified in the Eleventh Amendment, prevented Congress from authorizing such lawsuits by tribes against states.

1. Seminole Tribe v. Florida

The Eleventh Amendment provides that the "judicial power of the United States shall not be construed to extend to any suit in law or equity, commenced or prosecuted against one of the United States by Citizens of another State, or by Citizens or Subjects of any Foreign State." (*Seminole Tribe*, 517 U.S. 44). The Eleventh Amendment has been broadly interpreted to generally prosecute suits against the states, including against state officials acting in their official capacity without the state's consent. There are some exceptions, including Congress' limited ability to abrogate state's immunity from suit and what is commonly known as the *Ex Parte Young* exception (209 U.S. 123, 28 S.Ct. 441, 52 L.Ed. 714 (1908)), which holds that state sovereign immunity does not extend to state officials who are acting unconstitutionally (or contrary to federal laws), so that they may be sued for prospective injunctive relief despite the state's immunity from suit.

The Seminole Tribe, in 1991, filed a suit against Florida and Florida's governor, Lawton Chiles, under IGRA, alleging that the state refused to negotiate a tribal-state compact allowing the tribe to offer Class III games on its reservation. The *Seminole* case held that neither the Interstate Commerce Clause nor the Indian Commerce Clause authorized Congress to abrogate state sovereign immunity. Despite Congress' exclusive authority to deal with tribes, it still may not create a cause of action against the states under the Indian Commerce Clause (as it attempted to do through IGRA). In short, the *Seminole* Court held that a state could not be sued in federal court by a tribe under IGRA without the state's consent. The Court invalidated Congress' statutory compromise between state interest and tribal and federal interests over Indian gaming. The Supreme Court had cut the heart out of IGRA, creating situations where tribes had the right to have gaming, but had no remedy.

2. Tribal–State Compact Negotiations After *Seminole Tribe*

The *Seminole* decision left open the question of what should happen if a state fails to deal in good faith in negotiating a tribal-state compact. To the extent that *Seminole* held that IGRA's enforcement mechanism was unconstitutional, IGRA's severability clause severed that unconstitutional section from the rest of the statute, allowing the remainder of the federal regulatory scheme to remain effective (25 U.S.C.A. § 2721). Most courts that reviewed the severability issue after *Seminole* determined that the tribal-state compact requirement survive. Some went further, holding that the Interior Secretary's power to issue an administrative compact allows a tribe recourse when a state fails to consent to suit. After *Seminole*, the Secretary of the Interior initiated regulations which took effect in 1999 that set forth the procedure for the Secretary's promulgation of Class III gaming regulations in the absence of a valid tribal-state compact; but other courts disagreed. Prior to the Supreme Court's decision in *Seminole*, the 9th Circuit had already discussed and dismissed the notion that the states can be bypassed by turning "the Secretary of the Interior into a federal czar ..." *Spokane Tribe of Indians v. Washington State*, 28 F.3d 991, 997 (9th Cir. 1994), cert. granted and judgment vacated on different grounds 517 U.S. 1129, 116 S.Ct. 1410, 134 L.Ed.2d 537 (1996), dismissed 91 F.3d 1350 (9th Cir. 1996). The 1999 regulations were firmly rejected by the 5th Circuit in 2007 in a suit brought by the state of Texas. The Court explained that the new procedures deviated so significantly from the procedures laid down by Congress in the statute, IGRA, that they could not be considered valid. *Texas v. United States*, 497 F.3d 491, 507 (5th Cir. 2007) (citations and footnotes deleted), Cert. Denied by *Kickapoo Traditional Tribe of Texas v. Texas*, 555 U.S. 811, 129 S.Ct. 32, 172 L.Ed.2d 18 (2008).

F. Federal Government Regulations of Indian Gaming

IGRA uses its regulatory authority over Native American gaming interests according to the type of gaming activity that is invoked. However, the tribes maintain exclusive regulatory jurisdiction over Class I gaming, while Class II bingo falls under tribal regulatory jurisdiction with NIGC oversight. Class III casino-style gaming requires both tribal regulation and a tribal-state compact. The NIGC and the Secretary of Interior also have regulatory roles as regards Class III, although, it is still in dispute whether the Secretary has the power to impose Class III regulations when a state refuses to negotiate a tribal-state compact and also refuses to consent to be sued under IGRA.

1. Federal Agencies

The mission of the Interior Department is to fulfill the federal government's trust responsibilities to tribes. The Assistant Secretary of the Interior for Indian Affairs heads the Bureau of Indian Affairs

(BIA) which, *inter alia*, manages 55 million acres of tribal land held in trust by the federal government and administers federal programs that provide services to more than 1.5 million Native Americans. Under IGRA, only federally-recognized tribes may conduct tribal gaming, and only on federally defined Indian lands. Some states also give official recognition to tribes within their borders. However, tribes which have not been recognized by the federal government do not come under federal laws or programs, have very few rights and often live in abject poverty, even if they have been recognized by a state.

The NIGC is an independent federal agency, created by IGRA to have a role in regulating Indian gaming. The U.S. Attorney General also plays a role in ensuring compliance with IGRA and other federal laws related to gaming. The Attorney General heads the U.S. Department of Justice, which includes the FBI, which exercises criminal investigation powers that involve Indian gaming. The NIGC and the FBI created the Indian Gaming Working Group, which was founded in 2003 and coordinates federal resources in the investigation and prosecution of cases of national importance that impact on the tribal gaming industry. Also, the Treasury Department's Financial Crimes Enforcement Network (FinCEN) regulates financial laundering under the Federal Bank Secrecy Act (31 U.S.C.A. §§ 5311–5330; 12 U.S.C.A. §§ 1818(S), 1829(B), 1951–1959). Tribal casinos are subject to the Act's money-laundering controls.

2. Tribal Gaming Commission

Tribes typically create gaming Commissions to implement the tribal gaming ordinances and to ensure compliance with IGRA, tribal-state compacts, and other relevant tribal laws. The Commissioners suffer from the appearance of being captive regulatory agencies, since they are almost always members of the very tribe that owns the casino.

3. State Gaming Commissions

Since Class II and III gaming is allowed in states that permit such gaming, state gaming commissions sometimes play a role in determining the overall regulatory scheme of legalized gaming within that state's borders. State gaming regulators implement, monitor, and enforce state law and state public policy as regards all types of legalized gambling allowed in that state. But state governments, including their gaming commissions, have no power over Class II games on Indian land, except in the extremely rare situations where the tribe has consented to co-regulation. States cannot even indirectly limit Class II games, by, for example, allowing only bingo but not paper pull-tabs. Only if a state completely prohibits all bingo can the state prevent its tribes from operating any form of bingo, including pull-tabs and electronic bingo machines, allowed under IGRA. It is common for states in their tribal-state compacts to require that the state gaming commission be almost a full co-regulator of Class III gaming. Questions continue to arise as to the scope of the states' power, such as whether it can conduct surprise inspections of tribal gaming operations or whether it can audit the tribes' books.

G.   The Future of Indian Gaming

The prospects for the future of Indian gaming is intrinsically connected to a myriad of political, legal, and economic developments. The key question involved in the future of Native American casinos is the interaction and problems that tribes and states find themselves in as they attempt to determine how best to promote a positive solution for both parties through tribal gaming.

1.   The Future of Tribal Legalized Gambling Generally

With the current climate of economic distress, many states and localities look to Indian casinos as a means to jump-start job creation and economic development. Also, tribal-state compacts often contain revenue-sharing provisions in which tribes make payments directly into community funds for public education or other local services. The statute, IGRA, not only does not contemplate revenue sharing, but actually forbids a state to even attempt to tax a tribe's gaming revenue. However, the Secretary of Interior has approved revenue sharing, when the state has traded some valuable right, usually the exclusive right to have Class III gaming in a particular geographic area, to a tribe in exchange for a percentage of the tribe's slot machine revenue. Tribes are often willing to give up 25% of the hundreds of millions of dollars a casino can earn rather than fight the state for years and end up with 100% of nothing. Governors and state legislators become less opposed to Indian gaming when they see it will mean significant help in balancing the state's books. So, as the economic crisis starting in 2007 continues to linger, states and tribes are making deals for more and more Indian gaming, with a large share of the newly created revenue going to the state.

2. Tribal Economic Diversification

Because of experience, expertise, and revenue gained through tribal casinos, many tribes now look to other economic strategies to diversify, and then stabilize, the economy of the particular reservation; this is especially so, since it appears that tribal gaming is a political football. The goal of tribal gaming is economic diversification; however, it appears that the continued relative profitability of tribal casinos will assure that gaming is a staple of the many diverse Indian economics.

3. Law Reform

Congress may address the problems related to off-reservation casinos and other aspects of tribal gaming by giving states, localities, or other tribes a larger say in the process of banning tribes from seeking casinos across state lines. IGRA requires government negotiations between tribes and states. With the renewed local, economic interest, IGRA's goals of promoting reservation economic development and tribal self-sufficiency appear to lack focus in an increasingly muddied political landscape. It seems that there will be continued proposed amendments to IGRA in Congress that will tend to clarify the problems that are inherent between tribal gaming and state and local political units.

4. Tribal–State Compact Negotiations

Tribal–state compact negotiations now veer away from IGRA's requirements for allowable subject matter and detour into a discussion of political issues such as the abrogation of treaty rights or revenue-sharing with state or local governments. In a shift of priorities, tribes now find themselves negotiating with state and local officials over such topics as land, water grazing, hunting, and fishing rights; not to mention the increase in revenue-sharing agreements. It is also possible that Congress will amend IGRA to reflect the perceived imbalance of state and tribal bargaining in Class III gaming after *Seminole*. However, it is also likely that Congress will not interfere with the current state of tribal-state compact negotiations.

The great unknown with Indian gaming, as with so much of legal gambling, is what will happen with betting conducted on the Internet. Tribes which have had casinos for years often have the economic and political power to demand a seat at the table, and perhaps one of the few Internet gaming licenses a state will issue. But interesting legal questions arise whether allowing anyone else in the state to conduct online gambling breaches a tribal-state compact, allowing the tribe to withdraw from revenue sharing with the state. Under IGRA, tribes have the right to offer the same forms of gambling that are permitted in the state. If a state licenses Internet poker, that means that the tribe can also offer Internet poker. But are players limited to those physically present on Indian land, or can the game be offered to anyone with a computer in the state?

CHAPTER 9
CANADIAN CASINOS

A. Canadian Gambling Generally

Some form of gambling is available in each of the ten provinces (British Columbia, Newfoundland and Labrador, Alberta, Saskatchewan, Manitoba, Quebec, Ontario, Nova Scotia, Prince Edward Island, and New Brunswick) and three territories (Yukon, Northwest Territory, and Nunavut) of Canada. Technically, the provinces and territories own the casinos. Sometimes they run them, as with Lotto Québec running Casino Montreal, among others. Sometimes the provincial governments contract to have private companies run the casinos, as Ontario has done with Caesars in Windsor.

All other gaming in Canada also operates entirely under the authority of the provincial and territorial governments. Charities, First Nations (Indian tribes, often called "bands"), and private groups all must follow the guidelines set by the provincial governments.

The legal age to gamble varies among the provinces. For example, the required age to gamble in a casino is 18 in Québec, while it is 19 in Ontario. For lottery and scratch tickets, the standard legal age is 18.

Gambling in Canada has always been linked to the Canadian Criminal Code. In 1892, this code banned all forms of gambling; however, charitable games such as bingo and raffles were allowed in 1900. This was followed by horse racing in 1910; and in 1925, gambling events were allowed to take place at agricultural fairs and exhibitions. This led to the massive temporary casinos offering games like blackjack during the Calgary Stampede and other fairs.

A Criminal Code amendment was passed in 1969 that allowed federal and provincial governments to use the lottery in order to help fund worthy projects. Nineteen eighty saw the opening of Cash Casino, located in Calgary. It was the country's first year-round charitable casino. In 1990, New Brunswick became the first province to allow Video Lottery Terminals.

Gambling in Canada was originally entirely regulated under the federal Criminal Code of Canada. The seemingly minor adjustments that have been made to the gambling provisions of the Criminal Code from 1892 until 1985 have, taken together, permitted and facilitated gambling's expansion. This had led to the growth of major gambling industries that generate significant amounts of capital for both public and private sector interests.

The explosion of legal gambling in Canada is the indirect result of the 1985 Winter Olympics. The

Federal Government of Canada desperately needed money to fund the Calgary games. In a unique political accord, on June 11, 1985 the Federal Government of the country sold gambling to the provinces for $100 million cash, plus $24 million per year, adjusted for inflation. The first year-round commercial casino, Crystal Casino, opened in Winnipeg in 1989.

It looked like a good deal at the time. The provinces already had an effective monopoly on true lotteries. The federal government had tried to compete by starting its own game; but the rival lottery brought in more hard feelings than money.

The provinces also had control over all other forms of legal wagers. It was the provincial governments that licensed charities to run bingos and blackjack. Although the federal Minister of Agriculture oversees betting on horseraces, eight of the ten provinces had racing commissions to regulate the races themselves.

There was the small question of whether the federal government could, in fact, sell the control of legal gambling to the provinces. As a contract, the agreement was probably not enforceable. However, once the $100 million had been paid by the provinces the federal Parliament amended the nation's Criminal Code making the political accord a done deal.

Canada, unlike the United States, has one Criminal Code for the entire country. In the U.S. each state is free to make up its own criminal laws. The national Canadian Criminal Code, on the other hand, makes virtually all forms of gambling illegal everywhere. So how could the provinces buy the right to run lotteries and casinos?

The written constitutional law of Canada is very strict: certain areas, such as control of crimes and responsibility for Indian affairs, are exclusively within the power of the federal government. The provinces have only those powers given them under such documents as the British North America Act of 1867 and the Constitution Act of 1982. Although the written constitutions do not allow the federal government to delegate power to provincial legislatures, Canadian courts have helped create an unwritten constitution, one that is much more flexible.

In 1991 the Supreme Court of Canada upheld the provincial takeover of legal gambling in the case of *Furtney v. The Queen*, 3 S.C.R. 89. The Court ruled the political deal was not an illegal delegation of power from the federal government. Rather, it was a "vacation" in the strictest legal sense: the federal government had simply withdrawn from the field. Since there was now a legal vacuum, the provinces were free to act. The high Court added that the federal Criminal Code did not actually delegate any power directly to the provincial legislatures. Parliament was giving the power to regulate legal gambling to a province's lieutenant governor. Of course, it was, in fact, the provincial legislatures that were given the ultimate control over legal games of chance.

The law itself was a masterpiece of misdirection. Nowhere is the word "casino" to be found. Section 207 of the federal Criminal Code uses the term "lottery scheme." The government of a province could "conduct and manage a lottery scheme in that province." Provinces were free to license anybody, not just charities, to conduct a "lottery scheme" for charitable purposes. The provinces could continue to license fairs' gambling, now called a "lottery scheme." In fact, anyone could be licensed to run a "lottery scheme," at a public place of amusement if the prizes were less than $500 and the stakes are limited to $2 a bet.

What exactly was a "lottery scheme"? The law defined it as:

"a game or any proposal, scheme, plan, means, device, contrivance or operation ... whether or not it involves betting, pool selling or a pool system of betting other than

(a) a dice game, three-card monte, punch board or coin table;

(b) bookmaking, pool selling or the making or recording of bets ... on any race or fight, or on a single sport event or athletic contest; or

(c) a game or proposal, scheme, plan, means, device contrivance or operation ... that is operated on or through a computer, video device, or slot machine."

So, Canadian casinos opened without dice games. Some used roulette wheels with pictures of dice, so that they could offer craps. Eventually, the law was changed to allow all traditional casino banking games.

Did the federal government understand that it was selling not just true lotteries, but casinos? We all, unfortunately, have the tendency to believe that everything around us is as it always was and always will be. In 1985, gambling in Canada consisted of paper lottery tickets, low-stakes bingo, race tracks and small casinos run by charities. The federal government probably thought that was all it was selling to the provinces.

B.   Canadian Provincial Law

Gambling by territory in Canada can be summarized as follows:

Alberta—Casinos, lottery, horse tracks, and horse track racino. Charitable groups are licensed by the Alberta Gaming and Liquor Commission. Alberta has more gambling per capita than any other location in the country.

British Columbia—Casinos, lottery, horse tracks and horse track racino. Casinos are privately operated at the permission of the government, but the province receives one-tenth percent of the net gaming revenue from a "community" casino and one-sixth from a "destination" casino. They also have allowed bingo halls to begin adding slot machines. The Lottery is running Internet poker.

Manitoba—Casinos, lottery and horse track racino.

New Brunswick—Horse racing and lottery.

Newfoundland and Labrador—Horse racing and lottery

Nova Scotia—Casinos, lottery, and horse tracks.

Ontario—Casinos, lottery, horse tracks and horse track racinos.

Prince Edward Island—Horse track racinos and lottery.

Québec—Casinos, lottery, and horse track racinos; Internet poker.

Saskatchewan—Casinos, lottery, horse tracks and horse track racino.

Yukon Territory—Casino (non-profit) and lottery.

Northwest Territory—Lottery.

Nunavut Territory—Lottery.

C. Canada's Indigenous People and Gambling

In the United States, many Indian tribes have launched successful gambling enterprises that have provided the wherewithal to improve social and economic conditions on many tribal reserves. Canadian First Nation groups are acutely aware of how Indian tribes in the United States have improved their lot through gambling proceeds, but they have been denied in their own efforts to establish similar gambling businesses. The 1985 Criminal Code amendment gave exclusive jurisdiction over gambling to the provinces. This transfer of authority for gambling was seen by some as circumventing the right of First Nations to create and operate gambling ventures. But an examination of the constitutional laws shows that bands in Canada were not historically viewed as domestic nations, as tribes in the U.S. were. The Commerce Clause of the U.S. Constitution expressly gives the U.S. Congress the power "To regulate Commerce with foreign Nations, and among the several States, and with the Indian Tribes." ARTICLE I, SECTION 8, CLAUSE 3. Legally, this puts tribes on equal footing with foreign nations and the states. There is nothing like this in the documents that make up Canadian constitutional law. Instead, Indians are usually seen as citizens of the Crown who happen to also belong to a band, rather than citizens of a domestic nation, (who were only granted full American citizenship in 1924).

Some First Nations have opted to work cooperatively with provincial authorities to implement gambling establishments. Agreements between provincial authorities and First Nations with respect to gambling have been reached in Saskatchewan, Manitoba, Ontario, Quebec, and Nova Scotia. Policies within each province vary considerably. Some First Nations have negotiated a percentage share of revenues from established casinos, while others have been permitted to operate casinos on their reserves.

D. Internet Gaming

The legal discussion in Canada surrounding on-line gambling issues has been somewhat muted compared to the lively and often heated debates in jurisdictions such as the United States, Australia, and countries within the European Union. The Canadian law applicable to online gambling consists of a few provisions of the *Criminal Code* (Canada), R.S.C. 1985, c. C–46, and a handful of cases that fail to probe much beyond the surface into the often complex legal issues associated with online gambling. In 2010, most of the provincial lotteries announced that they would be opening Internet poker and other online games, and pooling players across the nation. British Columbia was the first to get up and operating, but had technical problems, which caused it to have to close down for a while. Loto Québec was the second to open games online. Virtually every other provincial and territorial lottery in Canada is looking at joining and most will soon have many forms of gambling available for their residents on the Internet. It is not yet clear whether these games will pool players with other legal jurisdiction in the U.S. and around the world.

E. Problem Gamblers

Problem gambling is taken very seriously in Canada. The Canadian Safety Council estimates that over 200 people per year commit suicide due to problems stemming from a gambling addiction (such as bankruptcy, domestic abuse, family break-up, assault, fraud, and theft). Help for problem gamblers is available, however, and numerous 24–hour hotlines are in operation throughout the country. In addition, the various provinces spend millions of dollars each year in an effort to educate citizens about the risks associated with gambling.

The range of services offered for problem gamblers in Canada include toll-free helplines, warnings about gambling addiction in gambling venues, self-exclusion policies for problem gamblers who lack the willpower to stay out of casinos, and liaisons with Gamblers Anonymous chapters in the region. Provinces with established problem gambling prevention and treatment programs allocate substantial ongoing funds to provide comprehensive services that include outpatient counseling, intensive day treatment, and inpatient residential care. In addition, they provide courses on problem gambling for health care professionals, public education about problem gambling, and annual conferences on academic and applied problem gambling concerns.

CHAPTER 10

INTERNATIONAL GAMBLING

A. Global Gaming Generally

Gaming is an international phenomenon with startling developments, such as Macau and Singapore now surpassing Las Vegas. Although mostly controlled by local rules and regulations, there are always national laws, and in some cases, international treaties and organizations (such as the World Trade Organization, WTO) which also control and shape local policies. The University of Nevada–Reno's Institute for the Study of Gambling and Commercial Gaming has published numerous books on the subject. One constant in international casino regulations is the need for change and control. Currently, there are about 50 countries that allow casino gambling, and many more jurisdictions that authorize lotteries, sports betting and Internet gambling.

B. Transnational Regulations in On-line Gambling

A general consensus is developing with regard to when a state or nation has the right to exclude Internet and other remote wagering originating in another state or nation. The legal terminology may vary, as will the specific legal doctrine applied in any particular case; but the overarching analysis remains the same. Recent decisions from courts, including the European Court of Justice ("ECJ") and United States Supreme Court; tribunals for international agencies, including the World Trade Organization ("WTO"); and announcements from the European Commission, establish a framework for determining when a jurisdiction may keep out foreign legal gambling. These decisions also illustrate how the United States seeks to impose a prohibition on overseas internet gambling while permitting Americans to bet from their homes and offices with U.S. operators.

A sovereign has the inherent power to exclude all foreign goods and services, including gambling. It expressly volunteers to give up some of this power when it joins a federation, such as the states of the U.S. or Australia, or when it signs a treaty. When signing a treaty, a sovereign state can pick and choose what it will admit. For example, while some governments expressly said that they would not allow foreign gambling when they signed the WTO treaties, the United States did not. Nations can also agree to let down their trade barriers through their actions, a doctrine known as comity of nations.

Gambling, however, is a morally suspect industry. It is one of the few areas where a state can unilaterally change its mind—if it has a good enough reason. A state needs to put forward some evidence to show it has a reasonable belief that it must exclude foreign legal gambling to protect the health, safety, welfare, and morality of its residents, and in doing so, will be excused from the commitments it made when it joined the federation or signed the treaty. So, if the United Kingdom has agreed to let in all commercial services from other member states of the European Union, it has the right to keep out large foreign lotteries, so long as it is doing so to protect the health, safety, welfare, and morality of its residents. *Her Majesty's Customs and Excise v. Gerhart Schindler and Joerg Schindler, Reference for a Preliminary Ruling: High Court of Justice, Queen's Bench Division—United Kingdom*, Court of Justice of the European Communities, Case C–275/92, Doc.Num. 692J0275, Reports of Cases 1994 I–1039 (Judgment Mar. 24, 1994). However, excluding foreign legal gambling merely to protect local operators from competition usually is not considered a valid reason to keep out foreign legal gambling.

Withdrawing from its treaty obligations to let in foreign gambling presents no problem for a state that completely outlaws all forms of gambling.

When the state attempts to exclude foreign legal gambling, while allowing local operators to take the same bets from its residents, the state's motive appears to be merely the elimination of competition to maximize revenue for local operators. Once a country has signed a treaty or a state has joined a federation, it will almost never succeed in allowing local gambling operations while excluding legal outsiders. Portugal was able to convince the European Court of Justice that it was allowing only limited local gambling, to divert its residents away from illegal sites. But the Portuguese gambling operation was small, without extensive advertising, and with all of its revenue going for worthy causes within the country. *Liga Portuguesa de Futebol Profissional, Bwin International Ltd. v. Departamento de Jogos da Santa Casa da Misericórdia de Lisboa*, ECJ, EU: Case C–42/07 (Judgment 8 September 2009).

Because operating an Internet gambling business is mostly prohibited in the United States, the majority of online gambling businesses now operate from smaller jurisdictions, such as Antigua, the Kahnawake Mohawk Nation of Canada, or Alderney, a group of islands in the English Channel. These jurisdictions embrace, regulate, and legitimize Internet gambling in an effort to make it a profitable business. There has been a recent shift, however, and more industrialized nations are beginning to legitimize Internet gambling, including England, Australia, and even Canada.

C. Casinos in Europe Generally

The burgeoning European Community mentality has not yet significantly changed the historical local traditions of gaming in Europe. Gambling is one of the very few areas where the European Court of Justice (ECJ) has held that member states still have the power to set their own rules, provided they do not discriminate against operators in other member states. Casinos, for example, are exempt from the nearly universal requirement of harmonization; meaning, for example, that countries do not have to pay the same wages as other countries. However, the European Community has influenced the style of casino operations; for example, gender discrimination among employees has been restrained or eliminated in most jurisdictions. But, local authorities still control such issues as the variety of gaming rules, local operational monopolies, limit the types of games that are permitted, and permit the exclusion of certain people from gaming.

In the past few years the ECJ has made it clear that being licensed by one member state in the E.U., such as Malta, does not automatically lead to being licensed by any other member state. Operators of Internet gaming sites pointed to the many rights given citizens of the E.U. under the Treaty of Rome and other agreements which created the European Economic Community and the European Union. These include the right of citizens of the E.U. to travel freely across borders and to establish businesses and ship goods and sell services in other member states. But, the ECJ has ruled repeatedly that gambling is one of the few areas of law and society where member states can make their own rules. This is justified on the grounds that gambling, particularly remote wagering, is somehow more dangerous than other economic endeavors, particularly to the vulnerable classes of minors and compulsive gambling, and more susceptible to infiltration by organized crime. Gambling also has a unique moral element, and the E.U. respects the rights of nations and states to decide upon their own standards of morality. The ECJ has even upheld the right of governments to keep their monopolies, but only if they are excluding legal gambling from other member states solely for the protection of their own citizens. *Liga Portuguesa de Futebol Profissional, Bwin International Ltd. v. Departamento de Jogos da Santa Casa da Misericórdia de Lisboa*, ECJ, EU: Case C–42/07 (Judgment 8 September 2009). The ECJ will not allow a country to exclude operators from other E.U. member states if the monopoly gaming operator is actively promoting its games, rather than merely trying to divert residents away from what it considers to be illegal foreign sites.

In Europe, virtually every nation has the same thing: casinos dominated by blackjack, roulette and slot machines; a state lottery, with sports betting; low-limit gaming devices in bars; parimutuel betting on horseracing; charity games, often bingo; and a growing market for Internet gambling. Many countries allow low-limit slot machines in amusement arcades, often called amusement with prizes ("AWP"). These are sometimes declared, by statutes, not to be gambling. In the United Kingdom, for example, slot machines paying out jackpots of no more than a few pounds were classified as AWPs and were available to children at beachfront amusement arcades for decades.

Gambling is seen in Europe, as elsewhere, as a painless tax, an easy way for governments to raise revenue when they most need it and cannot raise taxes. The economic crisis that swept the world beginning in 2007 has led to more legalization of gaming in Europe. Italy was hit by an earthquake which caused massive damage in the center of the country, right when it was considering legalizing Internet gaming. The online gaming was put on a fast track, licenses were issued, and the money started pouring in.

But, each country is allowed to create its own standards. For European operators, the differences are significant, since they concern issues such as tax rates and who may be granted a license. But in Asia, the differences among jurisdictions is much greater.

1. England

The United Kingdom has long allowed betting on horseracing, bingo and sports events, and authorized limited casino gambling in what were supposed to be clubs. In 1994, it took the first important gambling case to be heard by the European Court of

Justice, *Schindler*, winning the right to exclude West German lottery ads, because England had no legal large lotteries. Today, its lottery is among the largest in the world. Amusement halls are allowed to have Amusement With Prizes ("AWP") machines, low-limit slot machines that were defined as not being gambling. Betting on sports and races has spread from tracks to off-course bookmakers. Spread betting took off in the 1980s, allowing punters to bet on exotic propositions during a game, such as when will a ball first go out of bounds. Facing competition from AWPs and casinos, bookmakers lobbied for and won the right to operate their own gambling devices, called fixed-odds betting terminals ("FOBTs"). The most common FOBT is an automated roulette wheel. Casinos and most other forms of gambling are regulated by the United Kingdom Gambling Commission: AWPs, bingo, casinos, bookmakers and small lotteries; but not spread betting or the National Lottery. The U.K. is now working under what amounts to two separate licensing schemes: casinos licensed as clubs continue, licensed by the Gaming Board of Great Britain; but the Gaming Act of 2005 allows the United Kingdom Gambling Commission to approve much larger casinos.

That Act also is leading to changes in the regulation of Internet gambling. Its main stated purpose was add protections for vulnerable, minors and compulsive gamblers. So, England is dropping its legal interpretation, that Internet gambling is ruled by the foreign country that licenses the operation, to impose restrictions on anyone accepting bets from the U.K. The Government has announced it plans to require all Internet gambling operators taking bets from England from anywhere in the world will have to be licensed by the Gambling Commission. Presently, anyone licensed by a jurisdiction on the UK's "white list," like Malta, that meet the Commission's standards, can advertise for British bettors. The white list will be phased out; but operators licensed by those jurisdictions will be "fast tracked" to receive the new Internet gambling licenses.

Casinos in Great Britain were legalized originally for purposes far different from those behind legalization in Nevada or New Jersey. In England, gambling was seen as a social evil to be controlled, not a means of raising revenue for the state. In addition to a system of licensing and continuing supervision through on-sight surveillance and audits, Great Britain adds a superstructure of controls, paternalistic in their design, that completely overwhelm the basic system. For decades, the emphasis was consistently on limiting gambling and its perceived adverse side effects. To get a license, an applicant had to show that there was an unmet demand for legal gambling in a particular geographic area. Casino gambling was limited to private clubs, owned by British individuals and corporations.

Casinos were initially limited to two—literally just two—slot machines per casino. Players had to register in person 48 hours in advance. Casinos were not allowed to advertise or grant credit. In fact, players' checks had to be deposited, even if the player won and could redeem the check. The theory was that people would be embarrassed if their bankers saw many checks going through written to casinos, as if bankers read customers' checks. In the mid–1960s, under the loose rules and enforcement practices of the 1963 Betting, Gaming, and Lotteries Act, there were over 1,200 gaming clubs in England, many of them connected with organized crime. Parliament passed a strict Gaming Act in 1968. It contained a control system allowing nearly unlimited agency discretion and imposing pervasive paternalism to protect players from themselves. By 1972, the number of clubs was reduced to 120. These restrictions seem to have been successful in limiting the overt presence of organized crime and corruption. Criminal activity, in the form of direct ownership of gambling enterprises or protection rackets, has been stemmed. The illegal casinos have apparently disappeared and the growth of legal casinos has been severely limited.

The club system developed, in part, due to fairly strict class differences in England. Betting with bookmakers attracted primarily working class punters. Clubs, on the other hand, were private, with membership fees and dress codes, self-limiting to members of the upper class. In England, gambling clubs operate much as private nightclubs would: play is mostly at night and the clubs compete for the discretionary funds of a limited segment of the population. The number of clubs is limited so there has not been a dramatic impact on the entertainment industry. It will be interesting to see if the larger, more tourist-oriented casinos allowed under the new law will lead to more competition to existing gambling operators, and more cries to loosen the governmental restrictions they must bear.

D.   Casinos in Asia Generally

Because of political and religious prohibitions many countries did not allow gambling even though many of the people of Asia love wagering. Of course in the last ten years casinos have dramatically increased in these regions especially Macau, Singapore, the Philipines, Korea, Cambodia, and even to some extent Vietnam. In fact, Japan is the last major industrialized nation on Earth not to have casinos. Not that it does not have gaming devices. There may be as many pachinko and pachislo gaming machines in Japan as there are slot machines in the rest of the world combined. The tidal wave that devastated the country in 2011 makes legalization of casinos more likely than ever.

The explosion of legal gaming which is sweeping the planet has finally reached Asia and the Pacific. But it is developing in ways that are idiosyncratic. Government policy in Asia ranges from complete prohibitions of all forms, to legalization of some gambling, to successful efforts to out-casino Las Vegas.

The differences are due, in part, to the divergence in local culture and the forms and philosophies of the governments involved. You would not expect

North Korea to treat gambling the same as the Philippines. But, the differences are primarily the result of historic accidents. Legal gambling goes through cycles. When all gambling is illegal, the legalization phase usually begins with a breakthrough of some form that is considered innocuous. Often this is social gambling and low-stakes games for charity, which are either expressly made legal or often simply tolerated. In the English– and Spanish–speaking countries and Europe, this is commonly bingo. In China and Hong Kong, it was mahjong. Today, by local ordinance, mahjong played for money is legal in Hong Kong. In places like Zhuhai in southern China, there are signs on hotel saying that rooms for mahjong are available to rent by the hour.

A second breakthrough comes from the government operating its own lottery. These have come and gone for centuries. But even the most totalitarian regime will sometimes allow the traditional form, with paper tickets and once a week drawings. China, which purports to have no legal gambling, actually has authorized three lotteries for years, with tickets for sale from street booths—the China Welfare Lottery reported passing 70 billion yuan (US$10.2 billion) in sales for 2009. In 2007, it was the world's sixth largest lottery, and the China Sports Lottery was tenth. According to the World Lottery Association, China, aided by the introduction of video lottery terminals (VLTs), is now expected to be the second largest lottery market in the world.

A third form of wagering which has been tolerated historically is betting on horseraces. This was not seen as a problem when it was mainly for the rich, who could afford to own a horse or just to take a day off to go to the racetrack to make a bet. The invention of the telegraph, telephone and parimutuel machine in the 19th century led to new laws against bookmaking.

So, the recent expansion of gambling often comes against a background of small-stakes social and charity games, a state lottery and racetracks. This has been as true in Asia as in the rest of the world. But local customs and history have created situations unlike anything seen in the rest of the world.

Japan today has racetracks and one of the largest lotteries in the world. It also has more slot machines than any other country, except they are not technically slot machines, but rather pachislo machines. Physically indistinguishable from video slot machines, these now out-gross the more traditional pachinko machines, which also have gone hi-tech. These gaming devices are technically legal because they do not pay out in cash. Winners are paid in tokens and merchandise. There is always a convenient window nearby; sometimes literally a hole in the back wall of the building. Here, winning players can redeem their prizes for cash. The payoff is by a company that is supposedly independent from the parlor operator. Experts agree that at least this part of the operation is controlled by organized crime.

Gambling spreads when governments finds it difficult to argue morality, when the state itself is selling lottery tickets, licensing horseracing and at least tacitly endorsing social and charity games. Technology also plays a role, allowing off-track betting on horseraces and lotteries to move from paper tickets to online wagers, including cell phones.

But the major impetus for expansion is usually the legalization of a more attractive form of gambling in a nearby jurisdiction. The sight of all that disposable income, some from a state's own citizens, going across the border to another state, does more than anything else to weaken even anti-gambling lawmakers. No one would have predicted ten years ago that Singapore would be the next great casino market. And it would not be, if Macau, itself the result of a historic accident, had not shown how successful Las Vegas-style casinos can be.

It is doubtful whether the central planners of the People's Republic of China would have intentionally created places like Macau and Hong Kong. Macau always had casinos under the Portuguese. Hong Kong developed the world's largest racetrack, in terms of money wagered, under the British. On the mainland, on the other hand, gambling has been, and still is, one of the sins that can be punished by the death penalty.

1. Macau and Hong Kong

Hong Kong became a Special Administrative Region ("SAR") of the People's Republic of China in 1997, Macau in 1999. But the PRC pledged it would allow the capitalist systems of the two SARs to continue.

When Portugal controlled Macau, a single company, Stanley Ho's Sociedade de Turismo e Diversões de Macau, S.A.R.L. ("STDM"), had a monopoly concession on casinos. As with all monopolies, this restriction severely constrained the industry's growth. But three years after the turnover, the new rulers of Macau decided to issue more casino concessions and put them out to bid. This opened the door to foreign operators, and, more importantly, foreign money.

Unlike American casinos, the majority of gaming revenue came from table games. Traditional Chinese beliefs give the number nine great importance, so the domino game of pai gow, which translates as "make nine," and particularly the card game of baccarat, are of overwhelming importance, rather than slot machines.

The attraction for foreign operators was how much those tables made: STDM's 340 tables won on average approximately US$10 million a year. Las Vegas's gaming tables win only about $730,000. STDM's 11 casinos had revenue of approximately US$3.5 billion a year; at least that was the amount reported officially. And this was before the PRC more fully opened its border.

When the numbers for 2005 were counted, Macau surpassed the Las Vegas Strip in casino revenue, making it the number one casino market in the world. This would not have been possible if the PRC had not dropped its travel restrictions, allowing its residents to travel there without being part of a tour group. The exit and entry point between Zhuhai and Macau has become one of the busiest border crossings in the world. There are hundreds of millions of China's rising middle class who now have the money to spend on shopping and gambling, as well as visitors from Taiwan, Thailand and Hong Kong. By 2011, gaming revenue at Macau's casinos, growing at more than 40% a year, hit $33 billion, nearly three times the amount produced by all casinos in all of Nevada.

Stanley Ho's current holding company, Sociedade de Jogos de Macau ("SJM"), did win one of the three new casino licenses, but so did Steve Wynn and a Hong Kong group that issued a sublicense to another American, Sheldon G. Adelson, owner of the Venetian in Las Vegas. In May, 2004, Adelson opened the Sands, the first new casino in Macau in 40 years.

The Sands is a magnificent, western-style casino. Part of its enormous success has been the willingness of its management to test, and where necessary, to disregard accepted wisdom. For example, it was said that Asian gamblers would not play slot machines. They didn't in STDM's casinos. Of course, these were often isolated to grimy back corners. The Sands installed a few video poker machines. The devices have proven so popular that the casino ordered hundreds more.

The string of casinos being built in Macau, on the Cotai Strip, is intentionally designed to conjure up comparisons with the Las Vegas Strip. Laws have had to be changed. For example, the traditional Macau casino was nothing more than a room with table games. It made sense to keep out minors at the door. But hotel casinos have restaurants, shows and gamblers who bring their children. Legislation is necessary to let minors enter the buildings, even if they are kept off the gaming floors.

The biggest problems for operators like Adelson and Wynn are the strict Nevada laws, which forbid them to be associated in any way with illegal activities, especially organized crime. But the laws and traditions of Macau's casinos were originally built around different laws, institutions and traditions. When STDM bought the casino monopoly in 1962, it was a small industry offering only Chinese games.

The legal structure of the monopoly was the concession, derived from the Portuguese legal system. The structure had been created in 1937, when the Macau government legalized casinos and first gave the gaming concession to a single company. But the company and its successors, including STDM and SJM, were allowed to open as many casinos as they wished, limited only by the availability of land and the demands of the market. This created a unique situation: Macau is probably the only jurisdiction in the world that licenses the operators and not casinos.

The main danger here was that the concession holders were free to enter into as many partnerships as they liked; regulators gave little scrutiny to those partners, or even to who was actually running the casinos or sharing in the casinos' profits.

A second area of concern arose due to the establishment of the junket system. Credit reporting had always been poor in the People's Republic of China, and gambling debts are not legally collectable. Casinos were not allowed to issue markers. And the PRC has severe limits on taking or sending money out of the mainland, even to Macau. So, junket operators arose to make all of the arrangements to get high-rollers, and their money, to Macau. An elaborate system of dead-chips and separate high-stakes rooms was created to enable the junket operators to share in the money lost by mainland players.

This creates problems for present-day operators. The systems of concessions and junkets still exist. The fact that there is no limit on the number of casinos, except for arbitrary declarations by Macau's Chief Executive, creates economic uncertainties, since a concession holder does not have merely five other competitors, but faces literally an unlimited number of other casinos.

The idea of concessions was simply carried forward and expanded after Macau became a Special Administrative Region of the PRC, and the government in Beijing decided to end STDM's casino monopoly. Since Stanley Ho's SJM won one of the concessions, and continued the partnership arrangements of STDM, it was only fair for the other two companies winning the new concessions to also be allowed to operate more than one casino.

One of the successful bidders was a partnership between Galaxy Entertainment and Las Vegas Sands. When that partnership fell apart, the Macau government allowed Galaxy to have the concession, and drafted a new law, creating a sub-concession for LVS, since they could have had two casinos anyway. But, the other concessions now also had to be given the right to have sub-concessions. The three concessions had now turned into six, with no fixed limit on the number of actual casinos.

And all six concessions and sub-concessions are allowed to have revenue-sharing partnership deals with an unlimited number of unlicensed outside individuals and companies. The availability of partnerships has resulted in dozens of casinos being opened in a few years. Growth has been so explosive that when Macau's Chief Executive announced a freeze on new casinos and casino expansions on April 22, 2008, after the initial shock, there was a general sigh of relief. No one complained that this was not the way to run a casino jurisdiction. The Macau government, without hearings, votes or any public input, simply said these are the new rules. And no one is sure exactly what these rules are.

The second problem also continues: Junkets are at the heart of gaming revenue for Macau's richest casinos. They are so important, in fact, that junket operators were getting a larger share of money lost by high-rollers than the actual casinos. It is not clear, however, whether this money is all profits. Junket operators complained when the Macau government, at the urging of its casinos, put a cap on commissions, claiming that they have to give large kickbacks to losing high-rollers.

Visitors from the mainland still have trouble getting their money to Macau; gambling debts are still not legally collectable; and there is still very little fiscal infrastructure, since most Chinese do not have bank accounts, let alone credit cards and credit histories. So the junket operators bear the risk when they lend money for gaming.

Plus, business in China is mainly conducted informally among people who know each other, or the personal contacts of personal contacts. So it is extremely difficult for a U.S. company to break into this market without junkets, with their agents and subagents.

The PRC is committed to aiding the growth of the casinos in Macau and sports and race betting (and shopping) in Hong Kong. China hopes to have the best of both worlds. It can get all the jobs, tax revenue and economic growth from legal gambling, while keeping it somewhat isolated in its outer border regions of Hong Kong and Macau.

Macau casinos are now the number one casino development zone in the world. Not unlike Las Vegas, the Macau economy depends almost entirely on the gaming industry. But China is not Nevada.

Casinos in Macau are built on land owned by the government, operating under gaming concessions that expire within a decade. No one expects the government of Macau to say, when the time comes, "Thank you for building that billion-dollar integrated resort. It now belongs to the government." But having that legal right almost guarantees that the government will ask for significant payments for it to renew the land leases and gaming concessions.

2. Singapore

The opening of the Macau market was radically different from what is taking place in Singapore. Macau was a massive expansion of an already thriving industry. Singapore prohibited all casino gambling, and permitted only a limited number of gaming devices in halls designed for locals.

The two jurisdictions have different views of the role of law. Macau comes from the Portuguese legal tradition, where the emphasis is on general principals put into a code and then interpreted by officials. And, despite its power to govern itself in many areas, Macau is still a part of China. These forces sometimes lead to government by decree, such as when Macau's Chief Executive, Edmund Ho, simply announced that there would be a moratorium on new casino projects. Now, no one knows exactly how many casinos Macau will eventually have. Singapore comes from the English common law tradition, with its emphasis on the power of precedence and rules of law. Singapore knows exactly how many casinos it will have: two. And they have to be integrated resorts ("IRs"), meaning massive complexes with not just gaming and hotels, but conference halls and attractions for non-gamblers. To get the giant investments it was seeking, Singapore went further than any western state or country in announcing that it has frozen the tax rate on casinos for ten years.

Singapore has a strong tradition of social control and stability. When considering legalizing casinos, it took a step back and asked, "Why do we regulate gambling?" The answer is threefold—:

1) To keep the bad guys out

2) To prevent or at least lessen the negative social impacts, and

3) To fulfill the purposes for legalizing casinos in the first place.

Performing background checks and requiring investments of more than US$1 billion took care of the first. Singapore is taking care of the second by having more protections in place than any other casino jurisdiction, starting with the requirement that residents of Singapore cannot enter the casino unless they pay S$100 (about US$67) each day. And Singapore knew exactly why it was legalizing casinos. The IRs were expected to be and are magnificent draws to foreign visitors.

Macau was at a disadvantage here, because it already had an established casino industry built on a complicated system of junkets, private rooms and unreported credit. Gambling is still the main activity, and everything else is a distant second. Singapore had a clean slate. So the IRs have succeeded phenomenally. They are, in fact, generating so much revenue that every other country is Asia is now looking at establishing its own IRs.

E.   Casinos in Africa Generally

The premier gambling site in Africa is the Republic of South Africa, although of the continent's 50 nations, about half allow casinos. Even muslim North Africa's Egypt, Tunisia, and Morocco allow casino gaming. However, as with many other muslim nations, local residents are not allowed to gamble. Prior to the recent Arab uprisings, these casinos attracted wealthy Muslims from other countries. Of course, almost all of the casinos in Africa are designed, and sometimes restricted, to foreigners. Sun International is the dominant casino operation company and is based in South Africa.

Schedule 4 of the Constitution of the Republic of South Africa, adopted in 1996, expressly gives shared legislative competence to the national provincial legislatures over "Casinos, racing, gambling and wagering, excluding lotteries and sports pools." So, each of the nine provinces has developed its own gambling laws, with the understanding that the National Assembly has concurrent jurisdiction. Older national laws, like the Gambling Act of 1965, have been replaced, though cases decided under those statutes provide guidance in interpreting the newer laws, including the National Gambling Act of 1996, with amendments from later years, and the Lotteries Act of 1997. South Africa's legal gambling industry continues to grow, even during the world-wide recession, reaching gross revenues for 2011 of R17.14 billion (US$2.19 billion), with significant tax contributions to both the states and federal government. About 90% of the gambling revenue came from casino gaming. Gauteng is by far the largest casino state, contributing 41% of the nation's total gaming revenue, followed by KwaZulu–Natal at 19% and the Western Cape at 15%.

F.   Casinos in North America Generally

Casino gambling in Canada and the United States differs from province to province and state to state. Also, important to Canada and United States are those casinos that are allowed on the land of that country's Indigenous Peoples. With Nevada, of course, gaming dominates its economy. Gaming in Nevada is highly regulated. There are licenses for operators, landlords, gaming employees, junket representatives, information services, service industries, race books, and sports pools, disseminators, gaming devices, lenders, labor organizations, and gaming schools.

There is also casino gaming in the Bahamas and the Caribbean. The Bahamas and the Commonwealth of Puerto Rico are the two most successful casino jurisdictions in the region. Also, Aruba has eleven casinos, mostly around the capital of Oranjestad and all in large resort hotels. The islands nation of Antigua and Barbuda pioneered the licensing of Internet gambling and remains a leader in the field.

G. Casinos in South America Generally

Twelve of the twenty jurisdictions in Central and South America have casino gaming. A trend is that most governments now seek privatization of the gaming industry. Recently-passed free trade agreements with the United States and Panama and Colombia will undoubtedly increase investment in this sector. Columbia, for example, with decree 1905, has made a serious attempt to liberalize the casino industry by creating safety and security measures for would-be foreign investors.

Latin America has had a long history of recurring bouts of economic and economic instability. This makes long-term, and sometimes even short-term, predictions difficult. In the past, investors have been hit by occasional government expropriation, and, more often, runaway inflation.

Legal gambling generates enormous amounts of untraceable cash and requires strict regulation to prevent cheating. These are problematic in a region with a history of widespread corruption. Even today, many local residents believe that the police are venal. And some believe that the system is rigged from top to bottom. Some reformers oppose expanding legalized gambling, even when they acknowledge that it would create jobs and raise much needed revenue, because they fear the newly created wealth would go only to well-connected insiders.

The expansion of democracy throughout Latin America has eased some of this concern. Dictators can, of course, be pro- or anti-gaming. But they do tend to be corrupt, and to have ties with undesireables. The casinos that flourished in Cuba during the 1950s, under Fulgencio Batista, were notorious for their tie with organized crime, particularly Meyer Lansky. Fidel Castro closed them all down.

But the days of the strongmen, Spanish caudillos and Portuguese caudilhos, are fading. Even the Castro brothers will soon be gone. The imposition of Communism wrecked Cuba's economy, which depended upon tourism as much as agriculture. Within 10 years, Cuba will probably once again have legal casinos.

1.   The Argentine Republic—is a federation of 23 provinces and an autonomous city, Buenos Aires. This makes for interesting jurisdictional questions. For example, Buenos Aires has 24 separate authorities regulating, and sometimes operating, games of chance. Yet, there is a casino on a boat in the Puerto Madero barrio, which is undoubtedly in the city, which does not come under the city's control. This is because it floats on the Río de la Plata, and the river was declared to be under the jurisdiction of the federal government. The license for the floating casino caused a political stink, when the President of Argentina simply declared that he had the power to issue it, and renew it, to a close friend and supporter. There are large and small casinos throughout the country, the most in South America, more than 80.

Because each jurisdiction sets its own rules, regulation varies widely. Argentina faces the possibility of massive growth. Gaming machines are being introduced as bingos. And the governor of Buenos Aires has announced that he thinks selling additional casino licenses, without putting in additional controls or licensing, is a good way to raise money.

2. Federative Republic of Brazil—Brazil is the big prize, waiting for legal gaming. Not only the largest country in South America, Brazil is the fifth most populous country in the world. Yet, it has no casinos, and not much in the form of other gambling. As recently as 2007, there were 1,500 bingo halls with as many as 130,000 gaming machines. Most of these were licensed by the federal government, but many were state-licensed, or even unlicensed, yet allowed to remain open by court decree. Scandals, including bribed judges and politicians, led to a new federal law and the termination of all but a small handful, which are still litigating the issue. State lotteries suffered the same fate; the Federal Court ruled that the 1998 Brazilian Constitution forbad states and even local courts from deciding whether gambling was legal. Although the gray-market slot machines were closed down, also lost were hundred of thousands of jobs. Politically, this is a major problem. And it looks like it is about to be fixed. Bills, such as 270/2003, have been introduced in the Federal Legislature to bring the gaming back, and usually pass through committees with large margins. But despite the support of former President Luiz Inacio "Lula" da Silva, Brazil does not have casinos.

3. Republic of Chile—Chile is the present boom area of South American gaming, with a recently enacted casino law. Licenses are issued by the Superintendent of Gaming Casinos and are good for 15 years, and renewable. The licensing system is designed to be objective, looking not only into the background of the applicants and sources of money, but what the project promises to accomplish in creating jobs and promoting tourism. The statutory law limits the number of casinos to 24 and is designed to ensure that every region of the country will have at least one. In fact, in many cases, it is only one, giving the operators a legal monopoly. Also, Chile is normally friendly to foreign investors: It has a law that expressly states that foreign investors cannot be discriminated against. It will be interesting to see what happens when this law collides with the licensing law, which might favor local applicants.

4. Republic of Colombia—Colombia appears to be second, only to Argentina, in the number of casinos within its borders. James Kilsby, in GamblingCompliance.com, estimated in February 2008, that there were more than 3,000 casinos, bingo halls and slot machine parlors in Colombia. However, as WorldCasinoDirectory.com puts it, "this is difficult to authenticate due to political issues in the country." Colombia modernized its government with a new Constitution in 1991, creating changes and continuing uncertainty over exactly who has power for what. For the gaming industry, the most important development was the apparent increase in control over almost all forms of gambling given to department governors, municipal mayors and other local administrators. On the other hand, on May 30, 2008, Colombia President Alvaro Uribe signed Decree 1905 into law, giving the federal government's ETESA (Empresa Territorial para la Salud) the power to consolidate the country's legal gambling. ETESA is moving ahead, slowly, with the stated goals of instilling confidence in the integrity of gambling, eliminating illegal slot machines, and forcing consolidation. Major operators like Codere and CIRSA, and smaller ones like Thunderbird, as well as suppliers like Cyberview Technology and Synergex, and even Gtech, have either announced their intentions or already joined this growing market. Colombia looks particularly attractive, the more its neighbor, Venezula, suffers political and economic chaos under the unstable Hugo Chavez.

5. Republic of Costa Rica—Costa Rica is the home for much of the licensed Internet sports betting operations aimed at the U.S. market. Its land-based industry is limited to casinos, about 40 at present, which include slot machines and table games, including poker. The gaming industry in Costa Rica is relatively mature, yet still legally in flux, due to constantly changing legal requirements and interpretations. The present legal structure for gaming was set down in 1987, limiting casinos to hotels with at least three stars, with licenses granted by the Tourist Institute of Costa Rica. This law was designed to eliminating gaming rooms and slot machine arcades. Unlike most other countries, gambling is not a state or provincial matter, because the Supreme Court eviscerated the provincial governments: The seven provinces still have governors, appointed by the President, but there are no provincial assemblies. So, the control of gaming defaulted to municipalities. The city of San Jose used this power in 2000 to issue regulations covering video gaming machines. Meanwhile, the federal government continues to issue decrees, covering such things as opening and closing times. The unicameral national legislature is studying a proposal to bring more stability to the legal structure.

6. Republic of Ecuador—On paper, Ecuador has the traditional model of casinos, with both slot machines and table games, limited to expensive tourists hotels. In reality, years of running court battles have allowed gaming devices to be opened in arcades in many parts of the country. The 35 authorized casinos have been licensed by the Ministry of Tourism. The system, at the moment, is not too complex. However, Ecuador has decided to adopt many of the regulations of its neighbor, Peru. This will increase controls, but also costs to operators.

7. United Mexican States—Mexico allows sports betting, wagers on dog and horseraces, cockfights, lotteries, and bingo. But the big boom in legal gaming is electronic machines, commonly called Class II, due, in part, to confusion over what is and is not legal. In 2004, one of the co-authors, Prof. Rose, was hired by the Federal Government of Mexico to be an expert witness in the first dispute heard under NAFTA (North American Free Trade Agreement) involving slot machines. An American company, Thunderbird, complained that Mexico had closed down its gaming parlor while letting identical parlors remain open nearby. The legal dispute revolved around whether the machines were games of skill—the NAFTA tribunal agreed with Prof. Rose's analysis that they were not. But this did not necessarily mean that the locally owned competing gaming devices were also illegal. They might have been, or the police might have been bribed. But some operators were obtaining court orders allowing them to stay open, while the issue of what machines were allowed was being considered by all segments of government. Court decisions and decisions by federal ministries, as well as a 2004 federal Law of

Gaming and Raffles, have now led to some temporary stability, and the opening of Class II and even Class III (true slot machines) casinos. In 2008, a new organization was set up by the gaming operators. The operators understand their legal status; rather than call themselves "licensees," they chose the more correct designation "permittees": "Asociación de Permisionarios de Juegos y Sorteos," which could be translated as Association of Permittees of Gaming and Raffles. Casinos are booming throughout Mexico, though often their legality is questionable. A more complete regulatory system will undoubted develop in the coming years.

8. Republic of Paraguay—Under Law No. 1016, Paraguay allows all forms of gambling, so long as they are operated in accordance with regulations from the National Commission on Games of Chance. Expressly permitted are casinos, with table games and video games; all types of lotteries; raffles; bingo, using 90 numbers, not the U.S. 75; quinella; promotional sweepstakes; electronic games of chance; sports betting; horseracing; and, telebingo. Most of the licenses are awarded through competitive bidding. The Act expressly gives municipal governments the exclusive authority to determine the number and types of gaming allowed for electronic gaming arcades. Casinos, on the other hand, are limited to only Asuncion and six departments, and only departments with more than 250,000 people may have more than one casino.

9. Republic of Peru—Peru expressly allows slot machines—there are more than 60,000 in the country—and casino table games, lotteries and betting on horseraces. Issues have arisen because the law also expressly allows bingo. It also does not expressly prohibit sports betting and Internet gambling, so operators have taken this to mean they can operate without licenses. The regulation of gaming is complex and difficult to navigate. For example, some slot machines, found in arcades, come under one set of rules, while other slots, found in high-class hotels and restaurants, come under another. As another example, the government requires casino slot machines to be tied online to the Ministry of Foreign Trade and Tourism and Sunat, the tax authority. Gaming is supposedly for tourists. Casinos must obtain four separate licenses, and local governments have a great say in what can and cannot be done. Growth will probably be most noticeable with sports betting, which is still small, at the moment, although casinos and slots will continue to proliferate, since there is no law limiting their numbers.

10.   Republic of Uruguay—Like much of the world, Uruguay allows casinos, with table games and slot machines, and recreational halls, arcades with gaming devices. It also allows bets on horse and greyhound racing, including free standing betting parlors. There are presently 11 casinos and 26 recreational halls. Legally, this gaming can only be operated by the Directorate General of Casinos; the Municipality of Montevideo; and one private company, Baluma S.A., which operates what is technically the only privately owned casino in the country, in the Hotel Conrad Punta del Este Resort and Casino. However, the governments allow private companies as partners of both casinos and recreational halls, through joint operating systems. So, Codere recently announced that it was awarded a contract from the Montevideo Town Council which will lead to a $60 million Sofitel Montevideo Casino Carrasco and Spa.

11. Republic of Venezuela—President Hugo Chávez is a controversial figure. Rather than try to describe him, here is a quote from a typical proclamation: 1) The country must prepare for war with Colombia; and 2) His supporters should exercise and eat healthy because "there are lots of fat people" in Venezuela; "I'm not saying fat women, because they never get fat," he added. "Women sometimes fill out." A socialist, he can't quite figure out what to do about legal gambling. In 2007, the Chávez government imposed a three-year moratorium on imports of slot machines and greatly raised taxes on gaming operators. On September 9, 2008, his Ministry of People's Power for Tourism issued Resolution DM/No. 086, ordering the National Commission for Casinos, Bingo Halls and Slot Machines to stop issuing permits and licenses. Yet, on April 27, 2009, the Ministry repealed Resolution DM/No. 086, without comment. Chávez isn't much of a dictator; he couldn't even rig the election in 2007, where 51 percent voted against giving him more power. But this year, he did win the right to unlimited terms. Since he is only 55 years old, it will probably be many years before the legal gaming industry, particularly foreign investors and operators, come back to Venezuela in force.

H. Gambling in Australia, New Zealand and Oceania

Commercial casino gaming came to the greater Australian sub-continent in 1973 when the Australian State of Tasmania licensed the Wrest Point

Casino in Hobart. Soon thereafter, casino gambling spread across the region. Australia now has casinos in all states plus the Northern Territories. New Zealand has six casinos, the first license was granted in 1995, catering mainly to high-rollers, often from Asia, and local punters. Casino gaming has also spread to Tinian, part of America's Commonwealth of the Northern Marianas, and New Caledonia. In 2011, Fiji made news when Military ruler Voreqe Bainimarama over-ruled long standing objections to gambling from local chiefs and church leaders and authorized a large casino for Denarau Island.

Australia has one of the highest ratios of gaming machines to population in the world. Besides casinos, hotels and private clubs can offer "poker machines," called "pokies," which are not limited to video poker and can be any form of slot machine. This is in addition to bingo (often called "housie"), horse and dog racetracks and lotteries. All have a minimum age of 18 to gamble.

States in Australia were some of the first jurisdictions in large, developed nations to legalize Internet gambling. But, the federal government stepped in, declaring first a moratorium in 2000, and then enacting a statute, the Interactive Gambling Act ("IGA") in 2001, which took control away from the states. The IGA makes it a crime to accept bets from residents of Australia, with some significant exceptions; though it is not illegal for Australians to make those bets. Australia's online gambling includes state-licensed sportsbooks.

Australia is one of the leading jurisdictions when it comes to government and private studies of the gambling industry. Leading politicians and others are often concerned with the possible negative impact legal gaming can have on Australian society, especially compulsive gamblers. Restrictions are continuously being proposed, and sometimes adopted. But Australians are avid gamblers, living in a country with widespread opportunities to make a bet. The result is Australia has some of the highest per capita spending on gambling in the world.

The New Zealand Gambling Act of 2003, Public Act 2003 No 51, divides all gambling into four classes, plus there are long sections dealing with casinos and lotteries. The statute reflects the modern trend of requiring operators and government to look at the potential harm legal gambling can cause and to put into place safeguards to protect minors and problems gamblers. The Act was also designed to strengthen governmental controls and to put a cap on the amount of legal gambling in the nation. Virtually all gambling now comes under the control of the Department of Internal Affairs. As in Australia, New Zealand has enormous numbers of gaming devices, often called "pokies." Besides in casinos, they can be found in in hotels and bars, operated by charitable foundations, and sometimes as gray market machines in "fun parlours" and sports and social clubs. Since July 2009, all gaming devices must have "Player Information Displays." These tell the patrons how long they have been playing and how much money they have won or lost; they even encourage gamblers to take breaks. One study found these safeguards help limit the excessive betting of every group—except compulsive gamblers. Since problem gamblers are betting, at least in part, to relieve their anxiety, showing them how much they have lost increases anxiety and actually led to increase betting by the one group most at risk. In total, more money is now bet in New Zealand on slot machines then on horseraces or the Lotteries Commission's games combined.

CHAPTER 11

THE W.T.O. AND CROSS–BORDER GAMBLING

When may a state or country keep out foreign legal gambling? With recent decisions from courts, including the European Court of Justice and United States Supreme Court, and international agencies, including the World Trade Organization ("WTO"), we may now be able to answer that question, or at least make educated guesses, about most situations that might arise in most parts of the world.

Despite a broad commitment to the liberalization of trade in goods and services, Member States of the WTO retain legal authority to impose trade-restrictive measures "necessary to protect public morals." As a matter of first impression under WTO law, in April 2005 the WTO Appellate Body interpreted the term "public morals" as it is found in the General Agreement on Trade in Services (GATS). The Appellate Body held that certain U.S. laws prohibiting the cross-border-provision of Internet gambling services, alleged by the United States to be necessary to protect U.S. public morals, were inconsistent with U.S. obligations under GATS. The decision is consistent with rulings from around the world dealing with restrictions on gambling that is legal in another state or nation but that a local government wants to exclude.

A. Cross–Border Legal Gambling

The first question in any analysis of whether a government can keep out foreign legal gambling is: Is there a prohibition in place and does it apply to this form of gambling?

Governments almost never exercised their powers to their theoretical limits. First, most lawmakers simply have not thought about the issue. If they have, they rarely enact laws that would infringe on the sovereignty of other nations. Governments are reluctant to embarrass themselves by passing laws that cannot be enforced. And sometimes there are omissions created by historical and other accidents. Changes in the law follow changes in society. Lawmakers are reactive, rather than proactive. They wait until an actual problem has occurred before they take action, making laws that address that particular problem. Since different forms of gambling have spread to different jurisdictions at different times, the existing restrictions on gambling are a patchwork quilt of various statutes, regulations and court and administrative decisions usually with no connections with each other. Therefore, it is important to know what form of gambling is involved, and whether the jurisdiction where the bettor resides has a law covering that type of gambling, when asking whether cross-border gaming is prohibited.

The most dramatic recent example is the Wire Act, 18 U.S.C. § 1084, which used to be the federal government's main weapon of intimidation against all Internet gambling. Just before Christmas 2011 the federal Department of Justice announced that it had officially changed its interpretation of this law, deciding that it only applied to bets on sports events and races. So, prosecutors would have to find another statute, if they want to prevent a licensed overseas gaming operator from taking bets from America.

There are other potential statutory problems that must be overcome, if a jurisdiction wants to keep out foreign legal gambling. For example, there is often a strong presumption that lawmakers have not reached out beyond their jurisdictions' borders in enacting a statute. Therefore, any prohibition on gambling which does expressly state that it applies to cross-border wagers will be presumed to include only activities taking place with the borders of that particular government entity. In 1922 the United States Supreme Court reaffirmed this doctrine: If Congress intends a criminal prohibition to apply outside the United States, it must "say so in the statute." The only exception is the limited class of offenses committed directly against the federal government itself, such as the foreign theft of U.S. government property. Federal courts have consistently halted criminal proceedings when it was shown that the conduct was outside the United States and no statement of Congressional intent to intrude on the sovereignty of an independent nation could be found in the statute. See, e.g., *United States v. Velasquez–Mercado*, 697 F.Supp. 292 (S.D. Tex. 1988); and, *Ito v. United States*, 64 F.2d 73 (9th Cir. 1933).

Assuming a government has acted to prohibit cross-border gambling, the question arises whether that action was valid. In analyzing whether a jurisdiction has the power to prevent cross-border betting it is necessary to step back and analyze that government's legal relationships with other governments. These fall into one of two types: The first is the more common situation, where the state or nation has no relevant legal restrictions on its power. The second, which has become of great interest recently, are governments whose rights to exclude extraterritorial legal gambling are limited, due to some other law. These latter include states that belong to federations and are restricted under federal laws or the federal constitutions; nations that have voluntarily, if sometimes unintentionally, agreed to let in legal gambling from other specific countries under treaties; and the governments bound by the doctrine of comity, where out of courtesy and mutual respect, rather than because they are bound by a written document, states and nations recognize the laws of some other foreign states or nations.

There seems little doubt that a government normally can exclude outside illegal gambling and even legal gambling. A sovereign government by definition has power over its own territory and citizens. It is thus the inherent right of every sovereign state to protect its borders from intrusions. This right is so fundamental that it need not be spelled out explicitly in a constitution or statute.

The state's right derives not only from its right to continue to exist as an independent state, but also from the state's police power. The police power is the inherent right, and perhaps the obligation, of a government to protect the health, safety, welfare and morals of its citizens. In the European Union ("E.U.") it is called the "overriding public interest," which allows member states to take actions that violate the treaties creating the E.U. In the WTO it is called "necessary" actions, taken in violation of the WTO treaties for reasons of necessity, such as preserving public order.

The police power is most commonly connected with governmental action taken in emergency situations, especially where public health is endangered, as in a fire or an epidemic. But gambling, licensed or illegal, even legal lotteries, has always been held to fall within a state's police power. For example, the United States Supreme Court declared in *Edge Broadcasting*: "While lotteries have existed in this country since its founding, States have long viewed them as a hazard to their citizens and to the public interest ... Gambling implicates no constitutionally protected right; rather, it falls into a category of 'vice' activity that could be, and frequently has been, banned altogether." *United States v. Edge Broadcasting Co.,* 509 U.S. 418, 113 S.Ct. 2696, 125 L.Ed.2d 345 (1993).

Recent decisions have shown there are often limits on a state and nation's power to keep out goods and services it finds detrimental to its citizens' welfare. The laws under review almost always involve statutes and regulations enact by a jurisdiction which prevent companies outside the jurisdiction from accepting wagers from bettors who are physically within the jurisdiction. In other words these are laws expressly designed to prevent cross-border gambling, so long as the operator is outside the boundaries of the state or nation. It is common to find that legal gambling, including Internet gaming, is permitted by companies that are licensed by that same state or nation, or even that the government is running gambling games itself.

The major restrictions on a government's police power are created by the government itself: A state joined a federation and thus subjected itself to federal statutes and treaties and a federal constitution; a nation signed a bilateral treaty with another country or a multilateral treaty with possibly a large number of other nations and agreed to either allow in goods and services from its treaty partners, or at least to limit its criminal prosecutions of those partners' citizens; or a state or nation has had unwritten agreements for many years based on courtesy to respect the laws of other jurisdictions with similar legal systems, a comity of nations.

The wording of the tests may differ, and certainly the actual applications of the policies to real-world situations vary greatly, but the basic principals restricting a government's ability to exclude cross-border betting are surprisingly consistent and can be stated easily: A government that is obligated to let in goods and services of other jurisdictions must let in outside legal gambling, unless it can show that the exclusion is to protect its residents. Laws that merely protect the local gambling operations from outside competition are invalid. But even restrictions designed to limit gaming for solid reasons of protecting a society are invalid, if they discriminate in favor of local operators

There are a few precedents dealing with cross-border gambling prior to the explosion of Internet gaming. In earlier cases, the issue of whether a government may exclude legal gambling from its partners, mostly involved lottery tickets, which are easy to ship through the mails. But in addition there are other morally suspect industries producing goods and services that are routinely subjected to the police power of a state, such as alcoholic beverages and tobacco, that have also been the subjects of court decisions.

Although there has been some controversy on the issue, today there is little doubt that a government that has an absolute ban on a morally suspect commerce does not have to let it in, even if it originates in other states in its federation or treaty partners. So, if Utah wants to be a "dry" state and completely prohibit alcoholic beverages, it does not have to allow the sale of those beverages simply because the manufacturer or retailer is in another American state. A state or nation that makes it a crime to sell lottery tickets, with no exceptions, does not have to allow sister states or treaty partners to sell lottery tickets to residents. This was the situation in *Schindler*,[1] Europe's first important cross-border betting case. When the United Kingdom prohibited all large-scale lotteries, the European Court of Justice held that it could keep out advertisements for legal lotteries originating in the Federal Republic of Germany, another member of the E.U.

It is important again to emphasize that *Schindler* involved a government that had completely prohibited (at the time) the form of gambling under consideration. The case would be even easier if a government has outlawed all gambling. But the situation is radically different once a state or nation legalizes a form of gambling and attempts to keep out identical forms from sister states or treaty partners.

States can and do raise police power concerns to justify raising barriers to outside competitors while allowing the local businesses, or even the state itself, to operate identical businesses without restrictions. Sometimes the arguments work. But a court has to agree that not just companies in other states but those other states themselves may not be as concerned about issues like consumer health and safety. It is difficult, but not impossible, to convince

1. *Her Majesty's Customs and Excise v. Gerhart Schindler and Joerg Schindler, Reference for a Preliminary Ruling: High Court of Justice, Queen's Bench Division—United Kingdom*, Court of Justice of the European Communities, Case C–275/92, Doc.Num. 692J0275, Reports of Cases 1994 I–1039 (Judgment 24 March 1994).

a court that State A, which licenses gaming operations, is justified in keeping out a competing gaming operation licensed by State B in the same nation. For example, there have been a few land-based casino companies who have been licensed by Nevada regulators and yet found unacceptable by New Jersey regulators.

The more common situation is illustrated by an important case handed down by the Supreme Court of the United States. The states of New York and Michigan allowed their local wineries to sell wine online for delivery to local residents, but put up substantial barriers to out-of-state wineries. The Court rejected the states' police power justifications: "keeping alcohol out of the hands of minors and facilitating tax collection."

Justice Kennedy, writing for a 5 to 4 majority, said that the 26 states that allowed direct shipment of wine report no problem with minors. He concluded this was not surprising, since minors are more likely to consume beer, wine coolers and hard liquor than wine; minor have more direct means of obtaining wine; and minors want instant gratification. *Granholm v. Heald*, 544 U.S. 460, 125 S.Ct. 1885, 161 L.Ed.2d 796 (2005).

The WTO came to similar conclusions as to the standards to be applied when one member state claims it is excluding businesses that are legal where they originate from another member state for reasons of "necessity." The widely reported decision arose when Antigua filed a complaint against the United States for prohibiting cross-border betting by Antigua's licensed Internet gambling operations.

B. The Role of the WTO

The WTO is a treaty-based trade regime with 148 Member States currently representing some ninety-five percent (by value) of all international trade. The WTO contains a number of core agreements, including GATT, GATS, and side agreements on other matters, including sanitary and phytosanitary measures and technical barriers to trade. In signing these treaties, governments have to decide which goods and services they will let in, and which they want to continue to exclude. Many nations expressly included "gambling" on their lists of excluded items. Officials from the United States had so little interest in and knowledge of gambling that they did not even think to exclude it. The negotiators for the U.S. did include "sporting" on the list of foreign services that would not be allowed into the country. But this was undoubtedly to protect the politically powerful professional and college sports leagues. So, in trying to defend federal and state laws that prevent Antigua-licensed gambling sites from taking bets from America, lawyers for the United States argued that its listing of "sporting" included gambling. It did not work.

C.   The WTO and Antigua

In 2005, Antigua and Barbuda became the smallest World Trade Organization (WTO) member state to win a case against the United States, one of the WTO's largest and more powerful members. In United States Measures Affecting the Cross–Border Supply of Gambling and Betting Services, the dispute settlement system appellate body found that U.S. law restricting Internet gambling violated U.S. obligations committed to under the General Agreement on Trade in Services (GATS), which the country signed in 1994. After years of working its way through the WTO dispute settlement system's lengthy appeals process, the case has made Antigua a big winner, and has placed the United States in a tough position.

On June 22, 2007, Antigua requested authorization to infringe on U.S. intellectual property rights through suspension of its obligation under the Agreement on Trade Related Aspects of Intellectual Property Rights (TRIPS). An arbitrator eventually granted this authorization up to the amount of $21 million annually, though its remains unclear if the remedy is satisfactory.

The WTO dispute began after an American citizen, Jay Cohen, was arrested and imprisoned for taking bets through his Internet gambling site, World Sports Exchange Ltd., that he and some friends ran out of Antigua. Cohen was charged and convicted in U.S. federal court for taking bets transmitted over a wire in violation of the Wire Wager Act.

In 2003, Antigua requested a WTO panel, claiming that U.S. state and federal law illegally restricted the offshore supply of gambling and betting services in violation of its commitments under the GATS. The basic argument was that if the United States allowed any Internet gambling at all, then its WTO commitments required that it not impose any barriers to foreign companies seeking access to its market. While U.S. federal law contains no explicit prohibition of Internet gambling, it has several laws that aim to restrict such operations.

On June 8, 2006, Antigua requested consultations under Article 21.5 of the Understanding on Rules and Procedures Governing the Settlement of Disputes (DSU), in which the parties unsuccessfully attempted to reach a settlement of the dispute. The March 2007 report of the Article 21.5 Panel concluded that the United States had still not complied with the recommendations and rulings of the DSB.

On December 21, 2007, the arbitrator announced its decision that Antigua may request authorization from the DSB to suspend the obligations under the TRIPS Agreement at a level not exceeding $21 million annually.

D. The WTO and the Interstate Horseracing Act

The first WTO Panel to hear the dispute ruled that the U.S. had indeed agreed to let in legal gambling from other signatories to the GATS treaty. The U.S. had agreed to admit all foreign "Recreational, Cultural & Sporting Services," which included everything from circuses to news agencies, except "sporting." The Panel ruled that "sporting" did not mean gambling. So, all American federal and state laws that prevented foreign legal gaming from entering the U.S. market violated GATS. On appeal, Antigua made a technical mistake, and failed to preserve its claims against American state laws. But, the WTO Appellate Body ruled that U.S. federal laws did prevent Antigua's legal gambling operators from accepting American bettors. The U.S. then argued that it still had the right to exclude remote wagering, because allowing people to bet by phone and computer would endanger American citizens. The WTO Appellate Body agreed with most of the U.S.'s arguments. But, when Antigua pointed out that the U.S. has a federal Interstate Horseracing Act ("IHA"), which expressly allows Americans to participate in state-licensed off-track betting, the Appellate Body found America's laws did discriminate against foreign gambling service providers. In particular, the IHA, 15 U.S.C.A. §§ 3001–3007, allowed states to authorize cross-border betting on horseraces, but only with operators located in other states, not in foreign nations. In reaching this conclusion, the Appellate Body affirmed the Panel ruling that the U.S. measures fell within the scope of XIV(a), leaving undisturbed both its definition of public morals and its evidentiary approach to determine whether gambling could be considered an issue of public morals. Attorneys for the U.S. argued that the IHA did not allow out-of-state betting. This was rejected, since the IHA was expressly designed for cross-border betting. The Panel pointed out that even the U.S. agreed the IHA allowed in-state remote wagering on horseraces, which fatally undermines American arguments of the dangers of letting people bet from their homes and offices.

E.   The WTO and UIGEA

The Unlawful Internet Gambling Enforcement Act of 2006 ("UIGEA"), 31 U.S.C.A. §§ 5361–5367, added an extra problem for attorneys for the U.S., since it requires financial institutions to identify and block illegal Internet gambling transactions. But, the Congressional committee reports dealing with the UIGEA contain no references to WTO commitments or the Appellate Body Report. Congress seemed oblivious to the WTO Appellate Body Report when drafting the UIGEA.

In response to Congress's enactment of the UIGEA, a number of WTO member countries have suggested that the UIGEA, which was "rushed through Congress," represents U.S. indifference toward WTO, and, in fact, all foreign law. Antigua claims the new law flies in the face of the 2005 WTO ruling.

F. The WTO and the Wire Act

In 1961, Congress enacted the Wire Act, 18 U.S.C.A. § 1084, in response to the use of race betting over wires of communication, such as telephones and telegraphs. The Wire Act prohibits a person from engaging "in the business of betting or wagering" and "knowingly us[ing] a wire communication facility for the transmission in interstate or foreign commerce of bets or wagers." 18 U.S.C.A. § 1084(a). By denying gamblers access to "information and communications infrastructure," the Wire Act's framers hoped to eliminate illegal bookies. Beginning in 1998, the Department of Justice ("DOJ") began using the Wire Act to prosecute offshore Internet gambling operators, claiming that the Internet was a "wire communication facility." In response, the United States Courts of Appeals for the Second and Fifth Circuits determined that Internet gambling on sporting events and contests falls within the scope of the Wire Act, and that cross-border Internet gambling must be legal in both the jurisdiction of the operator and the bettor. *United States v. Cohen*, 260 F.3d 68 (2d Cir. 2001).

Antigua, on the other hand, interpreted the Wire Act very differently than the DOJ. In its complaint to the WTO, Antigua challenged U.S. federal and state laws, including the Wire Act, and claimed that they prohibited "cross-border delivery of gambling services." The WTO Appellate Body found in its report that the U.S. primarily used the Wire Act to ban remote Internet gambling from other countries, but not from within the U.S.

The WTO Appellate Body held that (1) the U.S. did not prove that the Wire Act governs online interstate horseracing conducted under the IHA, and (2) the IHA's provision allowing remote Internet gambling on horseracing is discriminatory against Antigua's licensed racebooks. The DOJ, nevertheless, continues to argue that there is no need to modify its interpretation of the Wire Act and the IHA. Of course, if the Wire Act really did still apply to wagering conducted under the IHA, racing commissioners in more than half the states would be guilty of felonies, for having approved interstate remote wagering on horseraces.

G. Possible GATS Violations

In June of 2003, Antigua filed a complaint with the WTO, claiming that certain U.S. federal and state laws violated the United States' free trade commitments entered into under the GATS. Antigua argued that "various U.S. actions against offshore online gambling amounted to 'an illegal barrier to trade in services.'" In its Request for Consultation before the WTO, Antigua listed a plethora of federal and state statutes, as well as a number of individual federal and state actions, that it claimed infringe on the free trade of Internet gambling services guaranteed by the United States under the GATS. In addition, Antigua claimed that the totality of the U.S. laws amounted to a "total ban" on the cross-border supply of Internet gambling.

The WTO's analysis focused on determining the nature of the United States' free trade commitments under Article XVI of the GATS, applying those commitments to the measures at issue, and then considering the United States' defense under the "public morals" exception of the free trade agreement.

Based on the WTO decision, it is clear that if the United States restricts foreign gambling suppliers' market access into the U.S. economy, it is in violation of its obligations under Article XVI of the GATS.

The WTO proceedings were based mainly on interpretations of state, federal and international law. There was little evidence introduced, other than Antigua's efforts to show that the U.S. was tolerating cross-state Internet betting on horseraces while prosecuting any foreign licensed operator who tried to take the exact same bets from Americans. It is interesting to speculate whether the results in the WTO would have been different if the tribunals had been aware of how much international horseracing wagers the U.S. tolerates, from sending California races live to be bet on in Mexico, to creating cross-border parimutuel pools with Canada on the Breeders' Cup race held in Toronto, to Hollywood Park accepting bets on races run in Hong Kong.

H.   The Future of the WTO and Gambling

On December 21, 2007, an arbitrator under the auspices of the Dispute Settlement Body (DSB) of the World Trade Organization (WTO) issued an award in the aftermath of the dispute between the U.S. and Antigua and Barbuda over on-line gambling services. The arbitrator permitted Antigua and Barbuda to seek retaliation in a sector that is different from where the U.S. violations occurred.

The arbitrator found that the annual level of nullification or impairment of benefits in this case is only $21 million per year. Thus, Antigua and Barbuda may request permission from the DSB to suspend obligations to the U.S. under the TRIPS Agreement for up to $21 million per year.

But the real impact has not yet been felt. President George W. Bush unilaterally, without the approval of the U.S. Senate, which must approve treaties, or of any foreign government, announced that the U.S. was pulling out its commitment under GATS to an open border on foreign legal remote wagering. Any country has the right to change its treaty commitments. But such a unilateral withdrawal triggers a short period in which any other signatory can claim that the change would cause them harm. So, Pres. Bush's actions led to multi-billion-dollar claims being filed against the U.S. in the WTO.

It remains to be seen how these claims will be resolved, and whether the U.S. has legally closed the door to foreign legal gambling.

CHAPTER 12

BLACKJACK AND THE LAW

A. Blackjack!!

Blackjack, or 21, is a unique casino game. Like all traditional casino games, blackjack is both a banking game and a percentage game. Players play every hand against a single opponent, the house, which has a fund of money, a bank, that is relatively infinite compared with the limited stakes and maximum bet size allowed players. And not only does the house participate in every hand, it has a statistical advantage. The easiest way to see this is when both a player and the dealer go over 21—the dealer wins, because the player has to act first.

But blackjack is unique because it has a strong element of skill that a significant number of players can gain a statistical edge. By careful play and betting, skilled card-counters and other advantage players can shift the odds into their favor in the long run. Like a casino, a card-counter cannot win every hand. But, like the casino, a skilled card-counter with a large enough stake to outlast a losing streak, will win in the long run.

There are many skillful card-counters and even competing systems. Although there were a few isolated earlier skirmishes, the battle began in earnest in 1962, with the publication of BEAT THE DEALER by Edward O. Thorp, Ph.D. But, the late Ken Uston is the closest thing blackjack players have to a patron saint. He filed suits in Nevada and New Jersey, seeking to allow card-counters to play in the casino. What he found was that when people use their brains to win in blackjack, casinos sometimes change their rules or make sure that these aficionados are kicked out. Today, jurisdictions vary on issues like excluding players solely because they appear to be card-counters, or taking counter-measures, like shuffling after every deal. In addition, the serious blackjack player, who grinds out a small advantage against the casinos, must also worry about the pit boss, casino security, the rules of the casino, the IRS, the DEA, the Department of the Treasury, the Gaming Control Board, Native American tribes, and occasionally, local police and prosecutors.

B. Card–Counters

Blackjack is not necessarily a game of skill, but it can be beaten by card-counters; next to cheaters, card-counters pose the greatest threat to a casino's finances. Casinos operate on a slim profit margin. The house has an advantage of approximately one-half to one and one-half percent over the average blackjack player on every hand played. The legal rights of the card-counters to play blackjack, and, of course, the casino's right to bar those card-counters, is one of the hottest issues in gambling law. Counters keep track of the cards played to determine how to play, and bet, on the next hand. They vary their bets so that they are risking the least amount when their chances of winning are the slightest, and vice versa. They vary their play so that they maximize the chances of beating the dealer on any individual hand. With perfect card counting and perfect rules, such as a single deck dealt down to the last card and the unlimited right to vary the size of bets, it becomes a statistical certainty that the player, not the house, will win in the long run, if the player has enough money to last through short term losing streaks.

Advantage players know and use counting, but have developed other methods of increasing their chances of winning. For example, a sloppy dealer will flash the bottom card of a deck or shoe when shuffling. If that card is an ace, a team of advantage players will cut the deck or shoe in such a way as to know exactly when that ace will be dealt. They will then play their hand so it will go to one of their team, who will make an enormous bet. Having an ace as his first card does not guarantee the high-roller will win, but it does increase his odds by 150%.

C.   The Big Number Theory

The so-called "Big Number Theory," as explained in the movie, "21," with Kevin Spacey as a profit-oriented M.I.T. professor, is one way to beat the casino system. But, you need lots of money, a crew, and players who play religiously by certain rules. In BLACKJACK AND THE LAW (by I. Nelson Rose and Robert A. Loeb), the "odds" in blackjack was viewed in this manner: "But flip the weighted coin a billion times, and you will see close to 510,000,000 heads and 490,000,000 tails; a difference of 20 million results in favor of heads. Maybe there will be only 10 million more heads than tails, maybe 30 million; but enough to make a significant difference if you are always betting on heads." Casinos are not really in the business of gambling, since they have a statistical edge and are not greatly concerned with whether any individual player wins or loses. So card-counters are not gambling; they know that if they play enough hands perfectly, they are going to beat the casino.

D.   Blackjack and Criminal Laws

The question is this: "Is card counting cheating?" In New Jersey, any person who "by any trick or sleight of hand performance or by a fraud or fraudulent scheme, cards, dice, or device, for himself or for another, wins or attempts to win money or property or representative of either..." is guilty of a crime. N.J.S.A. 5:12–113(a). A player who attempted to manipulate the reels of a slot machine by striking down on the handle with a forceful blow was arrested and his indictment upheld under this statute.

Nevada has two state statutes that make it a crime to cheat and to conspire to cheat. The anti-cheating statute makes it "unlawful for any person, whether the person is an owner or employee of or a player in an establishment, to cheat at any gambling game." N.R.S. 465.083. Cheating is defined to mean "to alter the selection of criteria which determine (a) the result of a game; or (b) the amount or frequency or payment in a game." N.R.S. 465.015. The crime of cheating requires a fraudulent intent. An example would be card crimping, or folding the edge of certain cards.

It is difficult to see how card-counting meets the statutory definition of cheating, if a single player merely keeps track of the cards played and varies his play and bets based on which cards are remaining in the deck or shoe. But a player who uses a mechanical device to keep track, or worse, has a hidden computer to tell him how much to bet and whether to hit or stand, would probably be guilty of cheating. In between, we have team play, where players are keeping track of the cards dealt in their heads, and then signaling to each other. Is that cheating?

E.   The Constitution and Blackjack

There is no constitutional right to gamble. But if a state legalizes one game, can it keep other games illegal? In *Palmer v. State*, 191 Mont. 534, 625 P.2d 550 (1981), the Montana Supreme Court was asked the question whether it was a violation of the constitutional provisions of equal protection to adjudge one game, poker, to be legal, while another game, blackjack, is deemed to be illegal. Here, the defendant brought a declaratory judgment action for purposes of determining the constitutionality of a statute that governs card games and authorizes specific types of card games. This Court ruled that the statute was constitutional; and that it did not violate equal protection. Also, this statute was not special legislation which discriminates against blackjack and those gamblers who prefer to play blackjack; and defendant lacked standing to challenge constitutionality of a statute which defined some games as authorized (e.g., poker), and some games as unauthorized, such as blackjack.

The case of *Marshall v. Sawyer*, 365 F.2d 105 (9th Cir. 1966), discussed the ominous repercussions of being included in a casino's "black book." This was a civil rights action brought by plaintiff, a gambler who was excluded from and refused service in a gambling casino after the gaming commission listed him in their black book. The Court of Appeals held that the exclusion of plaintiff/gambler from 15 or 20 casinos did not restrict his movements in the state so as to deny him due process. Also, ejectment of plaintiff from the hotel which operated the gambling casino did not deprive him of the constitutionally-guaranteed right of privacy or of equal protection where plaintiff did not attack the validity of the gaming commission regulation which led to his ejectment.

F. Blackjack and Anti–Cheating Measures

There are various methods that are used by casinos to counteract cheating and counting. Their main interest is to diminish or eliminate the player's advantage. A New Jersey Superior Court explicitly held that it does not matter that a casino's shuffling changes the odds in favor of the house, comparable to a card-counter, who may use discretion to determine when a favorable place in the shoe has been reached, it is also permissible for the casino to exercise similar discretion in deciding when to shuffle, as long as this discretion affects everyone at the table evenly.

1. Casino Countermeasures and Preferential Shuffling

It is controversial whether there is a right of the casinos to shuffle cards in blackjack whenever the remainder of the deck favors the players. The issue of casino dealers counting cards has been simmering for years, but the most recent problem is the result of technological breakthroughs. Casinos can now buy card-dealing shoes that read each card automatically as it is dealt. Casino chips and tables can be manufactured with embedded Radio Frequency Identification ("RFID") readers to keep perfect track of every wager. Card-tracking shoes and bet-tracking tables can be tied into computers programmed to recognize card-counting systems. The intent is to identify and defend against card-counters. In Nevada, that would mean asking the player to leave. In New Jersey, where counters cannot be barred, the casino would shuffle early.

But is that cheating, by the casino? For the sake of simplicity, image a casino that only keeps track of aces. Aces favor the player over the house. When the casino dealer gets a blackjack, the player loses his bet, but when the player gets a blackjack he is paid one and one-half times his bet. So the more aces and possible blackjacks remaining to be dealt, the better it is for the player and the worse it is for the casino. Off the top of the deck or shoe, the odds of getting an ace are one in 13, about 7.7%. Now imagine a casino dealer who is told to continue dealing only when the odds of getting an Ace are worse than that. If 13 cards have been dealt and no ace appeared, the dealer shuffles; if two or more aces have appeared, the dealer continues to deal. The odds of getting an ace will quickly become worse than 7.7%. Doesn't this change the odds?

Maybe this is being done as a counter-measure. But what about the other players sitting at the same table? Preferential shuffling hurts all players, not just counters. A casino can lose its license for "unsuitable methods of operation," including "dealing any cheating or thieving game ... either knowingly or unknowingly ... which tends to deceive the public or which might make the game more liable to win or lose, or which tends to alter the normal random selection of criteria which determine the results of the game." Regulation § 5.011(9)(b) of the Nevada Gaming Commission and State Gaming Control Board.

2.   Cheating and the Backroom

If you are caught counting cards, can you avoid being pulled into a back room and photographed? In Atlantic City, the casino cannot backroom you merely on the suspicion that you are a card-counter. In *Bartolo v. Boardwalk Regency Hotel Casino, Inc.*, 185 N.J.Super. 534, 449 A.2d 1339 (Ct. Law Div. 1982), the Superior Court of New Jersey held that a player could sue for false imprisonment after a casino pulled him into a back room and forced him to produce identification. The casino claimed it was immune from suit because it has the right under New Jersey law to detain patrons under certain circumstances. N.J.S.A. 5:12–121(b). The Court agreed that the casino has that right, but, the casino's power is greatly limited. The casino can detain patrons reasonably for a reasonable amount of time but only for the purpose of notifying law enforcement. The casino still must have probable cause that the patron was cheating. And card-counting is not cheating.

3.   Computers and Devices

Individuals and teams now use "star wars" weapons to gain an advantage over the casino by using computers. These teams include an inside man equipped with a belt buckle camera, a tiny transmitter, and a concealed receiver. Using the camera, the inside man focuses the zoom lens on the dealer's hole card, transmitting a video image to his confederate waiting outside in a van. The man in the van will feed the information into a computer to calculate the most advantageous play. The computer's decision would then be transmitted back to the inside man, through small electric shocks. This is cheating and it is illegal.

4. Identification

To confuse the watchers, the use of another name may be to protect one's freedom to engage in a totally legal activity (e.g., counting cards). That should be fine, however, making a false statement in an application for an official document, such as a passport or driver's license, is a crime in and of itself. Griffin Investigators, Inc., was a private detective agency that worked for the casinos; it published a collection of books containing pictures and descriptions of people who cheat in casinos. This raises interesting question of privacy, and liability when a mistake is made.

Richard Chen, a card-counter, bought $29,000 in chips with cash. When asked for identification, Chen used a fictitious Burma passport. By the time he had accumulated a total of $84,400, it was discovered that he was a known card counter. So, the Monte Carlo refused to pay and called in the Nevada Gaming Control Board. After two investigations, an agent of the Board told the casino it could give Chen the full $84,400. But the casino gave him only his original buy-in, kept his winnings, and filed a petition for reconsideration with the Board.

Notice how the regulatory system works in Nevada. Even though the Board's agent found that Chen did nothing illegal, it did not order the casino to pay. The regulators merely said the casino could pay the player if it wished.

The full Board decided that Chen had committed a fraud on the Monte Carlo, so he could not collect. Chen appealed the Board's ruling to the state district court. A player does not get anything like a full trial in a case like this, and the grounds for reversal are extremely limited. Courts can only overturn an administrative decision if the Board's action was "arbitrary, capricious, or contrary to law." So, the district court ruled in favor of the Board.

Chen won in the State Supreme Court, 3–1. But, he could just have easily lost. Three of Nevada's seven justices voluntarily recused themselves, meaning they did not take part in the decision, apparently because they were part owners of casinos themselves.

Justice Miriam Shearing wrote the opinion, pointing out that the casino asked for a player's identification when more than $10,000 in cash is involved not to detect card counters, but because it is required to do so by the government, to prevent money laundering. Although Chen lied, he did not commit a crime. And he won at blackjack because he could count cards, not because he presented a phony I.D. Change the facts or law slightly, and the player would be in big trouble. For example, using a phony Burmese passport is not against the law, but making a false statement on a U.S. passport can get you five years in federal prison.

Justice Bill Maupin dissented. He would have upheld the decision of the Board not only because courts give great deference to administrative rulings, but also because he felt Chen's fraud made it possible for him to obtain large denomination gaming tokens. More frightening is the language Maupin used. For example, he stated, without being contradicted, "Gaming establishments have the unquestioned right to protect themselves against so-called 'card counters' who have developed expertise in the game of 'blackjack.' " *Chen v. State Gaming Control Board*, 116 Nev. 282, 994 P.2d 1151 (2000). The Maupin dissent was prescient: jurisdictions, like New Jersey, are now allowing casinos to take counter-measures to protect themselves against card-counters.

5. The Federal Government Is Watching You and Your Money

Casinos are required to file reports with government agencies revealing the identities of their whales (i.e., high rollers). The extension by the Treasury Department of the Bank Secrecy Act to casinos is an example of the natural tendencies of a governmental bureaucracy to extend its power.

G.   Internet Gambling

Internet blackjack is casino gambling via home computers. Yet, it takes so long for the law to catch up with changes in technology and society, that it is not even clear whether a casino operator, sitting in another country, is violating any state law when he accepts bets via computer.

H. Indian Gaming

The National Indian Gaming Commission was established to oversee the enforcement of the Indian Gaming Regulatory Act (IGRA). IGRA divides all gambling into three classes. Class III includes banking card games, like blackjack. IGRA asserts that tribes must first get approval from the state, through a tribal-state compact, before offering any Class III game. However, the Act contains a "grandfather clause," allowing to continue unchanged as Class II any Indian card game played on or before May 1, 1988 in South Dakota, Michigan, North Dakota, and Washington.

The basic rule of IGRA is that a tribe may offer a form of gambling that is permitted in the state where the tribe is located, but self-regulates. For example, when South Dakota permitted blackjack with $5 limits, tribal casinos could offer it to non-Indian patrons with $100 limits. It was correctly predicted that in practice this means that wherever a state allows charities to run low-stakes "Las Vegas Nights" or has legalized low-stakes riverboat gambling, tribes can now demand the right to operate wide-open, high-stakes casinos.

I. Federal Gaming Commission

The National Gambling Impact Study Commission was born in 1996. The Commission's mandate was "to conduct a comprehensive study of the social and economic impacts of gambling in the United States." The bill creating the Commission required "to the maximum extent possible, fair and equitable representation of various points of view." But the Commission ended up packed with anti-gambling activists, individuals with ties to Nevada casinos, and others who knew nothing about gambling, such as the wealthy doctor who was named to the Commission because he was a big donor and lived next door to the Republican Senator who appointed him. As it relates to blackjack and card counting, the Commission remained silent.

J. The Late Great Ken Uston and the Legal Future of Blackjack

The late Ken Uston violated the Nevada trespass statute when he was "caught" card counting while playing blackjack. "Defiant trespass" occurs when an individual refuses to leave or returns to a place, like a casino, after he has been "read the riot act," that is, ordered out and ordered never to return. By his lawsuits, Uston sometimes established the rights of players to be in casinos. He was a successful blackjack player who challenged the rights of casinos to bar him from playing blackjack.

Uston was not successful in Nevada. There, casinos can exclude anyone for any reason, or for no

KEN USTON

reason at all. The only exceptions are statutory, designed to prevent businesses from discriminating on the basis of race, religion, etc.

The Supreme Court in New Jersey reached the opposite conclusion. The Court held that casino gaming had been so thoroughly and completely taken over by the state through statutes and regulations that the casinos lost the right of other private businesses to exclude whomever they wished. Only if the regulators had passed a rule allowing exclusion of advantage players could casinos exclude card-counters. In *Uston v. Resorts Int'l Hotel, Inc.*, 89 N.J. 163, 445 A.2d 370 (1982), the N.J. Supreme Court held that the N.J. Casino Control Act precluded casinos from excluding Ken Uston *qua* card-counter based on his method of playing blackjack.

Casinos in the two states reacted to the limitations put on them. Nevada casinos continued to exclude anyone they thought might be a card-counter. But New Jersey casinos, being prohibited from actually preventing an advantage player from playing blackjack, resorted to counter-measures that sometimes amounted to harassment: Some casinos now shuffle after every deal, make snide comments, or refuse to provide drink and other services. Card-counters have complained that drinks were actually spilled on them.

The New Jersey Supreme Court later approved more direct counter-measures. Atlantic City casinos can now reduce the maximum bet of a card-counter at a table to $10, while allowing every other player at the table to bet $500.

Now, some casinos are faced with the prospect of having to let card-counters play; and having to survive the lawsuits for wrongfully evicting counters. Other casinos now resort to eight-deck shoes and early shuffling, or even automatic continuous shufflers. In some case, counter-measures prove to be counter-productive: They do eliminate card-counters' advantage; but they slow down the game so much that they hurt the casinos' profit. When you have a statistical advantage, you want to play as many hands as possible for as long as possible. Hand shuffling after every deal can even discourage non-counters into trying other casinos.

CHAPTER 13

POKER AND THE LAW

A. "Poker Law" Generally

Poker is the best known non-banking or "round" card game. Unlike a banking game, in non-banking gambling games players play against each other, not against the house or any single player. In banking games, it is one player against all others; the banker collects all other players' losses and pays all other players' winnings. In poker, players' losses go to another player; there is no house (other than a house-provided dealer to facilitate the game, but not make any bets). The winning player wins all the bets, less the house's take. Any advantage the dealer gets by going last is only temporary, since the deal rotates, clockwise, to the next player after the round is over.

Casinos make their profit by beating their own customers at games of chance. Poker room operators, on the other hand, never participate in any hand. They make their revenue out of charging players for the right to participate in the poker games. This can be by renting seats, either charging per hand or every half hour, or by taking a percentage of winnings, known as "raking the pot.

Poker is also unique because players can win without having the best hand. Bluffing is fundamental to the game. Often, the pot winner will simply be the last player who has not folded his hand, even if the rank of that hand was lower than that of another player who was scared out of the pot.

Poker, both landbased and online, has exploded in popularity in recent years. This naturally raises the question: Is poker illegal? The answer is, it depends; the best answer is to check the laws of that particular state, assuming everything occurs in a single state. For example, the Oregon legislature passed a statute expressly exempting players in social games, like poker, from the prohibition on gambling, as long as the players do not help set up the game and the only money they make is from winning. But, a player at a commercial poker website is not so clearly protected.

B. Video Poker

Video poker machines can be found in bars and arcades from New York to Hawaii. They are usually not really poker, but rather banking games, with patrons playing on slot-machine-like devices against the house. The Permanent Subcommittee on Investigations of the United States Senate estimated that illegal gambling through "gray area" video devices is a multi-billion-dollar-per-year industry. These machines have become widespread; and raids are reported in the press regularly.

A video poker machine may look somewhat like a video arcade game, since it has a video screen and a coin slot. And it may look like poker, since winning or losing depend upon the poker hands displayed on the screen. But patrons are only betting whether they will achieve certain hands. They are not competing against other players but against the house, through the random number generator in each machine. Although players can discard and draw replacement cards, they cannot vary the size of their bets. And they cannot bluff.

Bars and other operators have attempted to get around the prohibition on slot machines by setting up video poker machines where the payouts are credits instead of coins. This will work in most jurisdictions, if there really is no way to win cash, such as cashing in the winning credits. One easy way to see whether credits can be redeemed for cash is the presence of a "knock-off switch." This allows the bartender to pay the winning player and knock off the free replay credits. Of course, even this video poker machine would still be considered a gambling device in jurisdictions where replays are considered prizes of value, if the device could be easily converted back to paying off winning hands, or if the bar owner is caught paying winners cash.

Jurisdictions differ on whether video poker machines are legal. For example, in *Gallatin Cty. v. D & R Music & Vending, Inc.*, 208 Mont. 138, 676 P.2d 779 (1984), the Montana Supreme Court held that electronic poker machines are in actuality illegal slot machines. The Court also declared that the machines did not qualify as poker under the Montana Card Games Act, M.C.A. 235–311(2), because the Act does not authorize playing the game of "poker" when a single player competes against the house. But the Illinois Court of Appeal, in *Yasin v. Byrne*, 121 Ill.App.3d 167, 76 Ill.Dec. 683, 459 N.E.2d 320 (1984), held that an electronic video game that simulates draw poker fell within the statutory exemption to the definition of gambling device.

C. Poker Tournaments

Casinos now host poker tournaments, and have found such events to be lucrative. Because of this, they are forced to take numerous precautions to prevent cheating. This includes rotation of decks, to prevent marking, rotation of dealers, to prevent collusion with players, a multitude of security cameras, to catch actions the other players might have missed, and even adding RFID microchips into the poker chips to prevent one player from giving some of their chips to another during breaks in play. Players who attempt to work in "kits" (hand signals to one another) rarely are successful in tournament play because these players need to be highly skilled to stay in the game long enough until they have the opportunity to play at the same table. Additionally, security cameras as well as other players at the table often can spot such collusion. This is one reason why allowing players to pick their tables and seats (instead of assigning them randomly) is a poor policy. By letting multiple friends sit together at a table, they can more easily cheat, ensuring their advancement to the next round. Collusion by players is also done through "chip-dumping," the process where one player intentionally loses large portions of his stack to another. This is done in order to give the second player a sizeable advantage over all others at the table because a large stack can be used more effectively than a small one to win hands. Players are much more likely to return for future tournaments when they believe the events are legitimate; this brings with it patrons eager to watch the tournaments and, in the case of televised shows, advertising for the casino.

There is money to be made in poker tournaments—tax money. Apparently, someone at the Internal Revenue Service has figured out that a lot of people in America are playing poker. And—this will come as a shock—some are not paying taxes on their winnings. So, the IRS has changed the law. Internal Revenue Bulletin 2007–36, went into effect on March 4, 2008, with a new rule requiring card clubs, casinos and even charities to either withhold 25% of the prizes of everyone who wins more than $5,000, or report those winners to the IRS on a Form W–2G.

The IRS accidentally created a problem for winners of small tournaments, and the cardrooms that run the games. Operators now don't know how, or even if, they are supposed to report players who win big, but less than $5,000. There are two ways of reading the new rule. One is that by limiting the rule to prizes over $5,000, the IRS is saying that winners of smaller prizes don't have to be reported. The other is that this is a special rule dealing with withholding, as well as reporting. So, cardrooms still have to sometimes report, but not withhold, smaller winners. There is a general regulation that seems to require anyone who pays anyone else $600 in a year to file a Form 1099. So, some cardrooms are issuing 1099s to tournament winners of $600 or more.

The Form W–2G for "Certain Gambling Winnings" is required for anyone who wins $1,200 or more at bingo and slot machines; $1,500 at keno; $5,000 from a state lottery and now from poker tournaments; or at least 300 times the amount bet at a track. Some cardrooms always have felt that they do not have to file any report when a player wins at poker. There is some justification for this position. Thirty years ago, Congress rejected having casino table games included with lotteries and slot machines for tax withholding. So they are still not reporting smaller wins. The IRS created this mess by declaring that an Act of Congress did not mean what everyone thought it has meant for 40 years. Without holding hearings or getting public comment, the IRS declared that a statute covering "sweepstakes, wagering pools and lotteries" includes poker tournaments. Even if a "wagering pool" should include tournaments, why only poker? More importantly, the term "wagering pool" is found in other parts of the tax code, and clearly means what we all know it means: pool selling on races.

D. Poker Clubs

Poker clubs, these days, are more often called "poker rooms" or betting exchanges. The largest poker rooms not connected to a conventional casino are the standalone card casinos in California. Every city and county in California is given the local option to decide whether it wishes to license legal card games. By state statute, Calif. Penal Code § 330, only certain enumerated games, including "21," and "banking or percentage games" are prohibited. The clubs may offer every other game. Years of litigation have led to sometimes convoluted case law and additional statutes further limited what games may be "spread," that is, offered to patrons, and how many time the card club can rake the pot. See, e.g., Calif. Penal Code § 337j. Other states, of course, have other rules, or complete prohibitions on commercial card rooms.

E. Texas Hold'em

In Texas Hold'em, commonly referred to as "Hold'em," each player is dealt two cards face down, and three community cards, called "the flop," are dealt face up in the center of the table after an initial round of betting. After the second betting round, a fourth community card, "the turn," is exposed, followed by another round of betting, and then the fifth and final community card, "the river," is exposed, followed by another round of betting. This game is *extremely* popular and the goal of every poker player and potential operator is to allow this game in states that already have licensed card clubs or card rooms. The problem is that even in those states that have legal card rooms, the play usually is limited, so the case must be made to allow Hold'em and not lose business to Nevada casinos (and other places) where Hold'em and stud poker are flourishing. In California, it took years of litigation and legislation to allow the card clubs, some of whom had been in existence for more than 100 years, to be able to spread Hold'em.

F. Poker: Skill or Chance: And the Legal Ramifications Thereof

The question of whether poker is a game predominantly of chance or skill is being litigated in courts all over the world. Anti-gambling laws are often limited to games of chance. Of course, if a statute outlaws all games of cards, or mentions poker specifically, then the issue of chance versus skill becomes much less important, although it can still arise when these statutes are attacked for violating state or federal constitutions.

The objective of poker, in its simplest form, is to be the player who wins any given hand and, ultimately to be the one with the largest stack, and the entire stack when tournament poker is concerned. But the subtleties of the game, especially the ability to bluff, make it extremely complex. Skill is thus involved in not only winning, but in winning more often and larger pots, and in losing less often and smaller amounts.

Expert players do not rely on luck; they use their skills to minimize luck as much as possible. For example, in the most popular form of poker, Texas Hold'em, because of the inherent uncertainties of the cards being dealt, players must hedge the risk involved with their hole cards and the community cards. A player's hole cards often dictate whether they will be involved in the hand from the start. The proper way to minimize the risk of a starting hand and the impact the community cards will have in later rounds is to have a rough idea of the statistical probabilities in a given situation. A weak starting hand typically should be folded because of its meager chance for any return. Similarly, if the community cards do not help, folding is the safest option to avoid losing needless amounts of chips.

Position, another immutable factor that players cannot control, is closely intertwined with the previous two factors. The general rule is that a later position allows one to play riskier hands. Another layer of skill is added to the game: the ability to win with an inferior hand.

Ordinary games of chance occupy the other end of the spectrum from poker. Here, winning depends on that game's underlying statistics and nothing more. A simple example would be a raffle, which pays the winner a prize when his number matches the one drawn. Comparing poker strategies with the raffle example, it is clear that not only can poker players do more with the arbitrary hands they are dealt, but they also need not rely on an immense number of players in order to receive a large payout.

This alternate viewpoint demonstrates a key difference between games of skill and games of chance, namely, that when given an element of control, a game normally dependent upon chance alone turns into a competition where each player utilizes the skills available to him to outmaneuver his opponents. Also, in poker, players do not go up against the house.

Poker was not the first activity to be met with hostility for being deemed a form of gambling. In *State v. Pinball Machines*, 404 P.2d 923 (Alaska 1965), an Alaskan court found pinball games to be a form of gambling, leading to the seizure and destruction of those machines for violating state law. In 1978, in *Progress Vending, Inc. v. Department of Liquor Control*, 59 Ohio App.2d 266, 394 N.E.2d 324 (1978), the Ohio Court of Appeals decided "ample evidence was adduced from which it can be reasonably concluded that skill in the play of pinball machines greatly predominates over chance in achieving a successful outcome of attaining the prize rewarded." While the *Progress Vending* court does not specify what makes the machines at issue games of skill compared to earlier models, it is likely that the use of flippers changed their minds.

This viewpoint parallels society in that capitalistic nations favor utilizing one's abilities to succeed in life. However, few courts have ruled that poker is a contest of skill. To do so might open the door to widespread, commercial poker rooms. But, to declare poker as a game of chance has sometimes required courts to analyze the game in a way that does not resemble reality. When a judge wants to declare poker as predominantly chance, he will often point to the possibility of a complete novice sitting down for a single hand and getting dealt a royal flush against a professional. Of course, nobody sits down for a single hand of poker.

What has come to be known as Jackpot Poker adds another level of complexity to the chance versus skill question. In modern Jackpot Poker, players contribute a small amount to a "bad-beat" sidepot. This is only won when a player has a spectacular, predesignated hand, like four of a kind, and comes in second, beaten by a higher four of a kind or a straight flush. A California court, in *Bell Gardens Bicycle Club v. Department of Justice*, 36 Cal. App.4th 717, 42 Cal.Rptr.2d 730 (1995), held that even if traditional poker tournaments are games of skill, the Jackpot feature makes the game illegal, because it had all the features of a lottery and private lotteries are illegal in California. The theory is that the Jackpot constitutes a lottery because the only way for a player to win is by matching his hand to a predetermined one with no action on the player's part, other than having his cards randomly dealt to them. The Court ignored the testimony that players had to take the Jackpot feature into account when playing this type of poker and declared Jackpot Poker to be illegal under the statutory prohibition on lotteries. Regular poker games were permitted to continue at the state's card clubs because their legality did not depend on whether they were predominantly luck or skill.

One of the biggest victories for poker player taxation was brought about by poker legend Billy Baxter. Baxter challenged the IRS and proved that his winnings from poker should be considered earned income for tax purposes. Baxter, who never held an occupation other than gambling, argued that his poker earnings constituted "personal service income" under 26 U.S.C.A. § 1348(b), subjecting his earnings to a maximum tax rate of fifty percent. The Government argued that Baxter's winnings did not constitute "personal service income" and therefore should be taxed at a maximum rate of seventy percent. The District Court of Nevada agreed with Baxter. The court found that any argument that Baxter's gaming income is not based upon his personal expenditure of time, energy, and skill is meritless.

G. Poker: Illegal Gambling or Permitted Activity

By failing to distinguish it from games of chance, poker is often viewed in the same light as lotteries or casino games.

Even if poker were a game of chance proponents are quick to argue the benefits of the game. They view poker as having positive social values because it provides a form of adult play, serves as a social adhesive, provides other social benefits, including male and now female bonding, and provides enjoyment to any group with a deck of cards.

But poker as a game of skill should be evaluated differently than games of chance. Some states have exempted certain skill games from criminal-gambling prohibitions. Many reasons exist for these exemptions.

Creating policy distinctions between contests of skill and games of chance may have a scientific as well as historic basis. A study published in the New England Journal of Medicine in June 2003 found that the cumulative risk of dementia was significantly lower for elderly persons who played chess, checkers, backgammon, or cards on a frequent basis compared to those who did not. These studies appear consistent with the reduction of the risk of Alzheimer's. The mental simulation created by playing bridge, a game comparable to poker in most significant ways, was found to stimulate the immune system in a preliminary study reported in 2001.

Yet poker is different. Variants like Texas Hold' em require so much skill that computer scientists have had great difficulty cheating computer models that can match wits with the best poker players. It is a game that exercises the mind and challenges the intellect. Whether public policy justifies the banning of games of chance is wholly irrelevant when talking about poker. The variables on both sides of the pragmatic equation are fundamentally different for poker than games of pure chance.

Many state governments have decided that some games that purport to be poker, like video poker, do not share the attributes of the traditional game and are prohibited. Governments also may see the need to regulate the game to assure that it is conducted honestly and fairly. Most have decided to take the commercial aspects of the game from operators by prohibiting all but social or charitable games.

H. Mathematics of Poker

Gambling games can be categorized as those of pure chance and those involving an element of skill. Games of pure chance include roulette, craps, keno, bingo, (traditional) slots, and lotteries. In these games, the outcome is determined by chance alone, and no strategy or skill can affect the long-run percentage of money won or lost. Casino games involving skill include blackjack, video poker, and many of the newer poker-based casino games such as Caribbean stud poker, let it ride poker, and three-card poker. In these types of games, the per-centage of money won or lost is a direct reflection of a player's level of skill.

In poker, over the long run, everybody gets nearly the same proportion of good and bad cards, of winning and losing hands. (Poor players probably see more losing hands because they stay in too long). Beginning poker players rely on big hands and lucky draws. Expert poker players use their skills to minimize their losses on their bad hands and maximize their profits on their good ones.

In any poker game, whether stud or draw poker or any of the countless variations that combine skill and chance, the more skillful player will win more and lose less money in the long run. Poker appears to have a greater skill element than any other card game, including contract bridge, pinochle and gin rummy. Poker is the one and only game where a skilled player may hold bad cards for hours and still win the money.

An objective observer would probably conclude that poker is a game of skill; luck and psychology also play a part, but unlike other casino games that rely entirely on luck, winning poker requires skill. A skillful poker player can change the odds in the game to his favor by using position, psychology, bluffing, and other methods to increase his chances to win the pot and increase the size of the pots he wins. The latest studies indicate that most rounds in tournaments are won by players who did not have to show their cards. In other words, the winning player won based on something other than having the best hand.

There are several components to the skill necessary to play poker well, including a knowledge and ability to use mathematics and psychology; assessing competition; reading hands; recognizing tells; exploiting position; and, money management. Good poker strategy and tactics require the use of a combination of all these skill components; deceptiveness and bluffing are also essential to the game.

I. Case Study: Hold'em Poker in California

Although California had legal card rooms, the play was limited to draw poker, low ball, panguingue, and pai gow. California lost business to the Nevada casinos, which allowed Hold'em and stud poker. The state attorney general's office had ruled that only draw poker is legal, and all forms of stud poker are outlawed, and playing an outlawed game is a criminal offense. To add to this, an assistant attorney general issued a memorandum that said Hold'em is a form of stud poker, and, therefore, could not be played for money in a licensed card club. If Hold'em is a form of seven-card stud, then it obviously is not illegal if all forms of seven-card stud are legal. In a series of successful test cases, Professor Rose was able to show that Hold'em is not a form of stud, nor is it a form of draw, but instead, it is a third form of poker, a community card game, and as such, is legal under state law. Hold'em is legal for two reasons: the first is simply that it is not illegal, and the second is that any form of poker is legal in California unless it is specifically listed in the Penal Code as a prohibited game. The fight to bring Hold'em to California card clubs is recounted in chapter 3 in I. Nelson Rose's GAMBLING AND THE LAW (Gambling Times, Inc. 1986).

J. Is "Online Poker" the Future of Poker?

The biggest event in the world of Internet poker took place not online but in a casino in downtown Las Vegas. On May 23, 2003, Chris Moneymaker won the World Series of Poker, and its $25 million top prize, at Binion's Horseshoe Hotel & Casino. It costs $10,000 to enter. Some players pay cash, but Moneymaker put up only $40; he won his entry fee through poker games played entirely online. Did Moneymaker break the law? The federal government's interest is pretty much limited to organized crime. What about state law? All states make it a crime to conduct some forms of unauthorized gambling, but about half the states also make it a crime to make a bet under some circumstances, even though no one is rarely charged with that crime any more. The only way for a player to know for sure is to check the laws of that particular state. No state has passed a law expressly stating that players can or cannot play poker online; so, interpretation is required.

Gambling permeates throughout American society. One cannot watch television without stumbling upon a poker show, listen to the radio without hearing the amount of today's lotto jackpot, or go to the Internet without encountering an advertisement for a gambling website. In every state, except Utah, to one extent or another, there exists some form of legalized gambling. With such an ever-pervasive culture of gambling in this country, why is Internet gambling the bane that needs to be eradicated from modern society? The Unlawful Internet Gambling Enforcement Act of 2006 is only the most recent legislation passed by Congress in an attempt to curb the ongoing "problem" that is Internet gambling. The Act is intended to prevent money going from players in the U.S. to operators of illegal online gambling.

The United States Department of Justice gave the legal online gaming community a big gift, made public two days before Christmas. President Barack Obama's administration declared, perhaps unintentionally, that almost every form of intra-state Internet gambling is legal under federal law, and so may be games played interstate and even internationally. Technically, the only question being decided was, "Whether proposals by Illinois and New York to use the Internet and out-of-state transaction processors to sell lottery tickets to in-state adults violate the Wire Act." But the conclusion by the DOJ that the Wire Act's "prohibitions relate solely to sport-related gambling activities in interstate and foreign commerce," eliminates almost every federal anti-gambling law that could apply to gaming that is legal under state laws.

So every state is now looking to join the provincial lotteries of Canada in authorizing Internet poker. In some cases, it will be run by the state lottery. But in most states, licenses will be issued, for large payments up front and a tax of at least 10%–20%. And once the states have legalized intra-state Internet poker, they will authorize pooling of players across state and even national boundaries.

CHAPTER 14

INTELLECTUAL PROPERTY AND GAMING

A. Intellectual Property and Gaming Generally

Intellectual property law encompasses ideas and subjects such as patents, trademarks, copyrights, trade secrets, trade dress as well as other subjects that relate to topics such as publicity rights, passing off, misappropriation, false advertising, and unfair competition. There are many aspects of intellectual property that apply to gambling, including patents for casino equipment and games, copyright issues in video poker, trademarks, and trade dress concerns in casino décor, logos, and packaging, etc. For example, the developers of a gaming video should always retain intellectual property ownership of the code, tools, and technology used in the creation of the game.

B. Patents and Gaming Generally

Patent law is governed by the Federal Patent Act, 35 U.S.C.A. §§ 1, *et seq.* If an individual discovers or invents any new machine, process, manufacture or composition of matter, they may apply to obtain a patent. An individual can secure a patent by filing an application with the United States Patent and Trademark Office (PTO).

The Patent Act defines a potential patent as any "new and useful process, machine, manufacture, or composition of matter" that includes mechanical, chemical, and electrical structures and processes. In order for an invention to be patentable, it must meet four requirements. An invention must be (1) in a subject matter category, (2) useful, (3) novel in relation to the prior art, and (4) not obvious from the prior art to a person of ordinary skill in the art at the time the invention was made.

A patent confers on the owner the right to exclude others from selling or using the process or product. A patent owner may sue those individuals who directly infringe upon the patent by using or selling the invention without the proper authority to do so. A patent lasts (about) 20 years from the date of the filing of the patent application with the PTO.

The Canadian decision in *Progressive Games, Inc. v. Canada (Commissioner of Patents)* ([2000] F.C.J. No. 1829 (C.A.); the Trial Division judgment may be found at [1999] F.C.J. No. 162 [collectively, "*Progressive Games*"]), is often cited in support of the proposition that ways of playing casino games are excluded from patentable subject matter, at least in Canada. The case involved an invention similar to Caribbean Stud, with players getting payouts for having certain poker hands dealt them, while betting against the house dealer. Another example, *CIAS, Inc. v. Alliance Gaming Corp.*, 424 F. Supp. 2d 678 (S.D. N.Y. 2006), was a patent infringement case that involved a patent on a system for detecting counterfeit items used in tickets for playing cashless slot machines in casinos. The Court granted the defendant's motion for summary judgment, dismissing the complaint on the ground that its accused systems did not infringe plaintiff's patent. But there have been many patents issued in the United States for "blackjack type games."

C. Intellectual Property and Internet Gaming

The foundation for the copyright laws is in Article I, Section 8 of the Constitution, which states, "Congress shall have power ... to promote the progress of science and useful arts, by securing for limited times to authors and inventors the exclusive right to their respective writings and discoveries." In October of 1998, Congress amended the 1976 Copyright Act by putting into effect the Digital Millennium Copyright Act of 1998 (DMCA), Pub. L. No. 105–304, 112, Stat. 2860 (1998), which grants legal protection against the circumvention of any Technological Protection Measures (TPM) that copyright holders have implemented to prevent reproduction of their creation. The gaming industry needs to approach application of the DMCA from the gaming culture's standpoint.

The Internet has increased gambling's popularity. Unlike brick-and-mortar casinos, the action at "virtual casinos" and in other forms of online gambling is nonstop and accessible to anyone with Internet access. Bets can be placed anonymously or pseudonymously, regardless of the bettor's age, sobriety, or finances. And, many Internet gambling sites operate from servers in foreign countries that are unsupervised by U.S. government regulators.

D.   Copyright and Gaming Generally

Copyright law protects original works of authorship embodied in a tangible medium of expression (*see*, the Copyright Act, 17 U.S.C.A. §§ 101 *et seq.* (1998)). Subject matter that may be copyrighted includes music, drama, computer programs, sound recordings, and the visual arts. Copyright protects the original expression of ideas, not the ideas themselves. A copyright term extends for the life of the author plus 70 years after the author's death. Gambling video games and Internet gambling certainly are protectable by the copyright laws.

E.   Trademarks and Gaming

A trademark is a type of symbol used by one to identify a particular set of goods and to distinguish them from another's goods. A trademark owner can prevent others from using the same or similar marks that create a likelihood of confusion or deception. Under trademark law, an individual can establish one's manufactured goods and services from another's (think, the Nike SWOOSH). Trademark law distinguishes between the following: (1) the right to use a mark, (2) the right to exclude others from using a mark, and (3) the right to register the mark. The Federal Trademark Act of 1946, which is commonly referred to as the Lanham Act, governs the registration and law of trademark as well as the remedies and enforcement procedure for trademark infringement. A trademark is defined as including "any word, name, symbol, or device or any combination thereof adopted and used by a manufacturer or merchant to identify his or her goods and also to distinguish from those manufactured or sold by others." The Lanham Act provides for the registration of servicemarks and certification marks, as well as trademarks.

A related aspect of trademarks is the phenomenon of domain names and cybersquatting. To locate an Internet's business web page, you must know its Internet address. The addresses are the key to effective communication; by typing in a certain series of letters, numbers, and symbols, which is referred to as an Internet domain name, the user can gain access to the intended website. Domain names usually are the company's nickname, trade name, abbreviation, ticker name, or catch phrases. Many problems exist because domain names are classified as trademarks.

A fairly typical scenario is a casino trademark license agreement, which, for example, was used between a Macau developer, owner, and operator of a casino, which was the licensee, so it could develop and operate a casino using the name "Hard Rock Casino." The first recital states that "Licensor licenses qualified Persons to develop and operate casinos, under the name 'Hard Rock Casino' and certain other trademarks, trade names, servicemarks, logos, slogans, trade dress, commercial symbols, and other intellectual property rights designated by Licensor from time to time."

The major obstacle to any online gaming operation is not the law or even the costs of doing business; it is getting customers. Add to this the limited number of ".com" and ".net" names available, and it is easy to see why there have been more lawsuits over brand names than any other issue. In *International Bancorp, L.L.C. v. Societe Des Bains De Mer et du Cercle Des Etrangers a Monaco*, 192 F.Supp.2d 467 (E.D.VA. 2002), the federal court was faced with a declaratory judgment trademark infringement action: "the owner of Monaco's famed gambling establishment, Casino de Monte Carlo, against an individual and five companies who have registered fifty-three ".com" and ".net" domain names that incorporate, in various ways, the name "Casino de Monte Carlo." In a detailed examination of the many factors that must be analyzed in IP actions, the Court found that the famed Monte Carlo Casino company had proved an intentional trademark infringement; a violation of the in personam provisions of the Anticybersquatting Consumer Protection Act, 15 U.S.C. § 1125(d)(1); but, no evidence of actual economic harm attributable to dilution of its trademark.

Similar issues were raised in *Rio Properties, Inc. v. Rio International Interlink*, 284 F.3d 1007 (9th Cir. 2002), with the additional twist that the operators of the Internet gaming sides could not be located for service of process. The Las Vegas hotel and casino operator Rio Properties, Inc., raised various statutory and common law trademark infringement claims in its complaint. Because the defendants listed no physical location for their company, and could not be found, even with the help of a private detective, the district court allowed the plaintiff to serve by email and regular mail. The trial court entered a default judgment against the defendant for failing to comply with the court's discovery orders. The Ninth Circuit affirmed the district court's decisions in all respects.

F. Case Study: Gambling and the Law®

The phrase, Gambling and the Law® is a registered trademark of one of this book's co-authors. It began when he used that phrase in his column, which appeared in *Gambling Times Magazine*. He went through the trademark process and it was agreed that the phrase was associated with him, mostly through his columns. He can now prevent others from using the same or similar marks that would create a likelihood of confusion or deception. For example, "Gaming in the Law" might cause confusion, but "Running in the Law" most probably would not.

G. Trade Dress and Gambling

Trade dress protection is available for non-functional features if they distinguish the goods' origin. The Lanham Act provides protection against the creation of confusion by the simulation of a product or service's "trade dress." Trade dress originally meant a product's packaging, but more recent court decisions have extended trade dress to include the configuration and ornamentation of the product. An example would be the coloring and signage of famous casinos.

H. Trade Secrets and Gaming

Closely related to the other causes of action in intellectual property is the area of trade secrets and the misappropriation thereof. Factors considered in determining whether trade secrets exist include (1) the extent to which information is known outside of the business; (2) the extent to which information is known to those inside of the business; (3) the precautions taken by the holder of the trade secret to guard the secrecy of the information; (4) the savings effected and the value to holder in having information as against competitors; (5) the amount of effort or money expended in obtaining and developing information; and (6) the amount of time and expense it would take for others to acquire and duplicate that information. There are many examples of trade secrets in gaming and gambling, which might include gaming manuals, methods of dealing cards, programming video poker games, etc. But the most valuable proprietary information for a casino is its list of whales and other high rollers.

I. Future Issues in Intellectual Property and Gaming

Intellectual property concerns are vital to the casino industry since technology steers the industry whether it is copyrighted slots with patented digital advancements, or new space-age developments in casino security. The Internet with online poker, etc., undoubtedly will create the most intellectual property issues.

CHAPTER 15

VIDEO POKER, VLTS AND OTHER MACHINES

A.   Video Poker and the Law Generally

A video poker machine looks somewhat like other video arcade games; it also has a video screen and, usually, a coin slot. In the typical machine, when a quarter is inserted, the screen displays five cards. There are buttons under each card so the player can keep those he likes and discard the rest in hopes of a better hand on the draw. The machines can be set for any payment; for casino machines, usually a pair of jacks or better is needed. Payments can vary from one coin for a pair, to hundreds of coins for a royal flush. In monopoly or oligopoly situations, casinos can increase their take by requiring that patrons have a higher hand, as with the two-pair minimum required for a win by the first casinos in Atlantic City. Again, operators can increase their take by changing the payouts, for example, by paying more or less on full houses and flushes. A "Full Pay" jacks or better video poker machine pays nine for one on full houses and six for one on flushes, often shown as a 9/6 payout. This is significantly higher than an 8/5 schedule, where the bettor only receives eight times his initial wager if he happens to get a full house and only five times for a flush. A video poker machine may look like poker, since players can discard and draw replacement cards, and winning or losing depend upon the poker hands displayed on the screen. But patrons are only betting whether they will achieve certain hands. They are not competing against other players but against the house, through the random number generator in each machine. They cannot vary the size of their bets. And they cannot bluff. In non-casino games, the payouts are credits instead of coins. One variation allows the machines to be switched from one computer program to another. The gambling program pays out varying amounts for winning hands. However, another program can be installed with a flip of the switch. The second program eliminates the possibility of winning free replays and thus is not a gambling device: there is no prize. Of course, the video poker machine would still be considered a gambling device in jurisdictions where replays are considered prizes of value, if the device could be easily converted back to paying off winning hands, or if the bar owner is caught paying winners cash.

Care must be taken to examine the machines in question and the applicable laws. In *Gallatin Cty. v. D & R Music & Vending, Inc.*, 208 Mont. 138, 676 P.2d 779 (1984), the Montana Supreme Court held that electronic poker machines are in actuality illegal slot machines. The Montana Card Games Act,

M.C.A. 235–311(2), also declared that video poker machines do not qualify as a game of "poker," and that the Act does not authorize playing the game of "poker" when a single player competes against the house. However, in *Yasin v. Byrne*, 121 Ill.App.3d 167, 76 Ill.Dec. 683, 459 N.E.2d 320 (1984), the Court held that an electronic video game that simulates draw poker fell within the statutory exemption to the definition of gambling device.

Under the federal gambling statute, the Johnson Act (Gaming Device Act of 1962), 15 U.S.C.A. §§ 1171–1178, video gambling machines are gambling devices, unless exempted by state law.

B. Video Lotteries

The current batches of video lotteries, often called Video Lottery Terminals or VLTs, are in actuality nothing more than slot machines, in practice, if not in law. The player often has to put money directly into a slot on the machines and some set amount, up to, let's say, $1,000.00, is paid directly to winners on the spot. The fact that winnings larger than $1,000.00 require trips to the lottery office does not make the devices non-slot machines. There is one difference between slot machines and video lotteries: both slot machines and video lotteries can be set for any payback; however, traditionally, slots are usually set to take about 15% of the amount bet—over time, they will pay back

85%. On the other hand, lotteries often pay less than 50% of the amount bet.

VLTs are legal in jurisdictions that make them legal. Almost always this is done by express action of state legislatures. Often there are additional requirements, such as that the terminals not have individual random number generators, but rather be linked to a central computer. It is necessary to examine the laws of the jurisdiction to know whether VLTs would be considered legal, as part of the state lottery, or illegal, as merely another form of slot machine.

C. Credit Card Play

Most gaming devices still do not accept credit cards. This is often a restriction imposed by law. But, cashless slot machines are proliferating. Slot machines, video poker devices and VLTs often come with, or can be converted, to cashless play. Patrons use their cash or credit cards to buy special casino cards from the slot cashier. These cards are inserted into the machines and winnings and losses are recorded electronically on the card itself. When a player wins, the machine plays the pre-recorded sound of coins dropping into a metal basin since the machine cannot pay out in coins.

D. Paper Slots

Paper instant winner cards have been around for decades. In the law, these are called paper slot machines. Gambling devices need not be mechanical; in the past, pull-tabs and punchboards were readily available at the local store in the hope of winning a prize. Today's version of the pull-tab is the rub-off card, given out by fast-food restaurants; paper bingo pull-tabs, available for a dollar each at most charity bingo games; and scratch-off lottery tickets, called scratchers. Of course, jurisdictions are free to change their laws. For example, in most states and under federal law on Indian land, a paper pull-tab is legally "bingo," if sold in an authorized bingo hall.

E. Internet Poker

The Internet poker market is worth something like $12 billion, with much of it coming from the United States. However, the Department of Justice (DOJ) issued online poker indictments on April 15, 2011. The DOJ alleged that the goal of this conspiracy was to violate the Unlawful Internet Gambling Enforcement Act (UIGEA), 31 U.S.C.A. §§ 5362–5367. The indictments also contained criminal and civil forfeiture allegations. The Internet poker sites, Poker Stars and Full Tilt, have entered into agreements with the DOJ that expressly permitted the return of funds to the U.S. players. However, other Internet poker providers, such as Absolute and Ultimate Bet, do not have an agreement with the DOJ that expressly contemplated a return of funds.

Interestingly, the DOJ did not mention the main federal statute used in its ongoing war of intimidation against Internet poker, the federal Wire Act, 18 U.S.C.A. § 1084. Instead, it said the gambling was illegal because it violated New York state anti-gambling misdemeanor statutes. A few months later, the DOJ announced that it had reassessed the position it had taken for half a century, and would limit the Wire Act to bets on sports events and races. This meant that the states are now free to legalize Internet poker intra-state, and even form player pools with other states and nations.

F.   Muddying the Waters; Case Study: Dwarf Den Poker Machine

Since raids on video poker machines have become commonplace, the manufacturers have countered by coming up with ways to hide the outward appearance of the games while continuing the way that the game was played. Accordingly, in an attempt to appear to be a non-gambling video arcade game, poker is now being played with harmless, non-threatening images that are not related to poker, such as dwarves, balloons, and castles, instead of cards. For example, Dwarf Den flashes the image of five dwarves on the screen instead of five cards. Dwarves come in four different colors and are numbered from 1 to 13. You can ''zap'' a dwarf exactly the same way you can discard a card on a regular video poker machine. Winning combinations are the same as in poker: ''Thin Twins'' is a pair of aces; all of the same color, Green Brothers, Lavender Gang is a flush; a Generation is a straight and, a family is a full house, and so on. Changing the images does not change the legal characteristics of the game unless the anti-video law is so poorly written that it outlaws only the specific game of poker when it is specifically played with the images of playing cards only.

G. Are These Latest Incarnations of Video Poker Gambling Devices?

The legal question is whether these latest inventions are gambling devices; that is, is a video poker machine a slot machine in the eyes of the law? There is no distinct line in determining what is a gambling device; however, the courts are in complete agreement about the traditional coin-in-the slot, three-reel, one-armed mechanical bandit, which, if operated and played for money, is most assuredly deemed a gambling device. But inventors are creating new devices all the time; and the question is how a court is going to tell whether a particular machine is a gambling device.

In the present "Third Wave of Legal Gambling" sweeping the nation—the third time in American history that gambling has been made legal almost everywhere, it is not enough to know whether a device can be used for gambling. Virtually every jurisdiction in North America now allows legal gambling. So, a video poker machine may be illegal under applicable law, or it may be legal as a Video Lottery Terminal, or as in states like Oregon, the State Legislature has simply declared that every liquor license holder may operate up to five video poker machines.

H. State Supreme Court Decisions That Attempt to Decide When Video Poker Is Poker

In *Mills–Jennings of Ohio, Inc. v. Department of Liquor Control*, 70 Ohio St.2d 95, 435 N.E.2d 407 (1982), the Court held that raw Poker electronic videogame machines were gambling devices *per se* as defined in gambling statutes, since the game played on the machine was the game of poker, which is defined in that state's statute as a game of chance. The Court held that the machine was an apparatus designed for use in connection with a game of chance which fell within the statutory definition of gambling device. (R.C. § 2915.01 (D.F.); *see also*, *Johnson v. Collins Entertainment*, 88 F.Supp.2d 499 (D. S.C. 1999) (video poker junkies alleged that owners and operated induced them to gamble excessively.)

CHAPTER 16

INTERNET GAMING

A. Types of Gaming

Most forms of gaming can be duplicated on the Internet in some fashion. Online and interactive gaming, often called remote gambling, is here to stay. Games and contests that employ some element of chance, whether in print, at point of purchase, over broadcast media, or on the Web, are visible everywhere and are thrown at potential customers, for any product or service. Gambling can be defined as any activity with three elements: consideration, chance, and prize. It can be described as payment of a price for a chance to win a prize. Technology has allowed remote wagering since the invention of the telegraph. Telephone betting, especially on sports events and horseraces, has been around for more than a century. But modern technology is bringing virtual casinos and lotteries and poker rooms into homes, schools and offices.

Online gambling operators operate on an account basis and require an initial "post-up" by credit card, debit card, money wire transfer or some other payment in advance. Many of these are licensed by foreign states and countries. But, legal remote wagering has been authorized on horseracing in more than half the U.S. states, more than half-a-dozen states allow players to buy lottery tickets over the Internet, and Nevada has statutes and regulations for intranet sports betting and Internet poker.

Sites that are technically not gambling are also proliferating. There are "free" games offered online, which are used as a form of marketing by various sites. Some of the most popular are online bingo games with small money prizes and lots of ads. Skill contests are spreading. But the fastest growing gaming may be operators like Zynga, offering social games, including poker that may cost money, but where winners cannot win prizes redeemable for cash.

1. Game Formats and Their Online Versions

Gambling has traditionally been divided into three basic formats based on style of play: lotteries, wagers, and gaming. Lotteries usually require a pooling of money to create the prizes and players are passive, merely buying tickets. Gaming, meaning participating in a game of chance, used to require going to a particular place, like a casino, to play. These games depend upon the generation of random numbers within set parameters: possible results are available from 52 cards, two dice, three reels, etc. Remote wagering on an uncertain future event has been technologically possible since the invention of the telephone and telegraph. A sportsbook depends on odds and payoff calculations that are measured against results that are transmitted in real-time. All these formats are particularly adaptable to the use of computer software and online communication. And modern inventions are blurring the lines between these classes. For example, if a state lottery can sell instant lottery tickets, i.e. "scratchers," through images on a video screen, is the device still a lottery, or has it become a slot machine?

2. Lotteries

Lotteries can be summarized as pooling wagers, betting on a winning number or token, which is then drawn by chance. The most common types of lotteries are those operated by governments. However, in practice, very few governments actually operate every part of their own lotteries. Most governments have contracts with private operators, obtained by the winning private company responding to the government's Request For Proposal ("RFP"). These companies supply the computers and are sometimes "turn-key operations," meaning they do literally everything, while using the state's name and endorsement so that it appears that the state is running the lottery.

The second most common form of lottery is the charity raffle, such as the Plus–Lotto. These used to require bettors to obtain paper tickets, in person or by mail. But, today raffles can be run online. If the only way a player can obtain a chance to win is by buying a raffle ticket, the game is a form of gambling, technically a lottery. If anyone can obtain

tickets for free, such as "donation requested" raffles, the scheme may be legally not gambling.

Although modern lotteries encompass almost every type of gambling, including those that are indistinguishable from slot machines, the most common
lottery games are the scratch-types and drawings.
State lotteries have adapted readily to use of the
Internet as a marketing tool for direct sales. Under
an official announcement from the Department of
Justice, state lotteries are now free to sell tickets on
the Internet, and to use out-of-state payment processors.

3.   Direct vs. Indirect Participation

The Web page of each state lottery posts daily
and weekly drawings. These are often some of the
most visited Internet sites on the World Wide Web.
However, some state lotteries now use the Internet
as part of their actual drawing, not just for advertising. There also are televised "semi-interactive" variations, as in the California State Lottery, where a
closed circuit TV service displays the winning numbers of a "scratcher" game.

4.   Parimutuel Betting on Horse and Dog Races

Simulcasting, which is shorthand for "simultaneous broadcast," is the broadcast of a live race to a
remote site, allowing bettors to wager at that site,
as well as at the original track. These simulcasts
require the instantaneous transmission of wagering
information so that bettors at one location cannot

have an unfair advantage. Most simulcast races have a merged parimutuel pool with all bets being treated as if they were actually placed at a single location. Simulcasting is betting on a horse or greyhound race not taking place where the bettor is located. The parimutuel industry divides simulcasting into two categories: inter-track wagers, where a person has to go to one track to place a bet on races taking place at another track; and true off-track betting, which includes OTB parlors, as in New York City, and at-home wagering. Because the bettor has to deposit money in advance, usually through a credit card, the racing industry calls remote wagering from homes and offices as Advanced Deposit Wagering, or ADW.

Betting on races over the Internet was a natural development for parimutuel wagering. Simulcasting to other tracks and then to stand-alone OTBs at fairgrounds and then in New York City had shown that there is no reason for bettors to be physically present at a track. The Internet seemed made for race wagering, because operators had already adopted computer technology. As with sports betting, the outcome of horse and dograce wagers can be independently verified.

The Interstate Wire Act, 18 U.S.C.A. § 1084, specifically forbids the taking of bets by interstate telecommunications facilities on sports events and races. The Wire Act was passed as part of Attorney General Robert F. Kennedy, Jr.'s war on organized crime in 1961. It was designed to go after "the Wire," i.e. the telegraph wire services illegal bookies used to get horserace results. David G. Schwartz, CUTTING THE WIRE: GAMING PROHIBITION AND THE INTERNET (Reno: University of Nevada Press, 2005). There is an express exception if it is legal to take the bet at the place where the bet originates, and at the place where it is taken. Congress may have only intended by this exception to allow information to be transmitted, not actual wagers. However, cross-border betting is virtually everywhere, and at least tolerated by the federal authorities.

The Interstate Horseracing Act ("IHA"), 15 U.S.C.A. §§ 3301 *et seq.*, expressly allows bets to go across state lines, if the states involved have made the parimutuel wagering legal. Due to a complaint filed against the U.S. by Antigua in the World Trade Organization, the Department of Justice has taken the position that the IHA only authorized individuals to bet with ADW operators in their home states, even if they do it by computer and even if the wagers are on out-of-state races. However, everyone else, including the WTO and state racing commissioners, who had read the IHA sees it as expressly authorizing interstate wagers. It was also clear that the target of the Wire Act were illegal bookies.

5. Sports Betting

Sports betting, as informal wagering, is a part of the fabric of American society. Sports wagering as an organized business is often associated with professional gambling and attempts to fix the outcome of particular games, such as the infamous 1919

"Black Sox Scandal." The introduction of the point-spread increased the fear of corruption, especially the possibility of corrupting collegiate athletes, which was the moving spirit behind the Professional and Amateur Sports Protection Act ("PASPA"), 28 U.S.C.A. §§ 3701–3704. PASPA was passed when the Delaware and Oregon State Lotteries started taking parlay bets on National Football League games. Congress wanted to prohibit any state or Indian tribe from offering new forms of sports betting. But it grandfathered-in all existing forms of sports wagering between January 1, 1976 and August 31, 1990, thus allowing betting on college or professional sports in at least the following states: Delaware, Montana, New Mexico, North Dakota, Oregon, Washington, and Wyoming. Additional states authorize parimutuel betting on jai alai.

The voters of New Jersey approved sports betting in November 2011. Suit has now been filed to have the PASPA declared unconstitutional, so that New Jersey's betting can begin. It is difficult to see how a federal court could uphold PASPA, since it is legally irrational to allow a dozen states to have sports betting, but prohibit it in all others. This may also be the only federal statute that ever prevented states from changing their public policies toward gambling.

Nevada has two operators taking phone and computer sports bets from residents. Other states will follow, especially if the PASPA is overturned. But unlike Internet poker, sports betting will always be purely intra-state, due to the Wire Act.

6. Futures and Proposition Betting

Betting exchanges allow bettors to find each other. For a set fee, the exchange will help a given offer of a bet to find a taker, and hold the stakes until the transaction is resolved. Thus, even though an agency relationship may have been formed, there should be no conflict of interest with either party to the proposition. An online poker room, by contrast, merely provides its e-services in return for the "rake" percentage, fee-per-hand, or fee-per-"seat" it charges, so no real agency relationship arises. But, even though the betting exchange does not take the wager itself, it clearly is in the business of betting, and is violating federal laws, like the Wire Act, 18 U.S.C.A. § 1084, that prohibit sports betting.

It is a logical progression to point out occasionally that legalized gaming is similar to trading on the stock and commodities markets. Many states, in fact, view trading as gambling. Ultimately, Congress enacted the federal securities laws, which allowed trading on national exchanges from being outlawed by state laws, 15 U.S.C.A. § 78bb. These days, individual investors with Internet access can legally become "day traders" on listed markets. Both online gamblers and online investors rely on software programmed "systems."

There is also network or multi-level marketing (mlm), which is supposed to be an arrangement of independent sales representatives, and differs from the standard independent sales organizations in that "override" or "downline" commissions are awarded to the initial organizers and early participants on the sales of later recruited representatives, and sub-representatives.

Prediction and experimental markets are expanding, at least outside the U.S. These allow you to put up money, and win or lose, when you make a prediction. They have proven amazingly accurate in forecasting real-world events, like who will win the 2008 presidential election. Legally, these are usually considered forms of gambling, and they may also violate federal and state securities laws. The Iowa Electronic Markets is one of the few legal prediction markets operating in the U.S. The IEM was created by the University of Iowa and has received two no-action-letters from the Division of Trading and Markets of the Commodity Futures Trading Commission, allowing it to operate and accept real money trading in predictions.

7. Casino–Style Games

Casino-style games are those games that are found in Nevada-style licensed gambling establishments. These games can include blackjack, craps, and roulette; slot machines, and video poker machines; and poker itself, which is classified as a casino game, under Nevada law. Landbased casinos are incorporating more electronics into their games, such as creating growing side-bet jackpots. Internet versions of casino games are becoming more and more indistinguishable from their real-world counterparts.

8. Banked vs. Non–Banked

Card games in particular can be classified as "banked," on the one hand, and "non-banked" or "round" games, on the other hand. In banked or banking games, the players compete against one player, usually the "House," i.e., the gaming establishment, rather than against each other. The term arises from the definition of a bank: in a banking game, there is a fund of money against which the players bet. The banker "fades" or matches, up to house limits, the bets made by the players. A percentage game is a game where the house participates as a player and has a percentage advantage. Banking games are usually also percentage games. That is, the house participates in the game, taking on all other players, with a percentage advantage in its favor. Casino games like roulette are typically only played as banking games.

9. Other Table Games

The non-banked or "round" games are played among individual players with no house participation and no single participant has a continuous advantage. Poker is the best-known round game. In non-banked games, like poker, the operator is not a player. Losses go to the other players, and not to the house; there is no house. Most states would not classify poker as a casino game. Brick and mortar, and online poker operators, derive their revenue from renting "seats," charging per hand or by taking a percentage of the winnings, known as "raking the pot." Internet poker has become a big business, which attracts both professionals and amateurs. Internet poker is the one form of remote wagering that is most subject to legislative attempts to either legalize or outlaw it.

10. Slots

Most slot machines in land-based casinos are set to deliver a random number on each of three or five "reels." Video poker machines are also extremely popular, displaying images of cards and allowing players to discard and replace some of the cards in attempts to obtain winning combinations. In the traditional slot, the bet, which used to be a coin, is inserted into a slot by the player. Slot machines make more money per square foot than any other business. Slots can now be replicated through Internet technology, allowing anyone's home computer to be turned into an exact duplicate, but without the coin slot.

11. Skill Games

By definition, skill games are not gambling, even if it is played for money and valuable prizes are awarded. Federal and state governments are free to decide whether a game is predominantly skill. This allows the governments some room to regulate. The result is a wide variety in the way that the same game is treated under the law. The appeal and action of games is a powerful marketing tool, particularly on the Web. Skills games, like sweepstakes promotions, lure advertisers to the possibility of increased "stickiness"—that is, visitors not only come to the page but stay, and eventually use the service, or at least read the ads. Online versions of all these games are offered by Internet gaming sites. Generally, a bettor contacts an online gaming site and establishes an account, funded variously by credit or debit card or, less commonly, bank wire transfers and checks.

12. Fantasy Leagues

Where fantasy leagues are permitted, it is often because there is an implicit understanding that it is a game of skill and not a form of gambling. Computers have made this form of gaming both possible and practical. The fantasy leagues are fictional teams created out of the statistics of real-world athletes. Certainly in America, fantasy football is the most popular form. Computer analysis of real-world statistics allow "team owners" to see how well their artificial teams are able to perform. These "owners" compete against one another by managing their teams online. There is little, if any, opportunity for genuine corruption in these virtual fantasy league scenarios.

In 2006, the Unlawful Internet Gambling Enforcement Act ("UIGEA") included an express exemption for fantasy games; which it defined as not being a "bet or wager." 31 U.S.C.A. § 5362. The UIGEA also expressly defers to such existing statutes as the Indian Gaming Regulatory Act ("IGRA"), the Wire Act, and the Professional and Amateur Sports Protection Act, none of which has been invoked against fantasy leagues. Under the UIGEA, the definition of unlawful gambling depends upon the substantive law of the states where the bettor and the operator reside; it is expressly made irrelevant if the wire happens to cross into another state that prohibits the type of gambling

involved. Many states have at least implicitly declared that fantasy leagues are predominantly contests of skill and not gambling. The UIGEA has had
the real-world practical impact of setting standards
for what fantasy games are permitted, even though
it expressly states that it does not change any
substantive law.

13. Video Games

Almost any game can be transposed into software
form. The term "video game" can be defined as
games that are available to play over computers,
including PCs, laptops, PDAs, and 3G mobile
phones; or dedicated platforms, including TV con-
soles or handheld devices whose central feature is a
video display and where player input, moves, and
results are shown in animated form. The overwhelming majority of video games are games of skill
and amusement games. While console-style video
game systems such as PS2 have long allowed multiplayer participation by allowing four handsets to be
plugged into one TV console, it was only in 1996
that PC-based games began to network online
which offers interactive play, instead of simply playing against the software. The assorted video/FRPG
combinations, applied to PCs, have been strengthened by digital technology until they have become,
in many respects, virtual worlds that are worlds
unto themselves. They are also known as "persistent games," or, probably more accurately, "synthetic worlds." The development of these "worlds"
begin with three interconnecting roots: (1) available

computer power has expanded, (2) Internet and broadband access has expanded, and (3) the creation of server-based mega programs.

14. Mode of Play

Another means of differentiating forms of online gambling is how the game is played; that is, with, or against, and whom. Most forms of commercial gambling involve patrons betting against the house. With casino and similar games, this is known as a house banking game. The most common forms of sports betting involve bettors betting straight up against the bookmaker. Here, the sports book acts as the house, setting the odds; collecting from losers and paying winners. The sports book makes its money in a manner similar to casino percentage games: it pays winners, less than full odds. For example, bettors often bet $11 to win $10; that difference is seen as a small commission, and is known as the "vig." Most traditional lottery games involve pools, where the prize was created by the bets, minus a share for the operator.

Almost all gambling games require some form of a random number generator ("RNG"). Today, formerly pure mechanical or electromechanical slot machines use internal computers as RNGs. An online establishment can simulate the game's probabilities through computerized RNGs. Now, there is sufficient broadband available to allow person-to-person ("P2P") games to be offered to the general public, often facilitated through betting exchanges.

B. Techno–Legal Structures Behind Internet Gambling

When a gambling operation is successful, it will create a greater demand for its technology. Accordingly, I-gaming's operations have served to speed up software development and the demand for broadband. I-gaming, an information-based service, owes its rise to the instant accessibility to the World Wide Web. The Web owes that accessibility to a direct connection to the telecommunications structures in place worldwide. The UK Gaming Act of 2005 assisted in the development from a "gray area" phenomenon into a legitimate branch of e-commerce. When a gambler connects to the Internet, that person will be using one of three basic technologies to hook up, whether wireline phone, wireless, or cable. Most American phones still connect to the outside world by way of a copper wire loop which leads to the nearest switch. Switches use two basic modes of operation: circuit and packet. Circuit switching creates a dedicated line between the two points for the duration of the call. The switch governs the connection. Packet switching converts the transmitted information into discrete digital packets, each of which is addressed to the receiver and coded for sequence.

1. ARPANET and the Transition to Public Use

The possibilities of Internet-like technology became apparent with the launch of ARPANET in

1972, which used phone modems for connections. With the development of e-mail and the World Wide Web, the stage was set for Internet growth to ordinary users worldwide. Ordinary people could now communicate, gather information, and do business worldwide, almost instantaneously. Growth was concentrated mainly in developed countries, which had the necessary telecommunications infrastructure and disposable income.

2. The Phenomenon of Digital Convergence

Upon exploration of the position and future of American gambling from an Internet perspective, it is obvious that larger concepts are involved. The emergence of computer and digital technology forces us to look at the national information infrastructure ("NII"). The NII consists not only of the obvious services like wireless telephones, broadcast TV and radio, and the Internet, but book publishers, newspapers and magazines, cable TV and modems, and even video rental outlets and movie theaters.

With the advance of digital technology, however, the difference between discrete forms, compositions, and even platforms began to disappear. All material became digital code, a string of ones and zeros, and could be deployed and used by a variety of digital capable platforms, according to convenience, marketing requirements, or other considerations. Books became e-books. Photographs, TV programs, and feature-length movies could become e-mail attachments, DVD discs, or Internet downloads at will.

3. The Impact of Technology on Legal Gambling

The most prominent distribution and access bottleneck for Internet services of all kinds, including gambling, is the part of the system known as "the last mile," which is the actual connection from the local exchange or service provider to the consumer. For the United States, this still means, in many cases, the same loop of copper wire that was in use a hundred years ago; coaxial cables in place for 50 years; and, microwave relay towers in use for almost as long. What makes Internet new—and what makes cyberspace a different place—is the new equipment and capabilities that have been hung on the ends of these old links and connections.

Much of the profitability of a legalized Internet gambling regime will depend upon the amount of government-imposed costs and restrictions it must deal with; this, in turn, will depend upon which regulatory regime its distribution technology is placed under.

If bringing I-gaming to a given neighborhood or user meant expanding wireless service, then that would require FCC certification of present or future public convenience and necessity. The Internet as it is now is open, "dumb," and democratic. As it was established, the practical result was that web enterprises of all sizes operated "end-to-end," that is, more or less on terms of equality. The Internet still is very open to innovation, experiment, and sheer coincidence. Since entry barriers are low, this encourages and rewards the introduction of new concepts, software, and applications—including those for online gambling. It also meant that it became next to impossible to pinpoint, isolate, or exclude I-gaming operators and their customers. The effort required to pick them out of the "end-to-end" environment was quite prohibitive.

C. Internet Gambling Law and Regulation in the Digital Age

Internet gambling has become an established fact of the global economy. The question for governments, at both the national and state level is what should be done about this phenomenon? The authorities can either try to prohibit Internet gambling within the territory they control or permit it in some form under a scheme of licensing, regulation, and taxation.

1. Theory and Practice in the United States

The essential reason that a government may seek to forbid its citizens and corporate entities from participating in Internet gambling is the issue of control. Until the advent of modern digital telecommunications, governments could assume with a fair degree of certainty that they controlled the flow of information, goods, and money across their borders. Even such advances at the telephone, radio, and television did not disturb this balance; these media needed complicated transmission facilities for widespread operations, which insured that their operators would be large businesses.

A genuine quandary arises, however, when other states license Internet gambling. For example, if a Los Angeles-based Internet betting service takes bets on California races that originate in New Orleans or Chicago, can California operators be prosecuted for violating the anti-Internet gambling laws in force in Louisiana or Illinois? While California law deems these bets to have been made in-state, the laws of the other state do not recognize such exemptions.

Where does a bet take place? For civil cases, the law of personal jurisdiction is fairly well established, at least in theory. *International Shoe* and its progeny state that an out-of-state defendant, say, an operator of an Internet gambling site, can be sued if it has minimum contacts with the forum state that do not offend traditional notions of fair play and substantial justice. For criminal cases, the theoretical standard is broader, holding a defendant can be tried if the crime has a foreseeable impact on a person in the forum state. Of course, in practice, there are not a lot of precedents telling courts how these standards should be applied against a site that does something like operate an online poker site open to players from all over the world. It's not even clear that mostly archaic state laws would even apply to such an out-of-state operator.

Sometimes the legal problem is solved by calling upon a higher law. So, when California authorizes at-home betting by phone and computer on horse-races, the bets are legal, if they meet all of the requirements of the Interstate Horseracing Act, a higher federal law. 15 U.S.C.A. §§ 3001 *et seq.* Federal law overrules state laws, under the Supremacy Clause of the U.S. Constitution. Of course, in this case, as with almost all federal gambling laws, express deference is given to the states to set their own public policies about remote wagering. As long as California followed the federal IHA to the letter and Congress had the constitutional power to pass the Act under its power to regulate interstate commerce, California's state-licensed operators are protected from being prosecuted in other states. But operators in other states, which had not complied with the IHA, and in foreign nations would be in violation of the federal Wire Act.

The operator of an online gambling business must be publicly accessible to succeed, and is therefore easily traceable. Where an Internet gambling operation is located within a given government's jurisdiction, it can be prosecuted for violations of that government's law.

For precisely this reason, online gambling businesses, barring occasional bold or naïve exceptions, take care not to locate their facilities in such places. States such as South Dakota, S.D. Codified Laws § 22–25A–7, Illinois, 720 Ill. Comp. Stat. § 5/28–1, or Louisiana, La. Rev. Stat. § 14:90.3, which have laws against (other people's) Internet gambling operations on the books, can close down operations found within their borders and usually those inside other states. But, U.S. state governments cannot, without a great amount of effort, act against gambling sites whose servers are outside the borders of the United States. And, while a gambling operation whose activities cross state and national borders may be found in violation of federal gambling or money laundering statutes such as 18 U.S.C.A. §§ 1084, 1955, 1956, etc., and face the possibility of prosecution under RICO, 18 U.S.C.A. §§ 1961–1968, the problem of obtaining jurisdiction over such violators remains.

2. UIGEA

The U.S. Congress finally passed UIGEA but only because it was tacked on to the SAFE Port Act. The story of how this bill became law shows that Congress did not even know what it was voting on. Almost no one in Congress has much interest in Internet gambling. When Bill Frist (R–TN), then-Majority Leader of the U.S. Senate, rammed the UIGEA through in the final minutes before Congress broke for its pre-election recess, the only members of either chamber that cared about online gaming were a few who were against it, and even fewer in favor.

The UIGEA is quite unusual in a number of ways. First, it could hardly be called an actual bill. There were no expert reports, no hearings. In fact, it was not even read before being passed. The UIGEA is essentially an inaccurate summary of a similar House bill (H.R. 4777) of the 106th Congress, which had passed the House and was pending in the Senate. This bill is now law; but with more than a few ironies. The Department of Justice and other opponents of Internet gambling were not thrilled with the UIGEA. No one had a chance to give any input or even to look it over for typographical errors. So, it does not accomplish the DOJ's main legislative goal, i.e., to clarify the Wire Act so as to clearly cover all forms of Internet gambling, especially online poker, casinos, and lotteries.

The UIGEA actually does only two things: It creates a new federal crime, receiving money for unlawful Internet gambling, for operators who are already violating other state or federal anti-gambling laws. And it called upon federal regulators to make regulations requiring money transferors to identify and block transactions to, but not from, unlawful gambling websites. The Board of Governors of the Federal Reserve System and the Secretary of the Department of the Treasury issued proposed and then final regulations, which went into effect on January 19, 2009. 12 C.F.R. Part 233 duplicated at 31 C.F.R. Part 132. These do little but call upon banks and other payment processors to do due diligence in setting up new commercial accounts.

But the UIGEA did have a real-world impact: It scared the publicly traded companies taking Internet bets from the U.S. out of the American market. With the departure of sites like PartyPoker, privately owned companies, such as PokerStars, took their place.

3. Regulation of Online Gambling Outside of the United States

Credit for developing the first comprehensive system for licensing and regulating Internet gambling should go to Trevor Garrett, Chief Executive of the Casino Control Authority of New Zealand. Garrett's idea was to give operators incentives to submit to a thorough examination of their owners and their computers, and to penalize operators who refused to be licensed. Australia, England, and other countries have adopted this model, for example, by allowing only licensed operators to advertise.

Garrett also wanted fees and taxes to be extremely low, to encourage applications and eliminate competition between countries. Few governments have been able to pass up the opportunity to raise revenue from this new industry by levying high licensing fees. In some cases, large operators have folded under the weight of heavy regulations and taxation. The result is that large, unlicensed operations still abound.

4. Internet Gaming in the Traditional Context of International Law

Legally speaking, a gambling transaction is a contingent contract. In return for a set amount of money (the bet), the player is promised a payment (the prize), provide certain conditions are met (Green Bay wins the Super Bowl, or France wins the World Cup). Because it is essentially intangible, gambling qualifies as a service rather than a good or commodity, although gaming devices are obviously goods. This contingent contract is a discrete item of commerce, which can be, and is, transmitted and traded interstate and internationally. *Champion v. Ames (the "Lottery Case")*, 188 U.S. 321, 23 S.Ct. 321, 47 L.Ed. 492 (1903). Within the United States, furthermore, the U.S. Congress has essentially plenary power over interstate commerce, with few constitutional restrictions. With the power to regulate a given activity comes the power to forbid it altogether.

5. Legal Framework of Cross–Border Betting

The answer to whether a country can keep out foreign legal gambling is extremely complicated and requires an examination of exactly what type of gambling is involved, the statutes and regulations that might apply, and the relationship between the governments of the operators and the bettors.

Under international law, a sovereign government has no restrictions on keeping out foreign legal gambling or any other commerce. But states that are parts of federal nations and countries that have signed trade agreements often cannot keep out legal goods and services from their sister states and trade partners. However, gambling comes under a government's police power, and thus is treated differently from almost all other legal commerce. A state or nation may choose to completely outlaw all gambling, or the type of gaming under consideration, and it is not required to open its doors to an activity that it considers immoral or dangerous. Once a government has legalized a form of gaming, it is more difficult for it to argue that it is excluding nearly identical forms of gambling because of its public interest concerns. However, it may be able to justify an exclusion of remote wagering, especially via the Internet, because there are additional dangers not present with bets made face-to-face.

D. Money Transfers and Taxation Issues Affecting Internet Gambling

Electronic remote gambling cannot function without electronic remote money. That having been established, we examine the how and why of transferring to, from, and away from players, operators, and governments. The first e-gambling sites used the natural choice: well-known international credit cards such as Visa and MasterCard. They offered worldwide coverage, acceptance, and ease of use, even online. In addition, they were and are ubiquitous: as of 2007, more than 984 million major credit cards had been issued to the U.S. domestic market, and consumers used them to ring up charges of $1.8 trillion annually.

American Express and Discover cards are examples of full-service credit card companies. They issue cards directly to customers and authorize merchants to accept them. These are closed-loop systems: the company in question owns and operates the system, handling, and approving all transactions. Credit card associations, such as Visa and MasterCard, on the other hand set policies and the individual member banks issue the cards and the specific rules of use.

Online gambling appears to be the largest single source of chargebacks in online commercial activities. In fact, a Chargeback Bureau now offers its services to gaming and other web sites that wish to identify and avoid chronic welchers and frauds.

Gambling can be taxed essentially in two ways: either as a charge per transaction or as a levy on profits. Often enough, of course, it is both. In the absence of other statutory guidance, the government where the bet took place is the government with the authority to tax the bet or the winnings. With Internet gambling, however, the bet can take place in more than one place.

Title 26, U.S. Code, commonly known as the Internal Revenue Code, requires that every person in the business of gambling who takes state-authorized bets pays a federal excise tax of 0.25 percent of the amount of each bet. If the bet is not state-authorized, the operator/bet-taker owes a flat two percent. 26 U.S.C.A. § 4401. Every such operator is required to register with the IRS and pay a special tax of $500 per year (the so-called gambling stamp), 26 U.S.C.A. §§ 4411, 4412. It is the operator's responsibility to keep a daily record of bets taken, 26 U.S.C.A. § 4403, and this is subject to inspection at any time. 26 U.S.C.A. § 4423. In accordance with long-standing policy, registration and/or payment may not be used against the operator in criminal proceedings. State lotteries, parimutuel bets, and coin-operated betting machines are exempt. 26 U.S.C.A. § 4402.

Even here, however, we return to the unanswered jurisdiction question. This tax applies to wagers accepted in U.S. territories, placed by someone who is inside a U.S. territory, or placed with a U.S. resident or citizen, or a betting pool or lottery she conducts. 26 U.S.C.A. § 4404. If a U.S. resident bets out to an offshore sportsbook, is the bet placed within the U.S.? Probably not. But is it considered placed by someone who is in the U.S.? That is more likely. Is the bet considered to be placed with a U.S. citizen? Only if that individual is very careless—it is already illegal for him to own or operate any part of an illegal gambling business. 18 U.S.C.A. § 1955. So, overseas non-American operators are probably not subject to the federal excise tax on gambling.

The Internet Tax Freedom Act, formerly known as S. 442, now Title XI of P.L. 105–277, the Omnibus Appropriations Act of 1998, is an application to the American online market of the Supreme Court's decision in *Quill Corp. v. North Dakota*, 504 U.S. 298, 112 S.Ct. 1904, 119 L.Ed.2d 91 (1992). In that case, the Court held that Quill, an office supply retailer could not be required to pay a use tax to the state of North Dakota for sales in that state, since Quill had no physical presence, sales force or retail outlet in that state. Quill did have a licensed com-

puter software program that some of its North
Dakota customers used for checking the company's
current inventories and placing orders direct. The
Court ruled that might be enough to meet the
minimum contacts test for personal jurisdiction, but
was insufficient to meet the substantial nexus required by the Dormant Commerce Clause. If North
Dakota could impose a use tax on Quill, it would
interfere with legal commerce from other states.

E.   The Problem of Advertising Inter-
net and Interactive Gaming

If it is still not clear whether, where, or when
Internet gaming is legal, then what about advertising it? Can an operator in jurisdiction A, where
Internet gaming is legal, run commercials on television or radio in jurisdiction B, where its legality is
in doubt? Can he send advertisements through the
mail or put up billboards there?

What is advertising? Legally, it can mean publicity of any kind. It is not necessary that it be paid
advertising, although, of course, most of it is. A Web
site or business may garner as much or more public
notice (and profit) from blogs and links and news
stories, as from a campaign of paid media exposure.
Broadly speaking, advertising is subject to the limits that apply to all forms of public speech: libel and
slander; false or misleading ads; misappropriation of
celebrities' names or likenesses; invasion of privacy
(e.g., using pictures of big winners without permission); various unfair trade practices, such as anti-

trust violations, passing off your product as another's, falsely maligning a competitor's product, use of bait and switch come-ons, etc. Some of these categories overlap; there may be both civil and criminal liability, and some fall under both state and federal jurisdiction. Under American law, the mode of delivery largely determines the rights and privileges of both the message and the messenger.

Fortunately for most legal analysis of advertising in the real world, the first test of whether government restrictions are constitutional is whether the product of service is legal. Since states almost always take the position that operators who take bets from their residents without being licensed by the state are illegal, it is a short step to ban all of the operators' advertising as well. There are very few foreign operators who would voluntarily enter a state to fight a ban on advertising, when by stepping into the state they could be arrested and charged with major anti-gambling felonies.

F. Legal Issues Confronting Online Gaming Operators and Players

1. The Jurisdiction Question

There are many legal issues that confront users and operators of Internet gambling. The first problem concerns a jurisdictional question; e.g., if four players who are residing in Tokyo, Sydney, Los Angeles, and London, play poker online against each other using a server in Antigua, what nation has jurisdiction? Legally, the Australian and the Brit can bet "out." Poker is not approved for play in Japan, but neither is it outlawed; the Californian, however, technically may be in violation of Penal Code § 330, but prosecution is close to zero. The operator will have no trouble in Australia and, provided that he has not advertised "illegally," the Brit will have no complaint. Japan also is unlikely to act against an Internet business from Antigua. The U.S. government's position is that the operator is violating American law because all Internet gambling violates the Wire Act. This, however, depends upon the Wire Act as covering all gambling of any kind, which is debatable, and the poker game violates the Wire Act. There also is now an official federal Department of Justice announcement that limits the Wire Act to bets on sports events. Federal and state prosecutions now depend upon finding a violation of state anti-gambling laws, which rarely even consider the possibility of out-of-state defendants. And, the Wire Act has an exception for bets that are legal on both ends. Online poker is not only legal, but also licensed in Antigua. So, criminal liability for the operator will depend upon whether an Antigua-hosted poker game could be deemed to be "a controlled game exposed for play" in California. And, Antigua would never extradite someone it licensed to operate an Internet poker site to stand trial in the U.S. for the very activity that it licensed.

2. Criminal Liability for Players

It is not against federal law to make a bet online. There is no federal statute that applies to gamblers, as opposed to operators. Gamblers, however, may be liable to criminal laws if they aid the operator in any way. This requires more than merely making bets, otherwise every purchaser of illegal drugs would be guilty of selling illegal drugs. Other legal theories of liability could include being part of a criminal gambling operation under the Organized Crime Control Act, U.S.C.A. § 1955, and conspiracy, 18 U.S.C.A. § 371. These also would require the player to do much more than merely place bets, such as helping collect losing bets from other players.

3. Civil Liability for Operators

A government official can shut down an Internet gaming operation by seeking an injunction from a court ordering the operator to cease taking bets from that jurisdiction. In suits by players against operators, injunctions also can be sought by private parties, such as losing patrons. Of course, trying to enforce an injunction overseas raises great difficulties, including facing unfriendly foreign laws and law enforcement agencies. And the Internet was designed to survive an atomic war; so unilateral action by American law enforcement agents is always going to be problematic.

In what has become known as "Black Friday," April 15, 2011, the U.S. Attorneys for the Southern District of New York were able to close down the five largest poker sites then taking money bets from America. They did this by obtaining a court order seizing the sites' names worldwide. This is obviously a dangerous, and probably illegal, precedent. First, it prevented players from reaching these sites in countries, like England, where the activities of everyone concerned was perfectly legal. Second, it opens the door to another country doing something along the same lines against U.S. companies. For example, the Islamic Republic of Iran could ask its courts to seize the domain name of every distillery, brewery, winery and even restaurant in the U.S. that uses the Internet to advertise alcoholic beverages.

4. Suits by Operators Against Players for Gambling Debts

Until recently, gambling debts were not collectible. Gambling debts were unenforceable; a gambling agreement would not be enforced in a court of law. The law concerning gambling debts had been fairly well-settled by the famous Statute of Anne in 1710 (Statute of Anne, 9 Anne, c.14, 4 Bac. Abr. f. 456), which now is part of the common law of every state (e.g., Nev. Rev. Stat. § 1.080).

For the online player, timing is important. Gambling debts, even legal ones, are normally not legally enforceable; this, however, does not mean that they are uncollectible. The courts left the parties where they found them: if the debt had not yet been paid, the winner could not get a court to help him collect; but if the debt had already been paid, the loser could not get his money back. Legally, this means that gambling debts are voidable, rather than being inherently void. The law of gambling debts stood for almost three centuries: illegal bets from a debt owed to a bookie, to a check written at a poker game, are void and unenforceable; but so were legal bets under the Statute of Anne. This is now changing, in the U.S. and in many other countries. But the rise of Internet gambling has caused the old system to return. It is so difficult, and expensive, to collect even large amounts in other countries that the practical reality is that the parties are left in the positions they were in when the dispute arose.

5. The Problem of the Compulsive Gambler

A study funded by the casino industry's National Center for Responsible Gaming released in December 1997 by the Harvard Medical School, Division on Addictions, showed the percentage of adults with gambling disorders in the United States and Canada has risen in the past 20 years, with teenagers yielding a higher percentage than adults. The American Psychiatric Association claims that there are about 2.5 million "pathological" or compulsive gamblers, unable to control their need for continual gambling, and another 3 million "problem gamblers," whose gambling disrupts any of their important life functions. The inclusion of pathological gambling in 1980 in the third edition of the American Psychiatric Association's *Diagnostic and Statistical Manual of Mental Disorders* (DSM–III) (later revised in DSM–IIIR and again in DSM–IV and DSM–IVR) as an official mental disorder, has changed the law's view of both gambling and gamblers.

Many, if not most, Internet operators have taken steps to protect their players and their own operations. It is very common to find warnings on sites about compulsive gambling and links to self-help sites. Operators put in safeguards, like allowing players to set a limit on the maximum they are willing to lose in any one session. These may help. Of course, a compulsive gambler, who is barred from one site, may simply take his remaining money to another to continue gambling.

6. Privacy and Information Security

Another inherent problem in Internet gambling is the question of security, for both the establishment and the player. In order to establish an account, a player must trust the online gambling operator with sensitive personal information, such as a credit card number and perhaps social security numbers. The establishment must protect its own accounts and operating systems against hacking and intrusions. Fairly sophisticated encryption is now necessary to protect transactions and the command access codes.

The anonymity of online gambling is one of its major attractions for bettors who wish to keep their activities from the view of other parties, ranging from spouses to the IRS. Since a gambling business is a financial institution for the purpose of regulation, a state-licensed online operator must balance a customer's privacy with government-mandated reporting requirements; and at the same time, comply with the requirements of state and federal privacy laws.

The unanswered question is whether state-legal sites, when they open, will be able to compete with foreign gray market and illegal sites. Although the legal sites will have the advantage of being able to advertise and take credit cards, the illegal sites will keep the players' information completely secret. This puts legal sites at a disadvantage, at least for larger bettors, who will know that their winnings from foreign sites will not be reported to the IRS.

G.   The Future of Internet Gaming

1.   Innovation and Regulation

The major question facing the future of all remote, interactive gaming beginning with Internet gambling, is whether the Internet represents something that is entirely new and different or whether even the newest digital innovations can still be analyzed and controlled in ways that the impact of inventions have been analyzed in the past and thus regulated by the law.

Use of cell phones (or mobile phones) for gaming purposes of all kinds is sure to increase, particularly outside the United States. The interplay of formats, functions, and platforms has increased, multiplied in a staggering manner. Today's Internet user, and Internet bettor, can choose to access the Internet from a phone, or make a phone call over the Internet. The caller may ''go on-line'' by way of a phone line (DSL), a cable company or wireless. Probably TVs, radio, computers, and cell phones eventually will merge into one central information and entertainment function receiving input from multiple networks and systems, and accessible to and by mobile and portable platforms offering the same functions.

2. Free Speech and the Right to Gamble

The reason that legal gaming has so few rights is that gambling traditionally is subject to state government's police power. Due to the history of gambling as a vice, with the potential to harm society, all gambling today, whether licensed or illegal, comes under the state's police power. Plus, it is doubtful that gambling itself can be said to be a form of speech. Only sites' right to advertise raise First Amendment issues, and these depend upon whether the gambling is legal both where the operator and bettor are, and whether the site accepts bets from that state.

3. The IMEGA Suit

On June 5, 2007, the Interactive Media Entertainment and Gaming Association ("IMEGA"), a nonprofit group based in New Jersey, filed an injunction against the enforcement of the Unlawful Internet Gambling Enforcement Act ("UIGEA"). The suit alleged that the UIGEA interfered with and had a chilling effect on the right to the expressive association of IMEGA members and their right to privacy. Additionally, it allegedly interfered with their protected commercial speech, and constituted an illegal and restrictive trade practice that directly harmed otherwise legal business interests. It also alleged that it violated the Constitutional prohibition against *ex post facto* laws and the separation of powers clause of the Tenth Amendment. But, the Court dismissed the suit for lack of standing, because IMEGA was one of the few businesses associated with Internet gambling that did not receive a threatening letter or subpoena from the Department of Justice.

4. UIGEA and Politics

There are very few members of either party who have much interest in Internet gambling, either way. A few in Congress want Internet poker and possibly other forms made legal; a few more want it clearly made illegal. When the Republicans controlled Congress and the Presidency in 2006, they rammed through the UIGEA. They then blocked Barney Frank (D.–MA) and Democrats from making revisions in that law. The political reality is that Congress now enacts almost no new substantive laws. Since the Republicans took control of the House of Representatives in January 2011, with only one or two exceptions, the only bills that have passed both houses dealt with naming courthouses and post offices, budget bills, and continuation of programs like the Federal Aviation Administration. Congress will not be passing a repeal or even amendment of the UIGEA, which conservatives would see as allowing gambling to enter peoples' homes. But it will also not pass a strengthening of the UIGEA or expansion of the Wire Act, which would step on states' rights to set their own public policies toward gambling.

Large Nevada casino companies, and their lobbyists, the American Gaming Association, want a federal law so that the big operators can take online poker bets from the rest of the U.S., and not have to compete against powerful local operators for a limited number of Internet gambling licenses in 50 separate states. But even if a federal law could pass both houses, Congress would still have to allow states to opt in or opt out. Congress would never impose a uniform policy for or against gambling on both Utah and Nevada.

5. ICANN

In 1998, the U.S. Department of Commerce turned the administration of the Internet over to a private non-profit group called ICANN (Internet Cooperation for Assigned Names and Numbers). Acting on the advice of its supporting organizations (Address Support, Protocol Support, and Domain Names) and membership, the elected board of ICANN oversees the creation and allocation of such things as URL domains (.com, .org, etc.) and helps formulate policy for the growth and maintenance of the worldwide net.

CHAPTER 17

SPORTS BOOKS AND PARIMUTUEL WAGERING

A. Sports Books and the Law Generally

Until the mid–1970s, sports betting was mostly limited to illegal bookies, who took bets in person or by phone. Their operations were fairly small; bookies would much rather have a few high-rollers as customers, rather than risk taking an illegal bet from an undercover cop. This is still true today for illegal bookies, although operators on college campuses often have almost retail operations. But, the legal sports betting business did not take off until the federal government lowered the wagering tax, and football began being televised into every home in the nation.

In 1954, Congress imposed a 10% federal excise tax on all sports wagers, legal and illegal. 26 U.S.C.A. § 4401 (now amended). This tax was so high that it was virtually impossible for even the best sports handicappers to win consistently. Licensed sports books were limited to Nevada. At the time these were called "turf clubs", and were limited in number and small in size, and not connected with large casinos. Individuals who worked in the industry during this time reported widespread tax evasion to get around this high tax. For example, a $1,100 bet to win $1,000 was recorded as merely $11 to win $10.

Sports books make their profit from the statistical advantage they have over their patrons. The most common wager is a multiple of $11 to win $10. If the sports book succeeds in having the same amount of money wagered on both sides of a match, it is guaranteed to make a profit. For example if Patron A bets $11 on his team and Patron B bets $11 on the opposing team, the sports book now has $22, but the sports book pays the winner, whoever he may be, only $21, his original $11 bet back and his $10 in winnings. The sports book keeps the additional $1.

It is easy to see why the 10% tax would be devastating, if it could not be passed on to the patrons. Of the $22 bet in the example above, the federal government would take $2.20, obviously much more than the sports book's expected $1 profit. But the 10% tax could not be passed on, because the patrons would no longer be betting $11 to win $10, but rather $11 plus 10% ($1.10) for a total of $12.10 to win $10.

Sports books allow patrons to make a wide variety of bets. The "hold" is the percentage that the sports book wins. A Ten Year Analysis of Sports

Betting Results from the Nevada sports books produced for the Delaware Sports Betting Proposal in 2003 found the Nevada state-wide handle ranged from a low of 2.48% to a high of 5.53%, with an average of 4.16%.[1] This was calculated by taking the total win for the ten years, $938,329,985, and dividing it by the total handle, $22,530,086,000. In other words, slightly more than $22.5 billion was bet, the sports books had gross gaming revenue of about $938 million, which means they kept 4.16% of the amounts bet.

Looking at a single sports book: If it has a handle of $10,000,000, the total amount bet in a year, and it holds 4.16%, it will win, or have gross gaming revenue, of $416,000. But when the federal excise tax on wagers was 10%, the federal government demanded $1,000,000 (10% of the amount bet, $10,000,000). If the sports book had to pay this, it obviously could not; it would be like imposing a 240% tax on gross gaming revenue.

In 1974, Congress lowered the federal excise tax on sports wagers to 2%. Nevada also has a sliding scale of state gaming taxes, with the top tax rate quickly reaching 6.75% of gross gaming revenue. NRS 463.370. The combined taxes were low enough to allow a few entrepreneurs to think about expanding the small turf clubs into true sports betting parlors. In 1975 the Nevada Legislature passed enabling legislation so that casinos could have sports books. But the tax rate was still so high that few

1. http://finance.delaware.gov/publications/Gaming/Sch _ 1.pdf.

casinos were willing to devote any of their valuable floor space to a form of gambling that generated so little to the bottom line.

In 1983, Congress lowered the federal excise tax on legal sports wagers to 0.25% (illegal sports bets still pay 2%). Adding in the Nevada state tax results in a wagering privilege tax of about 13% of gross gaming revenue for legal sports books. This much lower rate created an explosion of growth and capital expenditures for Nevada's sports betting industry. In 1973 there were only ten sports books with a total handle of $2.8 million. Twenty years later there were approximately 100 sports books with a total handle in excess of $2 billion. By the year 2000 there were about 157 sports books, with a total handle greater than $2.5 billion, generating more than $117 million in gross gaming revenue.

Football only became a prime at-home spectator sport with the start of Monday Night Football in 1970. Sports books not only became large and numerous in Nevada, they were viewed as profit centers and entertainment enticements for commercial casinos. By 1985 all of the small independent sports books were closed, replaced by multi-million dollar casino sports books with dozens of giant video screens and all the other services sports bettors could want, including easy access to other forms of gambling.

Other states began looking at legalizing sports betting as a way of raising revenue without raising taxes. The Oregon and Delaware State Lotteries started taking bets on National Football League ("NFL") games. Oregon's game, "Sports Action," and Delaware's were parlay bets, requiring bettors to beat the point-spread in three or more contests. The Oregon Lottery later took bets on National Basketball Association games as well.

The NFL, which hates and fears sports betting as a possible corruption of its sport, lobbied Congress to stop the proliferation. In 1992, President George H.W. Bush signed the Professional and Amateur Sports Protection Act ("PASPA") into law, putting a moratorium into law, 28 U.S.C.A. §§ 3701–3704. As a compromise with Nevada, which had legal sports wagering, states that had authorized sports wagering prior to October 2, 1991, were immune from the legislation. This compromise has since become known as the "Las Vegas loophole." New Jersey was given one year to legalize sports books for its casinos, but the State Legislature failed to act. PASPA prohibits any state or tribe from authorizing any new sports gambling.

Although there is some dispute, it appears that the following states were grandfathered-in under PASPA: Delaware, Montana, Nevada, New Mexico, North Dakota, Oregon, Washington and Wyoming. In *Office of the Commissioner of Baseball v. Markell*, 579 F.3d 293 (3d Cir. 2009), the Court of Appeals ruled that Delaware could only have the exact same forms of sports betting it had in 1991. This prevented Delaware's new sports books from taking bets on single events, limiting the state to the less popular parlay bets, where the bettor had to predict the winner in three sports contests. If other states are similarly restricted, then only in Nevada can state-licensed sports books or federally recognized Indian tribes take bets on single events; while New Mexico would be limited to Keirin, parimutuel betting on bicycle races. Alaska allows Calcutta pools, a primitive form of parimutuel wagering, on amateur and professional sports events, but does not appear to have had this in 1991, so probably violates PASPA.

Other states, including Connecticut, Rhode Island and Florida, have parimutuel betting on jai alai. PASPA expressly excludes both parimutuel betting on jai alai and horse and dog racing from its terms, allowing states to decide for themselves whether they want to legalize those forms of betting. A majority of the states have parimutuel betting on horse racing; dog racing, which has been criticized for animal cruelty, and jai alai are much less popular. Parimutuel wagering is usually done at the horsetracks themselves. However, simulcasting, allowing instant transmission of races and wagering information, allows both inter-track and true off-track betting ("OTB"). Remote wagering by phone or computer requires bettors to deposit money in advance, so the racing industry calls this Advanced Deposit Wagering, or ADW.

In November 2011 New Jersey voters approved amending their State Constitution to allow sports betting. The Legislature and Governor then enacted an enabling law in 2012. This revives a lawsuit to overturn PASPA that had been dismissed when New Jersey did not have an actual law attempting to legalize sports betting. It is difficult to see how PASPA can stand, since Congress has allowed almost a dozen exceptions to its supposedly complete ban on state-authorized sports betting, and is the only federal law that prevents a state from changing its public policy toward gambling.

In 1996, Congress established the National Gambling Impact Study Commission ("NGISC") to conduct "a comprehensive legal and factual study of the social and economic impacts of gambling." Although the NGISC was discredited, having become a political football with an incompetent Chair, Kay Coles James, it did contract for a few independent surveys, which appear to be accurate. The NGISC reported that the "vast majority" of American gamblers participated in recreational gambling and never experienced ill effects; that eighty-six percent of Americans had gambled at some time in their life; and that sixty-eight percent gambled at least once a year. And it concluded that gambling is inevitable. No matter what is said or done by advocates or opponents in all its various forms, it is an activity that is practiced, or tacitly endorsed, by a substantial majority of Americans. But, the Commission recognized the need for further study of the problems associated with sports wagering. Specifically, the NGISC wondered "how widespread the phenomenon of underage sports gambling is now, the relationship between sports wagering and other forms of gambling, and the ways to prevent its spread."

The NGISC found that the social costs from sports wagering included exposing student athletes to scandalous situations, serving as a gateway to other forms of gambling, and harming people and/or their careers. The Commission also suggested, without any evidence, that legal sports wagering in Nevada fueled illegal betting across the nation. As a result of these findings, the Commission recommended that Congress ban wagering on college and amateur athletics throughout the United States. As with all of its other recommendations, this one was ignored.

B. Sports Books and the NCAA

There have been some attempts to propose legislation to close the "Las Vegas loophole," but this would not stop illegal gambling, and will only cause a diminished respect for the rule of law in general among teens and adolescents.

A legal sports book makes it easier for illegal bookies to set lines and lay-off bets when action is heavy on one side or the other. The argument has been raised that Nevada thus probably facilitates illegal gambling on college sports. For this reason, supporters of the proposed legislation argue that a ban on collegiate gambling in Nevada will have a severe impact on illegal bookies and thereby protect the integrity of sports and student athletes across the nation. On the other hand, legal sports betting operators have been instrumental in uncovering attempts by criminals to fix sports and racing events, by reporting unusual betting patterns to government authorities.

It can be argued that Nevada sports books help the National Collegiate Athletic Association ("NCAA") uphold the integrity of collegiate sports. The NCAA has never uncovered a sports scandal on its own. Legal sports books have, however, been instrumental in monitoring the games for suspicious activity. In fact, it was a legal sports book that first alerted the FBI to the Arizona State basketball scandal in 1994. Chairman of the Nevada Gaming Commission, Brian Sandoval, pointed out, "there is nothing in the record that indicates legalized sports wagering in Nevada has compromised the integrity of any athletic contest at any time or place. Not one college sports scandal is the result of legal sports wagering." Nevada thus argues that it currently has all the incentive in the world to protect the integrity of collegiate contests, but a ban would remove the best policing and monitoring body that exists in gaming.

The former president of the NCAA, Cedric Dempsey, would like to stop newspapers across the nation from publishing betting lines (odds) because their publication sends a mixed message to students and the public at large about the legality of gambling. Although gambling on collegiate sporting events is legal only in a few states, the Las Vegas line (or point spread) is published almost everywhere, even where sports wagering is illegal. There are, of course, legal questions with trying to censor legal information. If point-spreads themselves cannot be kept out of the media, the NCAA believes it could accomplish the same result by outlawing all betting on college sports. Some evidence points to a different direction. And the trend is for more sports betting in the U.S., and particularly in other countries, not less.

There is no doubt that the publication of point spreads contributes to the popularity of sports wagering. It is a much harder case, however, to show that such publication causes people to think that gambling is legal; rather, people know that bookie operations are illegal but do not care very much about "friendly wagers," and never have.

Newspapers are certainly free to publish this information for any purpose, including non-gambling amusement purposes. People who look at point spreads published in the paper do so to increase their knowledge of sports, and not necessarily for wagering purposes.

The demand for lines on games exists for reasons beyond gambling alone. Fans want to know how one team stands against another, who is the underdog and who is the favorite. The Newspaper Agency Association indicated that it believed newspapers across the country would continue to publish point spreads for readers who actually have no intention of using them for gambling purposes, despite any ban that Congress may impose on legal wagering. In fact, the news media has used its First Amendment right to overcome the NCAA's attempt to keep point spreads out of the news; the NCAA withheld sports reporters' press credentials from newspapers that publish betting lines, but the NCAA, however, reportedly had to discard its initiative when the news media challenged the constitutionality of its actions.

C. Sports Books and State Lotteries

The federal government facilitated the spread of legalized gambling by loosening some of the restrictions that had been in place since the late 1800s, when federal legislation was used to bring the infamous Louisiana Lottery to an end. See, e.g., 18 U.S.C.A. § 1301 (prohibiting the importation and passing through interstate commerce of lottery tickets and related material); § 1302 (limiting the mailing of lottery tickets, advertisements, and related material); § 1304 (prohibiting lottery information from being broadcast over the airways); § 1084 (disallowing the use of wire communication in the promotion of gambling); § 1953 (similar to § 1084); 39 U.S.C.A. § 3005 (authorizing postal authorities to implement prohibitions). At first, these laws made it hard for states to run legal lotteries. See *New Jersey State Lottery Comm'n v. United States*, 491 F.2d 219 (3d Cir. 1974) (en banc), vacated as moot, 420 U.S. 371, 95 S.Ct. 941, 43 L.Ed.2d 260 (1975); *In re Broad. of Info. Concerning Lotteries*, 14 F.C.C.2d 707 (1968) (ruling that the ban on broadcasting lottery information applied to state lotteries); see also *FCC v. American Broad. Co.*, 347 U.S. 284, 293–94, 74 S.Ct. 593, 98 L.Ed. 699 (1954) (television and radio game show "give-aways" not prohibited by federal legislation restricting lotteries because no consideration was required to participate). In 1975, Congress resolved the confusion that these statutes raised with modern lotteries, and states were free to operate without fear of federal intervention. See 18 U.S.C.A. § 1307 (18 U.S.C.A. §§ 1301–1304 do not apply to state sponsored lotteries).

The NGISC found that in 1998 alone, legal sports wagering in Nevada sports books amounted to $2.3 billion. Estimates of illegal sports wagering are much more problematic. Some range as high as $80 billion to $380 billion per year in the U.S. which would make it the most popular form of gambling in the nation. The NGISC Final Report (1999) supported a complete ban on college sports wagering, but it also recognized that legalized gambling has become an aspect of everyday life. The NGISC stated that when left unregulated, gambling can produce a number of negative consequences; thus the most appropriate remedy is government regulation.

The PASPA eliminated state lotteries from coming up with new forms of sports betting. The restrictions are broad, 28 U.S.C.A. §§ 3701–3704 makes it unlawful for

(1) a government entity to sponsor, operate, advertise, promote, license, or authorize by law or compact, or

(2) a person to sponsor, operate, advertise, or promote, pursuant to the law or compact of a

governmental entity, a lottery, sweepstakes, or other betting, gambling, or wagering scheme based, directly or indirectly (through the use of geographical references or otherwise), on one or more competitive games in which amateur or professional athletes participate, or are intended to participate, or on one or more performances of such athletes in such games.

Sports betting that was already in existence was grandfathered-in: 28 U.S.C.A § 3704(1) provides that the new restrictions do not apply to: "[A] lottery, sweepstakes, or other betting, gambling, or wagering scheme in operation in a State or other governmental entity, to the extent that the scheme was conducted by that State or other governmental entity at any time during the period beginning January 1, 1976, and ending August 31, 1990." As a result, at least half a dozen states are exempt from the federal prohibition against state-authorized sports wagering.

Instituted in 1989, the Oregon game was based on selecting winning teams in NFL games, as adjusted by the point spread. There were also special bets on things like: total points by both teams, total sacks, total field goals, etc. As a state lottery, this game may be played only by purchasing tickets sold in Oregon. Moreover, the parimutuel nature of the game is not well-suited for gambling outside of a limited pool of bettors. A similar game is operated by the Delaware State Lottery in that state's newly opened sports books.

With millions of dollars bet on sports in this country every year, it is not surprising that there have been a number of scandals and incidents at the college level. In 1994, Northwestern University running back Dennis Lundy fumbled intentionally on the University of Iowa one-yard line during the third quarter of the game so he could win a $400 bet. Lundy also told authorities that he bet on five Northwestern games during his career, and that some of his teammates also bet against Northwestern in games. Arizona State point guard Steve Smith was coerced by organized crime bosses not to cover the point spread for many basketball games during the 1993–1994 season. Similarly, at Northwestern University, basketball players Kenneth Deon Lee and Dewey Williams were paid $4,000 to point-shave and fix the outcome of games against Penn State University, the University of Wisconsin, and the University of Michigan in 1995.

In 1999, the University of Michigan Athletic Department conducted a study of student athletes to determine the types of gambling activities in which student athletes engage. The university sent out 3,000 surveys to Division I football players, Division I men's basketball players, and Division I women's basketball players. The results of this survey showed that over 5% of male student athletes had wagered on a game in which they participated, provided inside information for gambling purposes or fixed a game in which they participated.

In 2001, Senator John McCain introduced the Amateur Sports Integrity Act (S. 718), to ban all betting on non-professional athletes. In response to

S. 718, Senator John Ensign introduced Senate Bill 338 (S. 338), the National Collegiate and Amateur Athletic Protection Act of 2001, on February 14, 2001. S. 338, 107th Cong. (2001). Ensign argued there was a problem with illegal sports wagering, but the problem would not be solved with the proposed legislation. See S. Rep. No. 107–16, at 16 (2001). Ensign argued that S. 718 did nothing to police illegal wagering and that it did not strengthen the existing penalties for illegal wagering. He argued that the proposed ban would only push the legal wagering into the illegal realm, resulting in an increase of scandals. Ensign's bill, S. 338, would have: (1) established a task force to enforce the existing federal laws that prohibit illegal wagering; (2) increased the maximum penalty for gambling violations; (3) had the National Institute of Justice conduct a study into the extent of teen gambling; (4) established a panel of law enforcement to conduct a comprehensive study on illegal gambling; and (5) required federally funded colleges to implement programs to reduce illegal gambling, inform students of university policy on gambling, and withhold scholarships from athletes who participate in illegal gambling. Both S. 718 and S. 338 and similar attempts at the federal level have failed to pass both houses of Congress.

D. Sports Books and Parimutuel Wagering on Tribal Land

PASPA applies to tribes as well as states. Since only a few states have grandfathered-in sports betting, the only federally recognized tribes which can take sports bets are those in Nevada, New Mexico, North Dakota, Oregon, Washington, Wyoming.

The Indian Gaming Regulatory Act ("IGRA"), 25 U.S.C.A. §§ 2701–2722, noted that "Indian tribes have the exclusive right to regulate gaming activity on Indian lands if the gaming activity is not specifically prohibited by Federal law and is conducted within a state which does not, as a matter of criminal law and public policy, prohibit such gaming activity." At § 2701(5). IGRA established three classes of gaming, each with specific requirements and restrictions: Class I gaming is defined as "social games solely for prizes of minimal value or traditional forms of Indian gaming engaged in by individuals as a part of, or in connection with, tribal ceremonies or celebrations." This type of gaming includes traditional "stick" or "bone" games, rodeos, and horseraces that are played as part of ceremonies, pow wows, and other celebrations. Class I gaming falls under the exclusive jurisdiction of the tribes and is unregulated by the federal government or any state.

Class II gaming consists of bingo and other bingo-like games (if played in the same location as the bingo) and non-banking card games that are authorized either by state law or not explicitly prohibited by state law so long as they are conducted in conformity with state laws regarding hours of operation and limitations on wagers. IGRA states that a tribe may conduct Class II gaming if it is "located within a State that permits such gaming for any purpose by any person, organization or entity (and such gaming is not otherwise specifically prohibited on Indian lands by Federal law)." The governing body of the tribe wishing to conduct the Class II gaming must adopt an ordinance that is subsequently approved by the Chairman of the National Indian Gaming Commission (NIGC). Explicitly excluded from the Class II classification are card games banked by the casino (blackjack, baccarat, and other similar games) and electronic banking games of chance of any kind, including slot machines. It is difficult to see how any form of sports betting would fall into Class II.

The IGRA defines Class III gaming as any type of gaming that is not included in Class I or Class II. Parimutuel betting on dog and horse racing, straight-up sports bets as with Nevada sports books, lotteries, slot machines, house banking card games, and other common casino games all fall under the Class III distinction. Just as with Class II gaming, a tribe may operate Class III games if it adopts an ordinance approved by the NIC Chairman and if the state permits "such gaming for any purpose by any person, organization, or entity." Unique to the area of Class III gaming is the requirement that the activities be "conducted in conformance with a Tribal–State compact entered into by the Indian tribe and the State."

E. Sports Books and Illegal Gambling

Jack Molinas was a famous college basketball player at Columbia and a professional basketball player who shaved points in college and with the Fort Wayne Pistons, and was suspended indefinitely from the NBA. He later became a lawyer but continued to pay college ballplayers to shave points and rig games. He was disbarred, went to jail, and was later murdered in what appeared to be a "mob hit." Of course, there were few, if any, legal sports books during Jack's era (he was expelled from the NBA in 1954 and was murdered in 1975).

Proponents argue that eliminating legal betting avenues would send more gamblers to illegal bookies, compounding the problems presented by illegal wagering. The "displacement" argument can be persuasive in some circumstances. But, it is not always true, when it comes to gambling. Legal gaming sometimes complements illegal gambling, not replaces it. For one thing, open promotion of legal gambling tends to remove much of the taint from illegal games. As such, people who would not have gambled illegally might be encouraged to do so. Moreover, by setting lines and stating odds, the legal game may make it easier to operate illegal games. The legal game also provides an easy way for the illegal operator to "lay-off" (thereby insuring against heavy losses) on popular wagers.

F.   Parimutuel Wagering and the Law Generally

Betting among individuals on the outcome of a future event or on the existence of a fact that is uncertain or unknown to the parties, with the bets all going into a pool, and the amount of pay-out determined by the amounts bet on each possible outcome, e.g., on each particular horse winning, is the basis for parimutuel wagering.

1.   Greyhound Racing

Parimutuel wagering on greyhounds is an established part of American gambling. Today, Americans can place bets on dog and horseraces in 43 states, buy lottery tickets in more than 40 states, gamble for charity in 47 states, and play at commercial casinos in 11 states.

In *People v. Monroe,* 349 Ill. 270, 182 N.E. 439 (1932), it was claimed that the state's Horse Racing Act is unreasonable in that it discriminates against dog races. There is a great difference between dog racing and horse racing. In dogracing, the dogs are turned loose on the race track, without human management or guidance, to run or not to run the race, according to their own will, mood, temperament, or instinct, and subject to being distracted by circumstances from efforts to win, while in horse racing, the horses are subject to human guidance, management, and urging to put forth their best efforts to win. There are also allegations of mistreatment of the dogs, such as killing greyhounds that don't win races.

2. Horse Racing

From the most primitive times, men have been accustomed to betting on horseraces, whether legalized or not, and no law has yet been devised to sufficiently curb the evils of unlicensed betting. It is a matter of common knowledge that among those evils has always been that of the "welcher," i.e., "one who at a race track makes bets or receives money to be bet and absconds without paying his losses or returning the money entrusted to him." Webster's New Int. Dict. State and county fairs where horseracing is carried on or OTB parlors operate differ from privately-owned licensed racebooks, in that those fairs are supported in whole or in part by public funds and are under the control of public officials.

Every event in life and the fulfillment of every lawful contract entered into between parties is contingent to at least some slight extent upon chance. No one would contend, however, that a contract knowingly and understandingly entered into between two parties is a gaming contract merely because its fulfillment was prevented as the result of the befalling of unknown or unconsidered forces, or by the issue of uncertain conditions, or by the result of fortuity. The parimutuel system of betting does not come within the definitions given above. While the amount of money to be divided is indefinite as to dollars and cents, it is definite in that the amount of money to be divided is the total stakes on the winning horse, less a given percentage to the management. The persons among whom the money is to be divided are not uncertain, as they are "those who bet on the winning horse." The winning horse is not determined by chance, alone, but the condition, speed, and endurance of the horse, aided by the skill and management of the rider or driver, enter into the result. The amount to be paid by a principal to an agent under a contract to be paid 10% commission on all sales made by him is dependent in some degree on chance and the happening of many uncertain and contingent events, but the defense that such contract was for such reasons a gambling contract could not be maintained.

Under federal law, parimutuel wagering on horseracing is not a lottery, because it requires some skill. The prohibition on "lotteries" found in many state constitutions may, or may not, apply to parimutuel betting on races and sports events. Cases arose in the 1930s, when many states relegalized horseracing in the face of the Great Depression, which involved questions of whether state legislatures had this power, or whether voters would first have to amend state constitutions. These questions are still being raised today, although the focus is usually on other forms of gambling, such as riverboat casinos and Internet gaming.

3. Jai Alai

Jai alai is a fast, indoor court sport popular in Florida and parts of New England. It is a game for parimutuel betting. It is sometimes called "Basque Ball," because it developed in the Basque areas of France and Spain. The game has a somewhat soiled reputation. Because single individuals and two-person teams compete against other small numbers of players, there is a greater chance of one person throwing a game.

Discharged professional jai alai player Edward Avilla worked at Newport Grand Jai Alai, in Rhode Island. At the end of 2001, he was not rehired. Although the players were covered by a collective bargaining agreement ("CBA"), it did not include a grievance procedure and the players were considered at-will employees. However, when Avilla learned that he was not rehired, he contacted a union representative. The union representative then spoke with the CEO of Newport Grand and the union president. The CEO told the union representative that Avilla was not rehired because he had too many inconsistencies as a player and had been accused of fixing games. Newport Grand ultimately decided it would rehire Avilla. However, when the players' manager threatened to quit because he believed Avilla cheated, Newport decided not to rehire Avilla. Avilla then attempted to play jai alai in Florida but prior to a tryout, he was accused of being the player that fixed games in Newport. Avilla accused Newport Grand of defamation. The defendants claimed that the statements made among the CEO, union representative, union president, and the players' manager was privileged. The trial court granted summary judgment in favor of the defendants, and the appellate court affirmed because the CEO had an interest in answering the union representative's questions regarding why certain players were not rehired. In addition, the plaintiff had not shown that there was any malice or ill will on the part of anyone at Newport Grand in making the statements about Avilla. *Avilla v. Newport Grand Jai Alai, LLC,* 935 A.2d 91 (R.I. 2007).

G.   On–Track Betting

Legal betting at racetracks, as opposed to illegal bookies or numbers, has been an established part of American gambling for hundreds of years. Now, many racetracks have simulcast betting where you can bet on races taking place at other race tracks, called inter-track wagering.

The difference between on-track betting and illegal off-track betting, is explained in *State v. Countdown, Inc.,* 319 So.2d 924 (La. 1975). The defendant corporation did not bet or wager but accepted money, carried it to the racetrack, placed the bets at parimutuel windows and returned betting tickets to its office to be retrieved by bettors. The corporation, therefore, was not engaging in "office of personal trust" that was prohibited by statute. LSA–C.C. art. 441. Since the corporation did not bet or wager but instead accepted money, carried the money to the race track, placed bets at parimutuel windows, and returned betting tickets to its office to be retrieved by the bettors, the corporation is not engaging in illegal off-track betting. LSA–R.S. 4:147, 4:149,

4:171. Many states fear that messenger services like this will not actually place the wagers, and have passed statutes expressly prohibiting agents from accepting bets, even if they are later bet at the tracks.

H. Off–Track Betting

Off-track betting ("OTB") is broadly defined as any wager on a race not taking place at the bettor's location. The racing industry distinguishes between inter-track wagers, where the bettors go to one track to place their bets and watch monitors showing races taking place at other tracks, and "true" OTB, either stand-alone sites or Advanced Deposit Wagering ("ADW") by phone or computer from bettors' homes and offices. All remote wagering requires that the operator know the results before the bettors; thus requiring simulcasting, where the racing signal is sent instantaneously to everyone at the same time.

The Supreme Court of Florida, in a matter of first impression, held that that state's Parimutuel Wagering Act prohibited a thoroughbred racetrack from enforcing an exclusivity agreement with an out-of-state track to rebroadcast simulcast signals of out-of-state races. Not only did the Act prohibit restricting another thoroughbred racetrack from rebroadcasting simulcast signals to other parimutuel facilities, it prohibited the track with the exclusivity agreement from stopping inter-track wagering on those rebroadcasts. *Gulf Stream Park Racing Ass'n,*

Inc. v. Tampa Bay Downs, Inc., 948 So.2d 599 (Fla.
S. Ct. 2006). In *Opinion of the Justices*, 353 Mass.
779, 229 N.E.2d 263 (1967), the Court allowed the
possibility of off-track wagering based on the transmission or communication of racing information, or
receiving or securing thereof, which if intended not
solely for furtherance of illegal gambling may not be
prohibited.

I. Anti–Sports Betting Laws

The most important federal anti-gambling law is
the Wire Act, 18 U.S.C.A. § 1084. It was passed in
1961 as part of Attorney General Robert Kennedy's
war on organized crime and designed to cut the
telegraph wire that allowed illegal race and sports
books to get the results of sporting events before
their bettors. In the 1960s and '70, Congress enacted additional laws, all designed to help the states
enforce their then-public policies of nearly complete
prohibition on all gambling. These include the Travel Act, 18 U.S.C.A. § 1952, the Interstate Transportation of Wagering Paraphernalia Act, 18 U.S.C.A.
§ 1953, and the Illegal Gambling Businesses Act, 18
U.S.C.A. § 1955. The Wire Act is still the main
weapon the federal government uses against illegal
sports betting on the Internet.

CHAPTER 18

LOTTERIES

A. The Concept of Lotteries

The law used to classify all gambling as being in one of three categories: Gaming, wagering and lotteries. The three were treated differently by lawmakers. Wagering was not much of a problem before the development of modern technology, because it was usually only bets between two individuals. Gaming and lotteries were of much greater concern. Gaming was considered both more and less dangerous than lotteries. Gaming created more of a risk to the bettors, because the games were fast, repetitive and conducted in hidden rooms, with players usually betting against a "house," which had the odds in its favor. In the 19th century probability theory was not widely understood, and both players and lawmakers often saw no difference between a cheating game which was rigged, and one which merely favored the house. The feeling of early Americans toward gaming rooms is shown in the slang of the era, which called them "gambling hells."

But gaming was also considered less dangerous to society than lotteries, because gambling games required that players go to a particular place and participate in the play of a game. Where only a few men could go to a casino at any one time, lottery tickets can be sold virtually everywhere. This distinction was recognized by the United States Supreme Court:

Experience has shown that the common forms of gambling are comparatively innocuous when placed in contrast with the wide-spread pestilence of lotteries. The former are confined to a few persons and places, but the latter infests the whole community; it enters every dwelling; it reaches every class; it preys upon the hard earnings of the poor; and it plunders the ignorant and simple.

Stone v. Mississippi, 101 U.S. 814, 25 L.Ed. 1079, 1080 (1880) quoting *Phalen v. Virginia*, 49 U.S. 163, 8 How. 163, 168, 12 L.Ed. 1030 (1849).

It used to be easy, or at least easier, to distinguish among the traditionally seen as three different forms of gambling: gaming involved a game with cards, dice or other equipment; lotteries were schemes involving paper tickets and a pool of wagers; and wagering was a bet between two individuals on some external event, like which horse would win a race. Due to accidents of history, a large percentage of anti-gambling laws focus on lotteries. Legal gambling has spread across the nation twice before. Lotteries were greatly responsible for the fall of the First and Second Waves. So, prohibitions on "lotteries" are found in state constitutions and federal laws from the 19th century.

So much time has passed, and so many cases have been fought in so many different parts of the country, that it is impossible today to come up with a common definition of what is a "lottery." There is not even agreement on who decides—Should the courts defer to definitions created by a state legislature, or ignore legislative attempts to legalize forms of gambling that the Supreme Court thinks is a lottery? Many of the disputes arose in the 1930s and '40s, when the rise of the Third Wave of legal gambling led to legislatures authorizing pari-mutuel betting on horseracing. More cases arose in the 1950s & '60s when charity bingo proliferated.

In general, the term "lottery" embraces all schemes for the distribution of prizes by chance, such as policy-playing, gift-exhibitions, prize-concerts, raffles at fairs, and various other forms of gambling. Of course, like all gambling, a lottery is composed of three elements: prize, consideration, and chance. Many cases focusing on whether an element is missing, such as in a no-purchase-necessary sweepstakes, which may or may not have consideration. But declaring that a lottery has to have these three elements, tells us nothing about whether a particular form of gambling is, or is not, a lottery.

Often, the question of whether an activity is one form of gambling or another is not as important as whether all three elements are present. For example, in *Glick v. MTV Networks, A Div. of Viacom Int'l, Inc.*, 796 F.Supp. 743 (S.D. N.Y. 1992), a television sweepstakes was deemed not to be an "unlawful gambling scheme" or "lottery" under New Jersey law; although the contest could be entered by calling a "900" number, for which there was a $2 charge, there were alternative cost-free methods of entering, and therefore, the sweepstakes did not require that participants risk "something of value," which is a necessary element to a gambling claim. N.J.S.A. Const. Art. 4, § 7, par. 2; N.J.S.A. 2A:40–1, 2A:40–6. Once it was determined that there was no consideration, it did not matter what the game was called. It was simply assumed that if there were consideration, the scheme would have been an illegal lottery.

Lotteries usually also require that there be a pool of money, formed from the bets of the lottery ticket buyers. Players do not have to go to a location to participate in the playing of a game. In fact, a lottery has traditionally been seen as not a game at all, but merely a scheme. Players were completely passive. Player participation was meaningless, because the outcome of a lottery was determined 100% by change.

The presence of legal lotteries in this country predates the American Revolution. Because there was only a rudimentary fiscal infrastructure, people often found it was easier to sell their property using a raffle rather than trying to get a bank mortgage. Colonies and states freely gave permission for individuals to run lotteries for worthy causes. George Washington himself ran a lottery to raise money for a road he wanted to build to property he owned in Appalachia. The First Wave ended when scandals closed almost all the lotteries by the start of the Civil War. Prohibitions on lotteries were written into state constitutions.

The Civil War devastated the South, which needed a way to raise money without heavy taxes. Reconstruction era state constitutions allowed Southern states to authorize lotteries. But scandals, particularly the Louisiana Lottery, also known as The Serpent, brought about cries for federal laws, which are still on the book. See 18 U.S.C.A. §§ 1301–1307. By 1909, all lotteries and almost all other forms of gambling had once again been prohibited in the United States.

The Third wave started with the Great Depression. In 1931, Nevada re-legalized casinos. States began reopening their racetracks. Charities began opening bingo games. Then in 1963, New Hampshire rediscovered the state lottery. It took nearly half a century, but now only a half dozen states do not have a lottery. They remain a popular mechanism for raising state revenues without increasing taxes.

B. Video Lotteries

With the introduction of video games for entertainment purposes in 1977, the gambling industry found another tool to market its product. Video gambling devices usually are referred to as "video poker" or "video lottery terminals" or "VLTs," in the various states that permit them. Essentially, these video machines replicate common forms of gambling, such as poker, blackjack, craps, and horse racing; or they are indistinguishable from slot machines. Players accumulate credits as they win and are able to redeem these credits for cash with the video poker operator. In addition, a pre-set pay-out percentage is programmed into each machine. If they are allowed, it is because under the laws of that particular state the video gambling device meets the legal definition of "lottery."

States and the federal government are free to decide for themselves what is, and is not, a lottery. Of course, almost all state courts, as well as the United States Supreme Court, agree that all gambling must have consideration, chance and prize. See, e.g., *FCC v. ABC*, 347 U.S. 284, 290, 74 S.Ct. 593, 98 L.Ed. 699 (1954). But many also define a lottery in exactly those terms. These prior poorly written decisions have led some courts to decide that "gambling" is synonymous with "lottery." In those jurisdictions, almost anything can be considered a lottery. This has resulted in the Kansas State Lottery actually owning the state's casinos, because the casino games were declared to be "lotteries." *State, ex Rel. Stephen N. Six v. Kansas Lottery*, 286 Kan. 557, 186 P.3d 183 (2008).

In other states, would a video poker machine be considered to be a lottery? The device does possess the three essential elements of consideration, chance and prize. Consideration is the stake, wager, or bet that gamblers risk losing if they are unsuccessful. In the context of video poker, the money deposited into the machine by the player constitutes consideration. Because a player must deposit money into the machine to begin play, consideration is the easiest of the three elements to establish. Likewise, the element of prize is rather simple to ascertain. A prize is something of value, usually money or property, that the player seeks to obtain by participating in the game. A video poker machine registers a running total of free replays or credits during the course of a player's time spent on the machine. When a winning player chooses to discontinue playing, the machine distributes a credit slip, which the machine operator redeems for cash. Because the credit slip represents a right to receive cash, it holds value and thus constitutes a prize.

Chance is the critical factor in determining whether video poker is a lottery. Generally, chance is defined as a lack of control over events or uncertainty as to the occurrence of those events. In other words, chance is present when we lack the means by which to effect a desired outcome.

Video poker lacks the human interaction that is critical in person-to-person poker. Specifically, video poker does not allow a player to mentally challenge an opponent by "bluffing" and "raising" during the progress of the game. Nor can a video poker player interpret the body language and facial expression of opponents as any truly skilled card player would attempt to do. In the standard game, with the odds in the house's favor even with perfect play and no progressive jackpot, player participation makes a difference, but not a big enough difference to make the game into a contest of skill. *See, United States v. 294 Various Gambling Devices*, 718 F.Supp. 1236, 1243 (W.D. Pa. 1989).

But having determined that the device has the three elements only means that it is a form of gambling. All lotteries are gambling, but not all gambling is a lottery. There must be additional tests to determine whether this game is a lottery or another form of gambling, such as gaming.

Nevada has always had a state constitutional ban on lotteries. This definition was tested in a friendly case in 1919. *Ex Parte Pierotti*, 43 Nev. 243, 184 P. 209 (1919). The Supreme Court of Nevada ruled that the Legislature had the power to legalize "nickle-in-the-slot machines," because, under the Legislature's interpretation, slot machines are not lotteries. The Court deferred to the decision of the Legislature, at least for purposes of looking at how the word "lottery" has been treated in the state. By pointing out that the Legislature consistently had separate laws over the various forms of gambling, the Court logically concluded that, at least under Nevada state law, lottery was not synonymous with gambling.

Of course, this leaves the question of how to distinguish one form of gambling from another. In Nevada, the test is whether gamblers can simply buy a ticket and wait at home to find out whether they have won, or whether they have to go to a specific place to participate in a game. Thus, bingo and linked progressive slot machines are not lotteries, and can be authorized by the Nevada State

Legislature. This leads to the interesting problem of what to do with keno, now that casinos allow players to buy tickets up to one year in advance.

Keno also shows how jurisdictions can differ, even on the exact same game. For while the Nevada State Legislature has declared that keno is not a lottery, the federal Internal Revenue Service has declared that it is. Various forms of gambling are treated differently for purposes of reporting and withholding for federal tax purposes. For example, there is a federal excise wager tax on certain wagers. As the IRS says in its official publication, "The IRS Gaming Tax Law and Bank Secrecy Act Issues for Indian Tribal Governments," "In general, the tax on wagering applies to ... wagers placed in a lottery conducted for profit (other than a state-conducted lottery)." The IRS then ads this Note:

> Pull-tabs, raffles, and tip jar games generally are taxable lotteries. Bingo (not instant bingo) is specifically excluded from the wagering tax. Keno may or may not be excluded from the wagering tax. The general rule is if it is a live Keno game, meaning all players are present and winnings are paid before the beginning of the next game, then it is not subject to the gaming excise tax. Generally, with Keno games over 20, the player may leave and collect his winnings at a later date (usually up to one year). This type of Keno game would be subject to the wagering tax.

In other jurisdictions, other tests may apply. One common test is the pure chance test. The English Rule holds that if an activity has some skill it may still be gambling, but it cannot be considered a lottery. A game of pure chance, with consideration and a prize, would almost always be a lottery. Certainly bingo would be, but betting on sports events or races would not.

Other courts have held that lotteries must have a paper ticket, or a pool of money formed by players' bets, or no player participation in a game. Each test could lead to a different result, depending upon the characteristics of the game.

C. Internet Lotteries

Lotteries outside the United States were among the first to use the Internet. The pressure on European countries to expand lottery coverage in neighboring markets has only grown with the adoption of the euro as the common currency. While some jurisdictions have barred non-nationals from participation in their draws, even online, the rule against accepting cross-border bets is not as pervasive as in the U.S. The difference between marketing online and online ticket sales is becoming both blurred and insignificant. Even Mainland China has experimented with direct online sales of virtual lottery tickets on a small scale.

Each state in the United States has its own web page, and uses it to post results of daily and weekly drawings, press releases, etc. There are, additionally, the "for fun" games, which are tutorials on how to play the real games. Faced with widespread maturing of markets and even declining sales, a number of American state lotteries have turned to using the Internet as part of their actual gaming, not just for advertising. About a dozen feature "second chance" drawings that partially or wholly use the Internet to give losing tickets another opportunity to pay off.

In 2006, four American states, New Hampshire, New York, North Dakota, and Virginia, began to offer subscription services to their respective state lotteries, available for purchase via Internet. In 2011, the federal Department of Justice, answering inquiries from the Illinois and New York State Lotteries, declared that it had changed its decades' old position on the Wire Act. It expressly held that state lotteries may sell subscriptions online, and may use out of state payment processors. This will open the door for state lotteries to sell individual tickets online as well. Lottery directors and legislators are looking at whether state lotteries can also offer poker online. But even without poker, there is about to be a major expansion of Internet gambling. Because a state lottery instant ticket, a scratcher, is indistinguishable from a slot machine if it is on a monitor.

D.   Lotteries in Tribal Areas

The Indian Gaming Regulatory Act ("IGRA") divides all gambling into three classes. Tribes may offer any Class II (bingo and poker) or III (all other gambling, including lotteries) permitted in the state. (For Class III gaming, the tribe must first have a tribal-state compact, which spells out the areas of co-regulation.) The question of exactly what gambling is permitted under state law, called the scope of gaming, therefore becomes of vital importance. In *Lac du Flambeau Band v. Wisconsin*, 770 F.Supp. 480 (W.D. Wis. 1991), the court held that the scope of gaming was not limited to the particular games expressly allowed under state law. At the time, the only forms of Class III gaming permitted under Wisconsin's Constitution were parimutuel on-track betting and a state lottery. But the federal trial court, looking at Wisconsin state court interpretations of what is a "lottery," ruled that the term included any game involving prize, chance, and consideration. Although these cases were decided when lotteries were outlawed, the legal definition held, now that there was a State Lottery. The State Lottery was only operating traditional lottery games. But, the Court said the inquiry is whether Wisconsin law prohibits other Class III gaming, including casino games. In *Lac du Flambeau Band*, the court's holding turned on the broad definition of "lottery" under state law rather than the conclusion that if a state allows one form of Class III IGRA gaming, it "permits" all Class III games under IGRA. But, since "lottery" includes any game of prize, chance and consideration, and there was now a State Lottery, tribes could open casinos in the state.

E. State Lotteries

The current recession shows the importance of state lotteries to public finance. Native American, commercial gaming and Internet gambling, along with lottery market and product maturity, have eroded the relative autonomy of state lotteries. Regardless, lotteries continue to make a substantial contribution to state governmental coffers. Lotteries are recession-proof.

Lotteries still have the potential to make an increased contribution to state coffers; this might include the privatization of lottery operations, legalization and expansion of video lottery terminals ("VLTs"), and higher price point strategies for lottery products. Because lotteries can operate any form of gambling permitted under their enabling statutes, all of the nation's state lotteries are looking into operating games over the Internet, now that the federal Department of Justice has announced that the major federal anti-gambling law, the Wire Act, 18 U.S.C.A. § 1084, applies only to bets on sports events and races.

F. National Lotteries

In the United Kingdom, the National Lottery Act of 1993 established a national lottery with the express purpose of raising money for good causes. It was initially run by a single corporate body, Camelot plc, whose license must be renewed every seven years. The Act requires the licensee to be a "fit and proper person," as judged by the regulator, the National Lottery Commission. The Commission has power under the Act to set and modify the conditions of the license. By § 4 of the Act, the regulator is under a statutory duty to ensure that the Lottery is run with all due propriety, that the interests of participants are protected, and, subject only to these stipulations, to maximize the revenue to good causes.

Other national lotteries have similar restrictions. However, the forms of gambling are often more extensive than those allowed in the United States. Most foreign lotteries, for example, offer bets on sports events and sell tickets over the Internet. Even in Canada, almost every provincial lottery is already operating Internet poker and other online games, or is about to.

G. International Sweepstakes

Games can be passive or active, exhaustive or non-exhaustive. In a raffle—the simplest form of a passive and exhaustive lottery—players are sold as many unique pre-numbered chances as they wish to buy, all of which are included in a draw to determine the winner(s). None of the unsold chances is included in the draw. If there is a single prize, this procedure will guarantee its winner; if there are many prizes, there will be only one winner of each prize. Such a lottery ensures a complete match between stakes, prizes, and contribution to any cause promoted by it, so there is no danger of a shortfall on either count, save that neither can be announced in advance with certainty. A variation on the raffle is the sweepstakes. Here, the player purchases a numbered chance, which does not in and of itself refers to a winning or losing number, but randomly identifies a constituent in some other chance event—such as a horse in a horserace— which, if it wins, gives the ticket holder a share of the prize money that is divided between all those tickets that refer to the winning horse. The player is allowed a chance to participate in a pool. The Irish Hospitals Sweepstakes of the late 1920s and early 1930s was famous, and to the British, infamous, since it siphoned money from the United Kingdom to the benefit of Irish hospitals. At one point, the Irish Sweepstakes was considered the largest smuggling operation in the world, since the tickets technically were not supposed to be sold in the United States. With the advent of legal state and national lotteries, sales dropped, until the Irish Sweepstakes eventually went out of business.

H. Agreements to Share

As in the movie, *It Could Happen to You*, many lottery winners feel jilted; and the courts then must ascertain if there was an "agreement to share" in some form. In *Pando v. Fernandez*, 127 Misc.2d 224, 485 N.Y.S.2d 162 (1984), rev'd. 118 A.D.2d 474, 499 N.Y.S.2d 950 (1986), modified, 124 A.D.2d 495, 508 N.Y.S.2d 8 (1986), the question was whether there was an agreement to share a \$2.8 million New York lottery with the caveat that the alleged non-winner pray for a victory; even though the agreement was oral, and extremely informal, both the trial court and the appellate court saw the agreement as a binding contract.

Also, an oral agreement to share lottery winnings was held to be valid in *Pearsall v. Alexander*, 572 A.2d 113 (D.C. 1990). In all, at least seven jurisdictions have addressed the same issues raised in *Pearsall* with regard to the validity of contracts to split lottery winnings. Four of those jurisdictions have held such contracts enforceable. In *Fitchie v. Yurko*, 212 Ill.App.3d 216, 156 Ill.Dec. 416, 570 N.E.2d 892 (1991), the Appellate Court of Illinois found such contracts to be valid. *Fitchie* involved a \$100,000 prize via a scratch-off ticket in the Illinois State Lottery and locals at a local coffee shop, who were promised by the winner to share with them any prize won in exchange for their help in scratching some lottery tickets. One of the plaintiffs actually scratched off the winning ticket and Yurko entered his name and the initials of the two plaintiffs on the back of the ticket. After Yurko collected the $100,000 prize, he refused to divide it with the plaintiffs. Plaintiffs, however, eventually prevailed; the Appellate Court of Illinois acknowledged the validity of contracts to split lottery winnings under a joint venture analysis where sufficient evidence existed to indicate that the parties formed a binding contract.

However, in at least three jurisdictions, the courts have held that contracts to split lottery winnings are invalid. In *Bloodworth v. Gay*, 213 Ga. 51, 96 S.E.2d 602 (1957), the Georgia Supreme Court held that the agreement between two parties to split the proceeds from the sale of an automobile won in a lottery was invalid. In *Talley v. Mathis*, 212 Ga.App. 330, 441 S.E.2d 854 (1994), the Georgia Court of Appeals followed the *Bloodworth* holding that a contract to split lottery winnings was illegal as a matter of law. In *Talley*, parties entered into the contract immediately prior to the creation of the Georgia State Lottery. Because the contract was illegal and violative of public policy at the time of formation, the court refused to require enforcement of the agreement.

With the spread of legal gambling, fewer and fewer courts are finding that gambling is against the forum state's public policy. The few cases where the argument can still be raised is when there is an agreement to share lottery winnings, and the trial is taking place in a state without a state lottery. It is even possible that a state with a lottery might hold such an agreement unenforceable. But legislatures are eliminating this problem by expressly stating that agreements to share lottery winnings are enforceable, or even requiring state lotteries to provide model lottery pooling forms.

I. Other Issues: Lost Tickets, Mistakes and Selling Future Payments

Other issues involving state lotteries have been litigated. Because the amounts involved can be so great, it is not unusual to find these cases fought all the way to the state's highest court. Many recurring issues have now been resolved through binding court precedents, or by explicit statutes and regulations.

A lottery ticket is a bearer instrument. This means that whoever has it automatically becomes the owner, like a dollar bill. It also means that a winning buyer cannot collect unless he has the actual ticket. Again, like a dollar bill, a court will not accept an affidavit from the former owner swearing that he had the bearer instrument but had lost it.

Because gambling is still against the public policy of every state, state lotteries are treated as merely exceptions to the law. Thus, their statutes and regulations are strictly construed. Lottery rules now commonly state that mistakes void the game. So, in the rare cases where state lotteries or their retailers accidentally tell someone who actually had a losing ticket that he had a winner, neither the lottery nor the retailer is required to pay.

When state lotteries were first authorized, very large jackpots were always paid out over time. This was done to protect winners from blowing all their money in the first year, and because income tax schedules used to be more progressive, meaning that the tax on one big prize might be much larger than the tax on the same prize paid out over a number of years. But many people, including the elderly, did not want to wait 20 years to collect all of their lottery winnings. Because statutes required payments over time, court were usually powerless to force the lottery to pay a prize in a lump sum, or even allow winners to use the future stream of payments as collateral for loans. Changes in lottery statutes have pretty much eliminated this problem, allowing big winners to decide for themselves whether they want the payments paid over time, or a reduced amount paid immediately.

CHAPTER 19

LEGAL GAMBLING'S RIGHT TO ADVERTISE

A. Right to Advertise Generally

Legal gambling's right to advertise is a somewhat "confused" area of law. State lotteries advertise on television, radio, and newspapers; however, legal charities' bingo games sometimes cannot even announce when a game is canceled on account of rain. Racetracks blanket the airwaves with commercials, and entire races, including the betting odds, are broadcast on television. But, licensed card clubs used to be prohibited from even broadcasting their business hours over the air. Until a ruling from the U.S. Supreme Court cleared the way, state-licensed casinos could not even broadcast commercials in the very state that issued the license. And state lotteries are still limited to television and radio in states with lotteries, which means that the Arizona and California Lotteries cannot broadcast commercials in Nevada.

The only way to ascertain whether a particular game can advertise in a particular manner is to study and research the specific laws involved, beginning with the actual statutes and regulations, both federal and state. Local city and county ordinances, regulations, and licenses can also sometimes apply. If a prohibition looks like it might prevent a legal form of gambling from advertising, the next step is to see if that prohibition violates freedoms protected by the United States and various state Constitutions. The control of gambling comes under government's police power, which is nearly limitless. But the U.S. Constitution gives Congress only limited power over state law issues in designated areas. And all constitutions protect the rights of individuals in areas like free speech and freedom of the press.

B.   Federal Anti–"Lottery" Laws

The tangled regulations impacting legal gambling's right to advertise emanate from a set of anti-lottery laws passed by Congress before 1900, and actions of regulators, particularly, the Federal Communications Commission ("FCC"), which regulates and licenses all broadcasters in the United States. Most legal gambling was outlawed by state statutes and state constitutional amendments prior to the Civil War. But, the Civil War devastated the South, so governments in the worst hit areas turned to state lotteries as a painless tax. The Second Wave crashed in the 1890s, primarily due to scandals connected to the Louisiana Lottery. That Lottery, known as "The Serpent," was legal—the operators had bribed the State Legislature for a license. And, being legal, it sold tickets throughout the nation.

Many states reacted by passing laws making it illegal to sell or even advertise a lottery, even if the lottery drawing took place in a state where it was legal. But states felt hopeless to prevent tickets from The Serpent from crossing their borders. So, the states asked President Benjamin Harrison and Congress for help.

The federal government used all the power it felt it had in preventing The Serpent from advertising in other states. Federal laws were passed, which in modified form are still around, preventing lotteries from using the U.S. Mail. When radio and then television were invented, these anti-lottery prohibitions were added to federal laws regulating those media as well. These are still on the books, codified in the U.S. Criminal Code sections entitled, "Lotteries," 18 U.S.C.A. §§ 1301–1307; the postal statute, 39 U.S.C.A. § 3005; and other federal statutes dealing with federally-insured financial institutions, 12 U.S.C.A. §§ 339, 1829a, 1730c, which contain some broad language relating to lotteries. Advertisements of a "lottery, gift enterprise, or similar scheme" cannot be imported or sent through the U.S. Mail. The federal government's prohibition on the use of the mails by lotteries was expanded to include broadcasting of lottery-related information as part of the Communications Act of 1934. The principal limit on broadcasting is found in 18 U.S.C.A. § 1304, which prohibits the broadcasting of "any advertisement of or information concerning any lottery, gift enterprise, or similar scheme ..."

The first rule of any statutory analysis is to carefully read the statute. But words may not always mean what one would first think. The definition of terms is important. For example, the federal prohibitions on gambling ads cited above should only apply to a "lottery, gift enterprise, or similar scheme." Unfortunately, the FCC has consistently ruled that most forms of gambling, including casino games, are "lotteries." Worse, the lawyers fighting for the right to advertise seem to have always conceded this point. On the other hand, the prohibition only covers "broadcasting." The FCC has also been consistent is declaring that cable television and the Internet are not broadcasting. You cannot run a lottery on cable T.V., but there do not appear to be any restrictions on advertising a legal Internet gambling website nor a licensed casino.

When the state lottery was rediscovered in the 1960s, the states asked Congress to carve out exceptions, so that the lotteries could advertise in their own states. Those exceptions were eventually extended to allow state-operated lotteries to broadcast commercials and use the U.S. Mails for advertisements in any state that also had a state lottery. State lotteries alone could advertise only in limited ways, such as broadcast advertisement within their own or neighboring states, but only if the neighboring state also has a state lottery.

But Nevada has no state lottery. Because the exemption was only for state lotteries, casinos licensed by the state of Nevada were told by the FCC that they could not advertise over the air, even in

Las Vegas. The problem arose because the FCC established regulations that decided, without any ostensible rhyme or reason, that many forms of gambling were "lotteries." A commercial for the Tropicana Resort was removed from broadcast television in Las Vegas, because in one scene the word "Casino" is seen reflected in a pool of water.

C. The Commercial Speech Doctrine

The First Amendment of the United States Constitution guarantees "Congress shall make no law ... abridging the freedom of speech, or of the press." Although the First Amendment is explicitly limited to acts of Congress, the guarantees of free speech and a free press have been expanded to include acts by state governments, through the Fourteenth Amendment. "No State shall make or enforce any law which shall abridge the privileges or immunities of citizens of the United States; nor shall any State deprive any person of life, liberty, or property, without due process of law; nor deny to any person within its jurisdiction the equal protection of the laws."

The Supreme Court has extended the protection of the First Amendment to purely commercial speech. In a series of cases beginning in 1975 the high court first implicitly, and then openly, stated that speech that was designed solely as an advertisement was entitled to at least some of the protections of the First Amendment. *Bigelow v. Virginia*, 421 U.S. 809, 95 S.Ct. 2222, 44 L.Ed.2d 600 (1975).

The Supreme Court has given the reasons it expanded the protections of the First Amendment to cover commercial speech. The Court "rejected the 'highly paternalistic' view that government has complete power to suppress or regulate commercial speech. People will perceive their own best interests if only they are well enough informed, and the best means to that end is to open the channels of communication, rather than to close them." *Central Hudson Gas v. Public Service Comm'n.*, 447 U.S. 557, 562, 100 S.Ct. 2343, 65 L.Ed.2d 341 (1980).

In *Central Hudson*, the Supreme Court developed a four-part test, apparently meant to be definitive, for measuring whether a government regulation of commercial speech is constitutional. 447 U.S. at 564. The test requires the following analysis:

1. Is the subject matter lawful and not misleading;

2. Is the asserted governmental interest substantial;

3. Does the regulation directly advance the governmental interest; and

4. Is the regulation no more extensive than necessary to serve that interest.

The Court has stated that the government's interest in restricting information about an activity that is legal is minimal at best.

The tests do not automatically mean that a government's restrictions on advertising legal gambling will be declared constitutional, or unconstitutional.

In *United States v. Edge Broadcasting Co.*, 509 U.S. 418, 113 S.Ct. 2696, 125 L.Ed.2d 345, the Court upheld the constitutionality of § 1304 as applied to advertising of Virginia's lottery by a radio broadcaster in North Carolina, even though there was no dispute that almost all listeners were in Virginia. The Court held that it was rational for Congress to draw lines, even in this case, where the broadcast tower happened to be in North Carolina, which had no state lottery at the time.

But then in *Greater New Orleans Broadcasting Association, Inc. v. United States*, 527 U.S. 173, 119 S.Ct. 1923, 144 L.Ed.2d 161 (1999), the Court threw out the FCC's restrictions on casino commercials broadcast in states that license casinos. In that case, the Court held the restriction on advertising was irrational, because identical casinos, which happened to be tribally owned, could air T.V. and radio ads. The Court held the statutes should be construed as narrowly as possible to preserve their constitutionality under the First Amendment. The Department of Justice reacted to the *Greater New Orleans* decision by announcing that it would not enforce the prohibitions on "lottery" broadcast commercials in any state, even those states that did not have state-licensed casinos.

The FCC was given the power to enforce the anti-lottery broadcast law, along with the general power to rule the airways. Congress delegated its power to the FCC, and now the FCC has much the same power, and limitations, as Congress. The courts have decided that it is unconstitutional for the government to completely suppress the advertising of a legal enterprise. Since Congress itself cannot violate a legal gambling game's right to commercial free speech, the FCC, which has only delegated power, also cannot restrict the legal gambling game's right to advertise.

D. Federal Agencies

Federal agencies still have some power to restrict the advertising of legal gambling. The *Edge Broadcasting* decision is still good law. The FCC has the power to impose the death penalty, taking a license, of a radio or TV station that broadcasts state lottery commercials from a radio tower in a state without its own state lottery. The FCC also has the power to regulate cable TV, but decided even before the *Greater New Orleans Broadcasting* case that casinos could advertise on cable TV, since cable ads are not "broadcasted."

The FCC does not have the power to regulate the United States mails, but the U.S. Postal Services and the U.S. Department of Justice do have that power. Presently, no federal agency regulates newspapers or the content of billboards, probably because neither medium involves interstate commerce *per se*. But newspapers used to have to print split editions, pulling all the advertisements for bingo halls and casinos from copies sent through the U.S. Mail. Operators used to have to spend large sums posting signs and taking out ads in newspapers that were hand-delivered.

The FCC staff has interpreted the term "lottery" to include all forms of gambling, including card games such as poker and blackjack; charity bingo, beano, and similar games; and all casino games, including craps, roulette, and slot machines. However, the FCC does allow information about betting on horse racing by interpreting handicapping as involving some skill. It will be interesting to see how the FCC and courts react to broadcast commercials for games like poker, once those begin to be run over the Internet by state lotteries.

E. Criminal Statutes That Allegedly Limit the Broadcasting of Casino Advertisements

Criminal laws are "penal" because they can lead to punishment and, as such, are strictly constrained; this means that if there is any doubt as to the meaning of a criminal statute, the law is to be interpreted as narrowly as possible. Federal and State statutes dealing with the broadcasting of lottery information and the corresponding FCC regulations must also be strictly construed, to not violate the First Amendment. The easiest way for regulators like the FCC and federal prosecutors to avoid constitutional problems would be to recognize that not all forms of gambling are "lotteries." The federal anti-lottery statutes are not just prohibitions on advertising; they prohibit "any advertisement of or information concerning any lottery...." (18 U.S.C.A. § 1304). The federal laws on lotteries are a complete ban on advertising and other information over the broadcast media and through the mail. But, if, say Internet poker, is not a "lottery" then it would not not fall under the anti-lottery statutes.

There are still state prohibitions on advertising activities, like some forms of gambling, that are not legal in that particular state. Perhaps because these are almost never enforced, there have been few, if any, court decisions on whether these state laws are constitutional.

F. Alleged Deceptive Advertising in *Franceschi v. Harrah's Enter., Inc.* (2011)

In *Franceschi*, 2011 WL 9305 (D. Nev. 2011), plaintiff claimed that he suffered injuries as a result of defendants' deceptive advertisements which lured California residents to gamble in Las Vegas; these marketing efforts included television, newspapers, and radio advertisements, California billboards, as well as direct solicitation by mail, email, and telephone. Plaintiff alleges that defendant's inducements were never intended to apply to "cardcounters." Ultimately, Plaintiff's complaint was dismissed. Of course, Nevada casinos are under no duty to admit all persons—including card counters—to play blackjack or any other game, *see, e.g., Uston v. Nevada Gaming Comm'n*, 103 Nev. 824, 809 P.2d 52 (1987).

G.   The Future of Advertising

It is possible that Congress will amend the statutes so that only illegal lotteries are prevented from advertising, and legal state lotteries can advertise even in states like Nevada which have no state lottery. But it is Internet gambling which is causing the biggest problems for both federal and state governments. Prosecutors have, for the most part, stayed away from going after advertisers, perhaps out of fear of the First Amendment. But there have been some attacks. When the CEO of BetOn-Sports.com, David Carruthers, was arrested changing planes in Dallas—he was going from his home in England to his offices in Costa Rica—the 27–page indictment included a charge against his advertising agency. One of the criminal counts was for fraud, for allegedly advertising in the United States that Internet gambling on sports events is legal.

Carruthers and BetOnSports entered into a plea bargain. So we do not know if a court would buy the idea that a site on the Internet can be arrested for advertising gambling that is legal in some jurisdictions, but not in others.

CHAPTER 20

CRIMINAL LAWS AND GAMING

A. Criminal Laws Generally

The piecemeal expansion of legalized gambling has been accompanied by a relaxation in the enforcement of those statutory criminal prohibitions still in effect. The true meaning of gambling laws and the effect that they have on restricting gambling activities are determined less by what the law says than by how local police and prosecutors conduct their daily affairs. State criminal enforcement usually reflects the national trend with a steady and substantial decline in gambling arrests. The few arrests that are made almost always result in dismissals, findings of not guilty, or the imposition of a minor fine. Illegal gambling, however, still flourishes; bookies continue doing a large business in illegal bets on single sports events and sports cards. The numbers racket, "policy," also flourishes. Off-track bets on the horses with bookies; card and dice games; and other forms of illegal gambling occur to a lesser extent. There are also those social bettors, about 20% of the population, who are probably breaking the law every year, by gambling among friends. Two parallel, marginally-competitive markets exist; one is an area of expanding gambling activities and the other is thriving illegal gambling that law enforcement officials, prosecutors, judges, and the public are either unable or unwilling to eradicate. This imposition of minimal burdens by local officials on the operators and bettors of illegal games has led to an unofficial policy of benign prohibition.

B. Law Enforcement and Illegal Gambling

Law enforcement involvement with illegal gambling can be characterized as follows: (1) law enforcement agencies often lack the resources to conduct thorough investigations of illegal gambling; (2) gambling is considered a low priority offense; (3) gambling-related corruption of police is sometimes widespread and weakens law enforcement; (4) many law enforcement officials believe that gaming laws are unenforceable and thus they ignore violations; and (5) penalties for gambling offenses are relatively light.

C. Arrests in Casinos for "Cheating"

There are few arrests for those who "cheat" in casinos. In some cases, there may not even be a specific statute on the books making cheating a crime. For years, county sheriffs who enforced the laws in many California cardclubs through contracts with cities, charged cheaters with burglary. The legal theory was that the cheaters were entering a building with the intent of obtaining money illegally. Of course, if any of the cheaters had had a great lawyer, that legal advisor might have moved for a dismissal on the grounds that there was no specific statute making it a crime to cheat at a licensed cardclub.

Of course, some operators would like to see any patron who is a regular winner locked up. But cardcounting in blackjack is not subject to the penalties of a criminal statute. Cheating in Nevada requires changing the criteria of the game. A player who keeps track of the cards played and calculates which cards must be remaining in the deck is not cheating. It is possible that under that definition even the use of a computer in card counting might not be cheating; since all of the information fed into the computer is available to all players. In fact, the Nevada State Legislature felt it necessary to enact a special statute making cardcounting computers illegal. NRS 465.075. Of course, using more advanced technology, like hidden telescopic cameras to spy dealers' downcards across a room is cheating. But, although it seems clear that the use of hidden "star wars" devices is illegal, there are few reported cases and often no firm criminal statute defining the alleged crime.

D. Gambling in Indian Country

There are a number of federal criminal statutes of general applicability that may pertain to tribal gaming; for example, sports bribery laws; lottery statutes prohibiting interstate mailing of lottery tickets; Gambling Ship Act; Wire Act; Travel Act; wagering Paraphernalia Act; Anti–Gambling Statute; and RICO. However, two federal statutes have specific applicability to criminal provisions that apply to Indian gaming: they are IGRA's criminal provisions, and the Johnson Act. IGRA created three federal criminal provisions, which are found in Title 18 of the United States Code; they are § 1166, "Gambling in Indian Country," which generally prohibits gambling in violation of state law on tribal lands; § 1167, which makes it a federal crime to steal money or property from a tribal gaming establishment; and § 1168, which applies to officers, employees, and individual licensees of tribal gaming establishments, making it a federal crime to embezzle or steal money from the facility. These statutes complement Public Law 280, which gave many states criminal jurisdiction over activities on federally recognized Indian lands in their states.

The Johnson Act prohibits the interstate transportation of illegal gambling devices (15 U.S.C.A. § 1172), as well as the possession or use of illegal gambling devices in Indian Country (15 U.S.C.A. § 1175; this portion of the Johnson Act is sometimes called the Indian Gambling Act). There are unresolved issues of whether the Johnson Act might apply to legal gaming devices on Indian land. But there is no doubt that slot machines and roulette wheels operated in tribal casinos without complying with the technicalities of IGRA, including first obtaining a tribal-state compact, is a violation of the Johnson Act.

E. Law Enforcement Discretion and Corruption

The problems of benign prohibition, particularly corruption, arise from the uncontrolled discretion the police and prosecutors have at their command. The police assume a role that they were not meant to assume when they are allowed complete discretion as to who will be arrested and when. An officer making a gambling arrest receives no support from the department, the public, or the judicial system. Repeated surveys show that there is general agreement in society for keeping anti-gambling laws on the books; but, most people do not want those laws vigorously enforced. They would simply like to have them there to be used against noisy neighbors and organized crime.

F. "Arrests" for "Internet Cheating"

Under present law, it is almost impossible for a state or the federal government to bring an overseas operator to trial. Extradition is also difficult. Some states have no criminal jurisdiction statutes *per se*, but rely on the Anglo–American common law. Generally, a given state criminal jurisdiction does not extend beyond its territorial borders. In *United States v. Cohen*, 260 F.3d 68 (2d Cir. 2001), an American citizen, Jay Cohen, was tried and convicted for violating the Wire Wager Act through Internet betting offshore. However, it is not against federal law to make a bet online. There is no federal statute or regulation that applies to a mere gambler, as opposed to an operator, even if the bets are made with an illegal bookie across a state line. But, they can open themselves to criminal liability if they aid the operator in any way, for example, by helping to collect gambling debts from other players.

G. Online Poker

As of June 7, 2006, it is now a felony in the state of Washington to play poker on the internet. The bill, S.S.B. No. 6613, has stirred up great anxiety in poker forums. Now, players are worried that they might get arrested.

In reality, this law has made little difference. In fact, the Washington State Gambling Commission has taken the official position that the bill merely "clarifies" existing law: "Although Internet gambling has never been an authorized activity in Washington, this law was passed to make it very clear that Internet gambling is illegal in Washington. This includes gambling on the Internet, operating an Internet gambling site, or facilitating Internet gambling in any way."

Prior to being amended by S.S.B. No. 6613, the law read: "Whoever knowingly transmits or receives gambling information by telephone, telegraph, radio, semaphore or similar means, or knowingly installs or maintains equipment for the transmission or receipt of gambling information shall be guilty of a gross misdemeanor ..."

This made betting by phone with a bookie a crime. But it is questionable whether playing poker on the Internet falls under this law.

Other Washington statutes make it a crime to participate in any form of gambling that is not authorized by the state or a pure social game. But there is at least some doubt as to whether these apply to the Internet at all, let alone to a game where the operator and all of the other players are in foreign states.

S.S.B. No. 6613 added the words "the Internet" and "a telecommunications transmission system" to the list. So, it clearly now is a crime to send or receive any gaming information online, which would include playing poker. Washington is probably the only state to expressly make it a crime to merely bet online. It certainly is the only state to make it a felony. (In Washington, a "class C felony" means a maximum penalty of five years in prison and a $10,000 fine.)

Washington made Internet gambling a felony so that a violation would create a federal crime: Racketeer Influenced Corrupt Organizations ("RICO"), 18 U.S.C.A. §§ 1961–1968. RICO requires that an organization commit two or more designated felonies in the prior ten year. Most state gambling crimes are misdemeanors. Washington officials also wanted to get greater help from other states in pursuing investigations against illegal Internet gambling. Law enforcement agents in other states are usually not anxious to spend their time helping with out-of-state misdemeanor investigations.

H. Money Laundering (of "Winnings," Legal or Not)

Since gambling in the past often was associated with organized crime, the governments learned to attack the flow of money in and out of the illegal activity. The Money Laundering Act (18 U.S.C.A. § 1956) is one of the most potent weapons in the U.S. government arsenal, and the passage of the USA PATRIOT ACT (P.L. No. 107–56, Oct. 26, 2001) has made this more so. This statute represents a particular hazard to American participants in the offshore gambling community, despite the fact that no conviction, proof, or even substantive allegations of actual money laundering has surfaced yet.

I. RICO and Gaming

Racketeer Influenced and Corrupt Organizations ("RICO"), 18 U.S.C.A. §§ 1961–1968, makes it a federal crime if you commit two other specified felonies within the last ten years. RICO along with conspiracy statutes, are the darlings of federal prosecutors. Penalties can be severe, and a RICO charge allows the government to seize all of a defendant's assets. To establish a claim under RICO, prosecutors or plaintiffs must prove that the owner of, for example, a video poker establishment, received a substantial source of business from gambling machines and has committed at least one other act that carries the possibility of imprisonment for more than a year. If found guilty of a civil RICO violation, machine owners must pay threefold damages to the plaintiff and the cost of the suit, including attorney's fees. *Gentry v. Yonce*, 337 S.C. 1, 522 S.E.2d 137 (1999).

Congress enacted RICO under Title IX of the Organized Crime Control Act of 1970 to combat organized crime. Today, most civil RICO suits have nothing to do with organized crime. However, *Gentry* simplifies plaintiffs' pleadings not involving fraudulent claims in civil RICO cases, contrary to Congress's intentions.

The other acts by the video poker machine operators and owners include offering special inducements to customers through logos on the machines offering a "jackpot" and receiving substantial gross proceeds from video gaming devices. Because video poker casino owners receive their monies from video gaming devices, *any* other act will subject video poker casino owners to RICO claims. Civil RICO suits are extremely damaging to owners of "gray-market" video poker casinos.

RICO is designed to go after the top bosses in organized crime, who usually do not get their hands dirty. It expressly covers owners and financiers of illegal businesses. Illegal gambling as a result of "organized crime" may trigger the application of RICO provisions. To establish the elements of a substantive RICO offense, the government must prove (1) that an enterprise existed, (2) that the enterprise affected interstate or foreign commerce; (3) that the defendant associated with the enterprise; (4) that the defendant participated, directly or indirectly, in the conduct of the affairs of the enterprise; and (5) that the defendant participated in the enterprise through a pattern of racketeering activities by committing at least the racketeering (predicate) acts, e.g., 18 U.S.C.A. § 1084 (Wire Act), 18 U.S.C.A. § 1952 (Travel Act), 18 U.S.C.A. § 1955 (illegal gambling business). RICO conspiracies are outlawed in a subsection that imposes no overt act requirement. They are complete upon the agreement to commit a RICO offense. Courts have held that you can be convicted and serve time for the two crimes, and then be convicted and serve additional time for RICO.

RICO also creates a new civil cause of action, and private companies have been suing each other charging RICO for such things as violations of the federal securities laws. RICO was intended to give federal prosecutors the power to reach organized crime bosses. But the law is so broad in its reach that it has been used against such "racketeer influenced corrupt organizations" as IBM. Under RICO, the prosecutor (or plaintiff in a civil suit) need only charge that two predicate crimes have been committed; there is no requirement that the defendant be convicted of those crimes.

J. Other Anti–Racketeering–Type Statutes

The racketeering statutes (18 U.S.C.A. §§ 1951–1955), including the Hobbs Act (§ 1951) and the Travel Act (§ 1952), make it a federal offense to travel or use any facility in interstate or foreign commerce, including the mail, with the intent to promote or carry on any unlawful activity. "Unlawful activity" is specifically defined to include "any business enterprise involving gambling," as well as alcohol and drugs. Section 1953 cover the interstate transportation of illegal wagering paraphernalia. Section 1955, part of the Organized Crime Control Act of 1970, makes it a federal crime to conduct or own a gambling business outlawed under state law. This new federal crime is limited to large-scale operations. The law also gives the federal government the right to seize and keep all money and property used in the legal business.

The federal anti-racketeering statutes are the prime weapons for both prosecutors and jilted competitors. They will be used to curtail "organized crime" elements and those businessmen that use gambling devices to make money. Actual knowledge is not a requirement *per se*. The case law seems to place much less emphasis on the "knowing" element. In particular, predicate offenses to § 1956 may not require nearly as clear a demonstration of "knowledge," which leads to the question of whether a series of general intent offenses can reach a "critical mass" sufficient to constitute a specific intent crime. For example, the Wire Act, 18 U.S.C.A. § 1084, a predicate act to RICO, and, therefore, to the money laundering statute, forbids the "knowing" use of wire communication facilities, even though this was not an essential part of either element of the substantive offense itself. Moreover, the same act also could be prosecuted under 18 U.S.C.A. § 1955 and the "knowledge" language there has been held also not to be specific intent. It would seem that in practice a conviction can be made from much less deliberate action and actual knowledge of wrongdoing than the statutory language would imply.

K. The Future of Criminal Laws and Gaming

There is a disparity between how the law treats gambling offenders more leniently than other criminal offenders. Since there has never been a comprehensive description of a city's gambling, no one has a precise knowledge of the consequences of enforcement policies; therefore, it is impossible to accurately assess the police role in gambling. Most cases against writers and runners are dismissed without judgment. This could be because these arrests are made improperly or the police testify in an imperfect way, or the district attorneys and the judges are corrupted or indifferent to these victimless charges. It is difficult to know whether corruption in these payoff schemes originates with the people who receive the money, at a higher department level, or elsewhere in city government.

CHAPTER 21
THE IRS AND GAMBLING

A. Gambling and Taxes

Casinos are certainly taxed, and lottery winners are also taxed (but not in Canada); big winners at casinos are taxed. If the lucky winner scores over $10,000 in a cash transaction, then the legal casinos are required to file additional forms with the Treasury Department.

Since with gambling the only commodity is cash, the government uses its taxing power to generate income, and to control the activity. In most other businesses, the paying and reporting of taxes are used solely to raise revenue; when it comes to gambling, raising revenue may be secondary to catching crooks. It is always easy to impose or raise taxes on what is viewed as a vice, the so-called sin taxes: alcohol, tobacco, and gambling. The idea is something like, the people should not be doing this any way, but we cannot stop them; so, why not allow the government to make some money? By making vice expensive, the government hopes to control and limit it. Of course, the laws of economics work for illegal activities as well as legal ones. If the taxes on legal gambling are too high, illegal operators will meet the unfulfilled needs of gamblers to place bets, without paying those taxes.

B.   Gambling Profits and Taxable Income

The problem, of course, is that the tax code is used here for some purpose other than raising revenue. In gambling, money changes hands so quickly and with so little documentation that the event is impossible to reconstruct without video or other recordings. For legal games, this means that, without documentation, the regulations are nearly powerless to control the flow of cash. Controversies continue to erupt over the tax regulations of legal games. The IRS fought for years to get the casinos to withhold on the tokes (tips) given casino dealers. And, the IRS apparently has never been successful in stationing agents in the cash counting rooms of the casinos. The Reagan Administration imposed regulations requiring casinos to file detailed reports on their high rollers. Additionally, the IRS will be able to inspect casino credit files on a routine basis. Pawn shops, stock and commodity brokers, travel agencies, and jewelers are required to file these forms. Yacht and car dealers are routinely reported to the government. The U.S. Treasury finally succeeded in forcing casinos to file currency transaction reports on large cash exchanges, and suspicious transaction reports on patrons who appear to have violated the law and are using the casino to launder money.

C.   The Bank Secrecy Act and Gaming

The attempt to bring casinos under the Bank Secrecy Act ("BSA") of 1970 (31 U.S.C.A. §§ 5311–5330; 12 U.S.C.A. §§ 1818(5), 1829(b), 1951–1959) reflects a current trend to use the taxing power solely to control. The government has flipped between using the tax code to raise money and using it to control criminals. As a result, there is a mishmash of tax statutes, revenue rulings, and court decisions that are inherently confusing. However, if the gambling tax is too high it will put the operator out of business; if it is too low, there is no incentive for the IRS to enforce the law.

An illegal game is not interested in obeying the laws, or, at least, does not want to get caught. The Treasury Department is mostly interested in going after big tax evaders. The tax money involved in illegal operations is insufficient to excite the IRS, nor is the underlying crime. Al Capone is one thing; neighborhood bookies are another thing entirely. While enforcing gambling tax laws, the IRS is subject to the same pressure as all law enforcement: The public wants anti-gambling laws to exist but does not want them rigorously enforced.

For legal gambling businesses, reporting laws are, at the very least, a nuisance. They take time and money for training staff to file the correct forms. And failure to obey all the intricacies of Treasury's regulations can result in large fines and bad publicity.

The extra burdens placed on gaming started with the passage of the BSA, also known as the Currency and Foreign Transactions Reporting Act, the "anti-money laundering" law ("AML") or sometimes "BSA/AML". Whatever the nickname, the Bank Secrecy Act is probably the most ironically named statute ever passed by Congress. Its purpose is anti-bank secrecy. As its main enforcer, the Financial Crimes Enforcement Network ("FinCEN") of the U.S. Treasury puts it, the BSA "requires U.S.A. financial institutions to assist U.S. government agencies to detect and prevent money laundering. Specifically, the act requires financial institutions to keep records of cash purchases of negotiable instruments, file reports of cash transactions exceeding $10,000 (daily aggregate amount), and to report suspicious activity that might signify money laundering, tax evasion, or other criminal activities."

Among its other requirements, the BSA and regulations promulgated under it by Treasury require every bank to photocopy and keep records which would enable the government to trace each check drawn for more than $100. Since banks don't read checks, this resulted in banks keeping permanent records of every check, no matter how small.

In addition, every "financial institution" had to file a report within 15 days of each transaction involving more than $10,000 in cash. Of course, $10,000 was considered a lot of money, when the BSA was passed more than four decades ago.

Banks didn't like it, and civil libertarians hated it, but the U.S. Supreme Court held the BSA constitutional in *California Bankers Assn. v. Shultz*, 416 U.S. 21, 94 S.Ct. 1494, 39 L.Ed.2d 812 (1974). The Court found the statute valid on its face, because the information being obtained from private citizens might prove useful in criminal investigations. Justice Douglas wrote a stinging dissent. He meant the following to be ironic, not prescient: "It would be highly useful to governmental espionage to have like reports from all our bookstores, all our hardware and retail stores, all our drugstores. These records too might be 'useful' in criminal investigations." 416 U.S. 21, 84, 94 S.Ct. 1494, 39 L.Ed.2d 812 (1974).

Ironically, it was the Administration of conservative Republican Ronald Reagan, who campaigned on getting government off the backs of citizens, which imposed those currency reporting requirements on casinos, in, appropriately, 1984. On January 1, 1985, Reagan's Treasury Department regulations became final, declaring that licensed casinos with gross gaming revenues of more than $1,000,000 per year were "financial institutions" under the BSA. This had the immediate impact that large casinos had to file Currency Transaction Reports, later renamed Currency Transaction Reports Casinos ("CTRCs"), with Treasury.

So, casinos outside of Nevada have been required to file CTRCs for more than 28 years, detailing the amount and the player's name, address, occupation and Social Security number, every time a player bought or redeemed chips, or even won a slot machine jackpot, and more than $10,000 in cash was involved. The currency reporting requirements were extended to tribal casinos effective August 1, 1996.

Nevada was able to win an exemption from the federal Treasury regulations only by putting in its own identical system, Regulation 6A. And those CTRCs, filed with the Nevada Gaming Control Board, were made available to the Internal Revenue Service anyway.

After the Islamist terrorist attacks on the U.S. on 9/11, the federal government took over completely. But the federal bureaucracy is much larger, and slower to change, that Nevada state regulators. It took years for Treasury to get rid of CTRCs on large slot machine jackpots. When these duplicate reports on slot winnings were finally eliminated, the number of CTRCs was cut in half.

But the CTRCs were not enough. Government investigators realized that data from legal gaming could be mined for even more information. So, FinCEN imposed a requirement that casinos act as police officers, and report mere suspicions that a crime had taken place.

The form is SARCs, Suspicious Activities Report by Casinos, and it differs significantly from CTRCs. CTRCs require casinos to ask the patron for two forms of identification. On the other hand, it is actually against the law for a casino to tell a patron that a SARC has been filed on him.

CTRCs are triggered by an actual cash transaction of more than $10,000, or a total of $10,000 in a 24 hour period. There is normally a similar requirement of a minimum of $5,000 for SARCs. But the casino is required to file a SARC if it knows, or *suspects*, or even *has reason to suspect*, that a transaction of any size involves funds derived from illegal activities. A casino will be fined if no SARC is filed when an executive has an actual suspicion, *or* with 20/20 hindsight when the casino employee *should have had a suspicion*. Since the usual $5,000 minimum also applies to a 24-hour-period, in practice a casino has to track a player and his spouse all the time, if anything looks suspicious.

All casinos and card clubs with gross annual gaming revenues in excess of $1 million must file CTRCs with the federal government every time a player has a cash transaction of more than $10,000. This includes players using currency to buy chips, deposit front money, pay off markers, make large wagers or collect large winning bets. The last is particularly interesting, because the original purpose of CTRCs was supposedly to track crooks who were using casinos for money laundering, like a drug dealer who bought gaming chips with $25,000 in small bills, made a few token bets, and then asked for a cashier's check for his remaining chips.

The U.S. Congress, which is supposedly the body that actually makes the laws, had established complicated rules for withholding taxes of gambling winnings, but only under special circumstances. For example, a sports book has to withhold 28 percent of the amount won, but only if it is more than $5,000 and at least 300 times as large as the amount bet. 26 U.S.C.A. § 3402(q), 26 C.F.R. § 31.3402. For years, the IRS has gone further by requiring casinos to report big wins at bingo, slot machines and keno, even though no money was withheld for taxes. 26 C.F.R. §§ 1.6011–3, 31.3402(q)–1.26 and 31.3406.

Today, a CTRC must be filed on every patron who cashes out for more than $10,000 in currency—no matter what the game and even if the player has lost money gambling. And every casino is covered, not just those doing more than $1 million a year in gaming revenue. Treasury gives the example of a small casino that makes less than $1 million a year having a patron come in with $15,000 cash. A CTRC is required. 31 C.F.R. § 1021.330(d).

The regulations also used to require that casinos obtain identification from the player before filing a CTRC. Today, a casino does not have to ask for a player's i.d. if it already has the patron's name, address and similar information. This eases the casinos' workload and prevents disruptions. But it also means high-rollers do not have to be told when the casino files CTRCs with the IRS.

The reason for the changes is simple: The Treasury Department has admitted that one of its primary goals is to go after untaxed cash transactions that have nothing to do with money laundering.

D. Wagering Tax Act

In 1952, Congress enacted the Wagering Tax Act, 26 U.S.C.A. §§ 4401–4424, which imposed a 10% excise tax on any wagering made in the United States and requires anyone engaged in the business of accepting wagers to register and pay a special occupational tax of $50.00 per year. Gambling operators were required to keep a daily record showing the gross amount of bets taken and the Act allows inspection of the bet-taker books "as frequently as may be needful to the enforcement of the law." However, payment of the federal tax did not prevent the states from imposing their own additional taxes.

Licensed parimutuels and coin-operated devices are exempted. The U.S. Supreme Court declared the Wagering Tax Act constitutional as a revenue measure in 1953; but 15 years later, the Court partially changed its mind. The Court concluded that the federal law was primarily a tool of law enforcement. It rejected the idea that a person could be convicted of violating federal anti-gambling laws based on the evidence that he was following the requirements of the federal tax laws by reporting his illegal gambling and paying the required special federal gambling taxes. *Marchetti v. United States*, 390 U.S. 39, 88 S.Ct. 697, 19 L.Ed.2d 889 (1968), *Grosso v. United States*, 390 U.S. 62, 88 S.Ct. 709, 19 L.Ed.2d 906 (1968). The Court also rejected the "silver platter doctrine," where federal tax officials were turning over illegal gamblers "on a silver platter," for prosecution of state anti-gambling laws.

E. Tax Regulation of Legal Games

State legislatures can restrict participation in gaming. The legislation can also impose heavy taxes on the gaming industry. Gaming is usually taxed at a rate higher than the rates imposed upon most other industries. Illinois imposes the highest gaming tax in the United States, 70% at the highest level. In Nevada, gaming tax revenues account for more than half of all public budgets.

F. Stamp Taxes on Slots

The federal government first imposed a stamp tax on slot machines in 1941. The tax was $10.00 for devices designed for amusement only, and $50.00 for gambling machines. The tax was raised to $100.00 in 1942, $150.00 in 1950, and $250.00 in 1951. The Gambling Device Stamp Tax Act was partially gutted by decisions of the United States Supreme Court in 1968, and was repealed by an act of Congress on November 6, 1978, effective July 1, 1980. Even before the law was terminated, it was virtually useless. The tax was originally applied only to coin-operated gaming devices, limiting the law to traditional coin-operated slot machines. Amusement devices were exempted from the gambling tax. Gambling pinball machines, where a player rolls balls in an attempt to line up a winning combination on a bingo card layout, were taxed only if an IRS agent happened to observe an actual payoff being made, which did not happen very often. These loopholes eventually were closed, but the damage to the law was irreversible.

G. Excise Tax on Wagers

The excise tax on wagers, the occupational tax on gambling establishments, and the registration requirement still exist in reduced form; they can be found primarily in §§ 4401 to 4424 of the IRC. These taxes on wagers once were administered exclusively by the IRS. On December 24, 1974, responsibility for enforcement was transferred to the Treasury Department's Bureau of Alcohol, Tobacco, and Firearms (ATF).

Following the Supreme Court decisions in 1968, holding that the Fifth Amendment right against self-incrimination applies to wagering taxes, criminal investigation under the wagering tax laws came to a virtual halt, with one major exception. Legal gambling operations continued to file reports and were routinely audited and investigated for skimming. Reporting by illegal operations dropped dramatically; about the only illegal gamblers investigated were those who filed false returns. The excise tax on wagers was reduced from 10% to 2% in 1974. The law was amended again in 1982 to lower the tax on legal bets to only one-fourth of 1%. Illegal bets are still subject to a 2% tax. Gambling operators must file a Form 730, Tax on Wagering, each month with the IRS to pay and report the excise tax on wagers.

H. Occupational Tax on Gaming Establishments

A completely separate occupational tax is imposed on anyone liable for the excise tax. The occupation tax was raised from $50.00 to $500.00 per year in 1974 but was lowered again to $50.00 for legal operators and their employees. Illegal gambling operators and their employees still have to pay $500.00 per year. If you qualify, you must file a Form 11–C and pay the occupational and excise taxes due. It is important for everyone associated with a gambling business that accepts wagers to register and pay the occupation tax. This includes employees who deal with the public. The penalties for non-registration can be severe. Willful refusal to pay is a crime.

I. Taking Gambling Losses and Expenses Off Your Taxes

Can the IRS have a man stationed in every casino full-time? As regards big winners, the answer is yes since the man is the gambling establishment itself. The IRS requires that a form be filed when a gambling establishment withholds gambling winning, so the government will know who the player is so as to collect any taxes owed. The law transforms the gambling establishment into an enforcement arm of the IRS; and the operator of an illegal game who will not report to the IRS when one of his players wins big will now find himself investigated by the FBI and subject to federal prosecution.

Form W–2G, "Statement for Certain Gambling Winnings," is a four-part form that identifies certain big winners to the IRS. Copy A of the form is sent to the IRS; Copy B is given to the winner to file with his federal tax return if the 20% tax has been withheld; Copy C is for the winner's records; and Copy D is kept by the gambling establishment. The IRC requires that everyone—from individuals and corporations to states and the federal government—must withhold 20% in certain cases before paying gambling winnings. The 20% withholding is to ensure that the federal government gets its tax share. Nonresident aliens and foreign corporations are subject to 30% withholdings.

CHAPTER 22

THE COMPULSIVE GAMBLER

The idea that compulsive gambling is a disease is in direct conflict with the dominant view in the law that gambling is a vice. Under the traditional view, individuals who gamble to excess are morally weak and deserving of punishment. The recognition of "pathological gambling" as an official mental disease or disorder by the American Psychiatric Association in 1980 created an irreconcilable contention: American law never punishes an individual for being sick. The most dramatic disputes have been over the insanity defense; but, the disease argument has been raised, sometimes successfully, in other criminal cases, to mitigate sentencing, in attorney disbarments, tax cases, bankruptcies, divorces, personal injury claims, and most significantly, in claims against casinos.

A. Vice or Entertainment or Disease

The sociopathic gambler exhibits antisocial behavior. The idea that an individual cannot control his desire to gamble is changing the way the law treats gambling and gamblers. The change goes deep, to the fundamental way society views all gambling activity.

A new view of gambling is coming into direct conflict with the old. Helped in part by the advent of state lotteries, where the state itself is promoting gambling, gambling is becoming viewed as merely another form of entertainment. But legal gambling runs head-on into the majority view, written into the law, that gambling is a vice. In Nevada, for example, the only legal businesses that were not allowed to generally advertise until relatively recently were licensed casinos and brothels.

B. Pathological Gambling Disorder

Pathological gambling disorder is an affliction that can destroy the lives of individual gamblers and their families, their employers, and the general public as a result of the relationship between the pathological gambling and the need to secure the monetary means to finance their gambling habit. This can certainly lead to criminal offenses. This disease is in the nature of an impulse control disorder, with features that are similar to substance addiction; with the "substance" being the insatiable urge to gamble.

1. Substantive Criminal Law

The on-going change in society's view of gambling, from sin to vice to disease, is most clearly illustrated in the area of sentencing. In the prevailing traditional view, evidence showing a criminal defendant has a gambling problem actually makes it easier to impose a harsh punishment; it answers the question of motive. On December 31, 1987 the Nevada Supreme Court upheld a sentence of 50 years for a compulsive gambler who passed five bad checks. *Houk v. State*, 103 Nev. 659, 747 P.2d 1376 (1987).

As the mental health community began to recognize the existence of compulsive gambling, the courts slowly followed. In 1980, the West Virginia Supreme Court, in discussing the concepts of rehabilitation, used a hypothetical example of a compulsive gambler, "It would be necessary for the lawyer to demonstrate that he is no longer a gambler and that he has taken affirmative action to cure himself of the vice of gambling." *In re Smith*, 166 W.Va. 22, 270 S.E.2d 768 (1980). The next year, the Supreme Court of California acknowledged a lawyer's illegal activities were the result of a gambling "addiction" with which he was attempting to cope, but ordered disbarment rather than suspension, noting that "there was no assurance that his control attempts were successful." *In re Petty,* 29 Cal.3d 356, 173 Cal.Rptr. 461, 627 P.2d 191 (1981).

2. The Insanity Defense (*M'Naghten Rule*) and Responses to John Hinckley's Acquittal

The mental disease must have had a prescribed relationship to the defendant's behavior. The various tests differ in their definitions of those incapacities that have exculpatory significance. Even a major mental disease is not a sufficient basis for exculpation under the insanity defense. The crucial issue is the existence of a casual link: whether the criminal conduct is related to the mental illness, in the sense of proving the nexus.

The major tests are the M'Naghten rules, the irresistible impulse test, and the Model Penal Code test. The M'Naghten rules consist of a cognitive inquiry: whether at the time of the offense the defendant was unable to know the nature and quality of the act committed or whether the act was right or wrong. (*See Daniel M'Naghten's Case*, 8 Eng. Rep. 718, 722 (H.L. 1843)). The irresistible impulse test focuses on the volitional capacity of the defendant, namely the capacity to exercise will to make choice. The Model Penal Code test combines the cognitive inquiry and the volitional inquiry. The defendant must have suffered from a mental disease or defect, and, as a result of the disease he must have lacked substantial capacity to appreciate the criminality of his conduct or the lacked substantial capacity to conform his conduct to the requirements of the law.

Following the acquittal in 1982 of John Hinckley, Jr., who tried to assassinate President Reagan, based on the insanity defense, a movement began to demand the modification of the insanity defense, and many experts called for the abolition of the violation tests, arguing that the cognitive inquiry is a sufficient basis for exculpating defendants who due to severe mental disease were unable to know right from wrong. In 1984, Congress passed legislation eliminating the volitional prong from the federal insanity defense, and many states followed that trend. A compulsive gambler would, today, have difficulty proving he was not guilty be reason of insanity, since he does not know the difference between right and wrong. He would even have problems in the few states that still have the volitional test, except for the crime of illegal gambling.

3. Sentencing

The concept of pathological gambling is used as a basis for mitigation in sentencing. Courts have been much more receptive to mitigating claims, compared to exculpating ones. Some courts are willing to mitigate sentencing based on pathological gambling disorders, on the premise that punishment should comport with culpability, and that some defendants, while not legally insane, deserve less punishment due to reduced mental capacity not amounting to complete lack of control over behavior.

In federal courts, sentencing procedures are carried out under a mandatory structured scheme: the Federal Sentencing Guidelines, issued following the Sentencing Reform Act of 1984. The Act created a commission whose role was to promulgate sentencing guidelines to be followed by federal district judges. The goal was to create uniformity and reduce disparity in sentencing, while maintaining flexibility for extraordinary circumstances.

The diminished capacity guideline—§ 5k2.13 of the Federal Sentencing Guidelines—permits downward departure from presumptive sentences for nonviolent offenses if the offender had a significantly reduced mental capacity. In this amendment, the sentencing commission embraced the view articulated by the Third Circuit in *United States v. McBroom*, 124 F.3d 533 (3d Cir. 1997), where the court ruled that the guideline's phrase "significantly reduced mental capacity" includes a volitional component. The main issue that remained open was whether the downward departure should be limited to charges where the underlying offense is illegal gambling or whether it should extend to charges where the underlying offense is not illegal gambling, such as theft crimes.

4. Sentencing Guidelines

Pathological gambling is also a voluntary behavior and highly correlated to increased propensity to commit crime. The First Circuit, upholding a district court's decision to depart downward based on the diminished capacity guideline, stated that "the general purpose of deterrence would be ill-served by discounting appellant's sentence on the basis of a gambling addiction because such dependence would be akin to drug or alcohol addiction." *United States v. Harotunian*, 920 F.2d 1040, 1047 (1st Cir. 1990).

In another case, a court refused to grant a downward departure based on a gambling addiction and rejected the defendant's contention that gambling addiction should be distinguished from drug and alcohol addiction. The court stated that: "defendant has not convinced the court that pathological gambling disorder can be distinguished in any principled way from abuse of drugs or alcohol." (*United States v. Katzenstein*, 1991 WL 24386 (S.D.N.Y)).

Making pathological gambling addiction a factor for departure under the Sentencing Guidelines creates an unjustified distinction between it and the guidelines' treatment of drugs and alcohol use.

5.   Disorder as a Basis for Mitigation in Sentencing

Conflicts between the old and new views divide not only jurisdictions but single courts as well. A divided New Hampshire Supreme Court voted against reinstating a disciplined lawyer. Chief Justice King would have allowed the disbarred lawyer to reenter practice since the criminal activity of theft was related to compulsive gambling and the lawyer had now rehabilitated himself. (*In re Carroll*, 127 N.H. 390, 503 A.2d 750 (1985)). However, one appellate court nearly avoided the issue by calling information of a convicted defendant's gambling problem merely opinions that did not have to be included in the trial court's finding of fact, and then buried this decision by refusing to publish its judgment. (*Johnston v. United States*, 815 F.2d 78 (6th Cir. 1987)).

Different courts weigh the factors differently, even within the same court system. A trial judge in New Jersey sentenced a compulsive gambler to 364 days in jail and to pay $150.00 per month as restitution for embezzling $720,600.22. The appellate court reversed, stating the trial judge had not given sufficient consideration to the crime and what the interest of justice demanded. The higher court remanded, indicating that the judge should impose a much more severe sentence. (*State v. Jones*, 197 N.J.Super. 604, 485 A.2d 1063 (1984)). The higher court may have been influenced by the fact that full restitution would take over 400 years, not including interest.

Judges, like laymen, can become highly emotional when debating whether compulsive gambling is a disease. The defendant in a New York case had been convicted of 50 counts of grand larceny, having taken $120,000 from his employer over a six-year period. The trial judge sentenced him to make restitution, attend Gamblers Anonymous and no jail time. The Calendar Judge considered the sentence too lenient and took the position that he had referred the case solely for trial and not sentencing. A higher court had to step in to straighten out the conflict between the judges representing the old and new views of compulsive gambling. (*Agnew v. Rothwax*, 121 App. Div.2d 906, 503 N.Y.S.2d 808 (1986)).

C. "Pathological Gaming" as a Protected Disability

In the past, individuals who experienced adverse consequences from gambling were viewed simply as people with gambling problems. This view changed profoundly following the 1980 inclusion of the disorder in the *Diagnosis and Statistical Manual Disorders,* Third Edition (DSM–III). The disorder is classified today in the Fourth Edition of the *Diagnosis and Statistical Manual of Mental Disorders* (DSM–IV) as one form of an impulse control disorder.

1. Definition

The controversy focuses on whether pathological gambling is some form of an impulse control disorder, or whether it is some form of addiction, akin to alcohol and drug dependence, despite the absence of substance. Although formally classified as an impulse control disorder in the DSM–IV, pursuant to its primary inclusion as a form of an impulse control disorder in the DSM–III in 1980, considerable contemporary evidence supports the characterization of pathological gambling as a form of addiction.

2. "Pathological Gambling" Included in DSM–III (1980)

The American Psychiatric Association has accepted the approach that pathological gambling is some form of a medical psychological problem by including it as a "disorder of impulse control." The DSM–III criteria were criticized for their single dimensionality, their emphasis on external consequences, and their middle-class bias.

3. "Pathological Gambling" Included in 1987 Revisions of DSM–IV

The DSM–IV definition attempts to operationally define the disorder. The definition includes ten criteria that describes both the individual attributes of sufferers and the social consequences that result from their behavior. Also described are associated features and disorders, specific culture and gender features, prevalence, course, familial pattern, differential diagnosis, and exclusion criteria. The ten criteria focus on three dimensions: damages or disruption, loss of control, and dependence.

The DSM–IV definition of pathological gambling focuses on the features of an impulse control disorder by classifying it as one of five different impulse disorders under a category called "Impulse Control Disorders Not Elsewhere Classified."

What is less clear is the dysfunctional nature and causal aspects of pathological gambling. There is considerable consensus that gambling involves control disorder, as defined by DSM–IV as "the failure to resist an impulse, drive or temptation to perform an act that is harmful to the person or to others." This definition implies a loss of control over behavior.

Nonetheless, empirical evidence in this area is inconclusive, and a variety of problems were identified in the methodologies researchers have employed. Moreover, researchers have not established that differences in impulse control characteristics predate the onset of gambling disorders, a necessary condition to establish a causal relationship.

While many researchers have focused on the impulse control features of pathological gambling disorders, others suggest that there is little evidence that loss of control is a distinctive feature of pathological gambling. Researchers argue that there are dangers in misdiagnosing pathological gambling, and there is serious disagreement as to whether pathological gambling actually results in a loss of self-control.

4. The *Frye* Test

The debate in the literature with respect to the proper psychological definition and clinical characterization of pathological gambling, creates problems for the admissibility of psychological testimony that are different from traditional scientific testimony. Additional hurdles arise on the use of experts' psychological testimony in criminal trials where the defendant raises pathological gambling as a defense or a mitigating factor.

As for the test for admitting psychological testimony, there are two evidentiary standards: *Frye* (Frye v. United States, 293 F.2d 1013 (Cir. D.C. 1923)) and *Daubert* (*Daubert v. Merrell Dow Pharmaceuticals, Inc.*, 509 U.S. 579, 113 S.Ct. 2786, 125 L.Ed.2d 469 (1993)) tests. *Frye* governed federal and state courts until 1993, and *Daubert* replaced it, and since then 24 states incorporated it into their jurisprudence. Sixteen states and the District of Columbia still adhere to *Frye*, and the rest of the states employ a hybrid of the tests.

According to *Frye*, novel scientific knowledge must have gained "general acceptance" in the scientific community in order to be admissible. This has been considered a stringent test because it excludes new scientific theories that have not yet gained acceptance in the general scientific community, even when they are based on sound methodologies.

Daubert was intended to revisit *Frye* by adding other factors courts should consider when faced with novel scientific theories. Once it is established the witness is qualified to serve as an expert, the judge must ensure that the scientific testimony is both relevant and reliable. In doing so, the following nonexhaustive factors must be considered: whether the theory can be tested, whether the theory has been subjected to peer review and publication, the known or potential rate of error and whether the theory is generally accepted.

While the issue of whether to admit psychological testimony is not dependent upon whether the jurisdiction applies the *Frye* or the *Daubert* standard, there are some consistent reasons why psychological testimonies are rejected. Lack of "general acceptance" is often given for rejecting psychological testimony. Other reasons include lack of expert qualification, lack of relevance or applicability, and inappropriate interference with witness credibility.

D. The Compulsive Gambler After *Caesar's Riverboat Casino, LLC v. Kephart* (2010)

In *Caesar's Riverboat Casino LLC v. Kephart*, 903 N.E.2d 117 (Ind. Ct. App. 2009), rev'd. 934 N.E.2d 1120 (Ind. 2010), the Indiana Supreme Court was asked to determine whether casino patrons have a common law cause of action for damages stemming from the consequences of gambling losses. In *Kephart*, a casino sued a patron for unpaid counter checks; the patron, a pathological gambler countersued for damages because the casino knowingly enticed and encouraged the patron to gamble.

Caesar's allegedly knew of Genevieve Kephart's addiction. On March 18, 2006 Kephart traveled to Caesars after receiving an offer of free transportation, hotel room, food, and alcohol from Caesars. In a single night of gambling Kephart lost $125,000 through the use of six counter checks provided to her by Caesars.

The Court found that in this case, not only does the statutory scheme cover the entire subject of riverboat gambling, but also the statutory scheme and Kephart's common law claim are so incompatible that they cannot both occupy the same space. As the sole regulator of riverboat gambling, the Commission had adopted detailed regulations at the Legislature's direction. The Court held, "In sum it appears to us that by unmistakable implication the Legislature has abrogated any common law claim that casino patrons might otherwise have against casinos for damages resulting from enticing patrons to gamble and lose money at casino establishments."

The Court held that this common law obligation, as applied to casinos, was abrogated by implication because the Indiana Gaming Commission, pursuant to statutory directive, created a program whereby persons may voluntarily place their name on an exclusion list that would prevent their being permitted to gamble, to receive direct marketing, or to receive casino credit privileges.

E. Tax and Bankruptcy Law and the Compulsive Gambler

Federal and state tax laws have great impact on everyone, particularly gamblers. Beyond the financial burdens, the law imposes criminal sanctions for failure to file returns or pay the amounts owed. The compulsive gambler by definition cannot keep adequate financial records, file the proper government forms, or send the government the amount owed.

The most worrisome case for the compulsive gambler is the definition of income under the Internal Revenue Code (26 U.S.C.A. § 61), which would make the gambler liable for practically every dollar obtained in any manner, including through winning bets, theft or embezzlement. Gambling losses can only be deducted up to the amount of money won, (26 U.S.C.A § 165(a)), so a compulsive gambler who has been misappropriating funds from his employer to pay his gambling debts could find himself with no assets while facing an enormous tax bill.

The federal courts have come to the protection of the compulsive gambler's spouse. The Internal Revenue Code protects an "innocent spouse" from liability where the spouse can prove that he or she did not know or have reason to know of the other spouse's failure to report gross income. (26 U.S.C.A. § 6013(e)).

A Gam–Anon member testified that this support group for spouses of gamblers taught its members not to question the gambling spouse regarding finances and had encouraged them to accept, without question, any money offered by the gambler. The gambling spouse had kept secret his lucrative narcotics trade. The court of appeals held the innocent spouse rule applied; the Gam–Anon spouse was not liable for the taxes on this nonreported income, except the sums she received in excess of their reported income. *Ratana v. C.I.R.*, 662 F.2d 220 (4th Cir. 1981).

Issues similar to the law of taxes have arisen in bankruptcy courts, for similar reasons. Of course, even noncompulsive gamblers do not keep records, but the compulsive gambler is not able, by definition under DSM–III, of obeying all of the requirements of the federal bankruptcy code. Some federal courts have found that compulsive gambling will indeed excuse the bankrupt while other courts have held the opposite.

F. Compulsive Gambling and Family Law

Now that compulsive gambling is gaining acceptance as a mental disorder outside of the individual's control, the law is becoming more lenient in its treatment of compulsive gamblers involved in divorce proceedings. This change in attitude matches a general change in the law of divorce; the overwhelming majority of jurisdictions today allow no-fault divorces, eliminating the acrimonious accusations common to a "fault" system.

G. Gambling Debts and Claims by Third–Parties

The growing conflict in the law over how to deal with compulsive gambling is coming to a head in cases involving legal gambling. The legal gambling industry would suffer a terrible financial blow if this doctrine were generally accepted. Their immediate concern is cases in which a gambler argues that he is not liable for his gambling debts because he is a compulsive gambler. Casinos in particular rely upon liberal credit policies; if any player could raise compulsive gambling as a possible defense, collection of small debts would become extremely expensive and many large debts would be uncollectible. However, every form of gambling, from racetracks, through state lotteries, to stockbrokers would be open to suits whenever anyone lost money.

One argument that has not succeeded is that the gambler was incompetent to make a contract at the time he borrowed money from the casino. This would require an expert witness to testify that during gambling sessions the gambler did not really know what he was doing.

The law, as represented by reported cases, still protects the casino, *Duff v. Harrah South Shore Corporation*, 52 Cal.App.3d 803, 125 Cal.Rptr. 259 (1975), is the only reported case involving a suit for tort damages arising out of a casino's allowing a compulsive gambler to gamble. The court held the casinos did not breach a duty to the gambler, who committed suicide, by allowing him to cash checks above his limit.

Wynn v. Monterey Club, 111 Cal.App.3d 789, 168 Cal.Rptr. 878 (1980), is the only reported case where a court allowed a legal gambling establishment to be sued in contract for allowing a compulsive gambler to gamble. However, the facts and legal theory of the case are unique. The plaintiff had agreed to pay off his wife's gambling debts on the promise from a California card club that it would deny her further check cashing privileges. The club allowed her in and cashed her checks, resulting in severe financial losses for her husband and eventually a divorce. The court rejected the argument that under California law the club could not exclude anyone.

H. The Future of Compulsive Gambling and the Law: Sin, Vice, or Disease?

Law trails society. Changes occurring in the social order in America inevitably lead to conflicts and eventually to changes in the law. The changes that are taking place in contemporary society in the way we view gambling give us a unique opportunity to observe this slow and painful process at work. The idea that compulsive gambling is a disease has been given great credibility due to its recognition by the American Psychiatric Association.

Some of the most important changes in the law will come in the field of legal gambling. Legal gambling, the fastest growing industry in the United States, is often dependent upon freely given credit. As the legal games spread and win the right to use the court system to collect their debts, more and more gamblers are going to be sued and more and more innocent third parties are going to be the victims of robbery, embezzlement and fraud; and more gamblers will kill themselves. The gambling establishments are not always going to be able to settle all of their lawsuits. Casinos can limit their risk by taking precautions; in many cases this means not allowing certain players to gamble at all, or at least not for credit.

Inevitably, the courts are going to have to decide whether casinos, race tracks, and lotteries owe some degree of legal responsibility for the harm created by compulsive gamblers. The answer will depend upon whether the court views gamblers as being in control of their own destiny or accepts the idea that sometimes gambling, like a fever, is merely a symptom of a disease.

INDEX

References are to Pages

415

NATIONAL COLLEGIATE ATHLETIC ASSOCIATION (NCAA)
Sports books, 322–325

NATIONAL GAMBLING IMPACT STUDY COMMISSION, 60, 238, 321–322, 326

NATIONAL INDIAN GAMING COMMISSION (NIGC), 141–142, 153
Blackjack, 237
Minimum Internal Control Standards (MICS), 141–142

NATIONAL INFORMATION INFRASTRUCTURE (NII), 292

NATIONAL INSTITUTE OF LAW ENFORCEMENT AND CRIMINAL JUSTICE, 24

NATIONAL LOTTERIES, 353

NATIONAL LOTTERY ACT OF 1993, 353

NATIONAL LOTTERY COMMISSION, 353

NATIVE AMERICANS
See Tribal Gaming

NEBRASKA BINGO ACT, 97

NEBRASKA PICKLE CARD LOTTERY ACT, 97

NEVADA
Anti-cheating, 229
Cardcounting computers are illegal, 372
Common law, 15
Constitutional ban on lotteries, 82–84
Gaming Control Board, 83, 108–109
LTRCs, 388

NEVADA GAMBLING
Generally, 105–119
Blackbook, 116–117
Everyday activities, 112–116
Gaming Commission, 108
Investigations, 115–116
History, 105–109
Licenses, 114
Types, 114–115
Local ordinances, 117
Regulations
Generally, 111–112

†